im Coates
of history.
The Sta-
Os in the
House of Lords *we get a hilarious recreation, directly from Hansard, of a nutty debate that took place in 1979 ... This is inspired publishing, not only archivally valuable but capable of bringing the past back to life without the usual filter of academic or biographer."* **Guardian**

"The Irish Uprising is a little treasure of a book and anyone with an interest in Irish history will really enjoy it. Its structure is extremely unusual as it is compiled from historic official reports published by the British government from 1914 to 1920 ... For anyone studying this period of history The Irish Uprising is a must as the correspondence and accounts within it are extremely illuminating and the subtle nuances of meaning can be teased out of the terms and phrasing to be more revelatory than the actual words themselves." **Irish Press, Belfast**

"Voyeurs of all ages will enjoy the original text of the Denning report on Profumo. It is infinitely superior to the film version of the scandal, containing such gems as: 'One night I was invited to a dinner party at the home of a very, very rich man. After I arrived, I discovered it was rather an unusual dinner party. All the guests had taken off their clothes ... The most intriguing person was a man with a black mask over his face. At first I thought this was a party gimmick. But the truth was that this man is so well known and holds such a responsible position that he did not want to be associated with anything improper.' " **Times Higher Education Supplement**

"Very good to read ... insight into important things ... inexorably moving ... If you want to read about the Titanic, *you won't read a better thing ... a revelation."* **Open Book, BBC R**

"Congratulati .... *and reissuing such an enjoy* .... *n Garden]* **The Specta**

D1293279

uncovered editions
www.uncovered-editions.co.uk

Series editor: Tim Coates

Managing editor: Michele Staple

New titles in the series
Attack on Pearl Harbor, 1941
The Cuban Missile Crisis, 1962
Letters of Henry VIII, 1526–29
Mr Hosie's Journey to Tibet, 1904
The St Valentine's Day Massacre, 1929
The Trials of Oscar Wilde, 1895
UFOs in America, 1947
The Watergate Affair, 1972

Already published
The Amritsar Massacre: General Dyer in the Punjab, 1919
Bloody Sunday, 1972: Lord Widgery's Report
The Boer War: Ladysmith and Mafeking, 1900
British Battles of World War I, 1914–15
The British Invasion of Tibet: Colonel Younghusband, 1904
Defeat at Gallipoli: the Dardanelles Commission Part II, 1915–16
D Day to VE Day: General Eisenhower's Report, 1944–45
Escape from Germany, 1939–45
Florence Nightingale and the Crimea, 1854–55
The Irish Uprising, 1914–21
John Profumo and Christine Keeler, 1963
The Judgment of Nuremberg, 1946
King Guezo of Dahomey, 1850–52
Lord Kitchener and Winston Churchill: The Dardanelles
    Commission Part I, 1914–15
The Loss of the Titanic, 1912
R.101: the Airship Disaster, 1930
Rillington Place, 1949
The Russian Revolution, 1917
The Siege of Kars, 1855
The Siege of the Peking Embassy, 1900
The Strange Story of Adolf Beck
Tragedy at Bethnal Green
Travels in Mongolia, 1902
UFOs in the House of Lords, 1979
War in the Falklands, 1982
War 1914: Punishing the Serbs
War 1939: Dealing with Adolf Hitler
Wilfrid Blunt's Egyptian Garden: Fox-hunting in Cairo

uncovered editions

THE ASSASSINATION OF JOHN F. KENNEDY, 1963

THE REPORT OF THE WARREN COMMISSION, SEPTEMBER 1964

∘⦅◈◈◈⦆∘

London: The Stationery Office

© The Stationery Office 2001

Applications for reproduction should be made in writing to
The Stationery Office Limited, St Crispins, Duke Street,
Norwich NR3 1PD.

ISBN 0 11 702748 0

Selected extracts have been taken from the final report of the
Warren Commission, presented to the President of the United
States in September 1964 and published by the US
Government Printing Office as *Report of the President's
Commission on the Assassination of President John F. Kennedy*.

A CIP catalogue record for this book is available from the
British Library.

Cover photograph shows President J. F. Kennedy and his wife
Jackie in the presidential limousine in Dallas on 22 November
1963. © Bettmann/CORBIS.

Diagram of Dealey Plaza on page viii prepared by Sandra
Lockwood of Artworks Design, Norwich.

Typeset by J&L Composition Ltd, Filey, North Yorkshire.
Printed in the United Kingdom by The Stationery Office,
London.
TJ4267 C30 10/01

About the series

Uncovered editions are historic official papers which have not previously been available in a popular form, and have been chosen for the quality of their story-telling. Some subjects are familiar, but others are less well known. Each is a moment in history.

About the series editor, Tim Coates

Tim Coates studied at University College, Oxford and at the University of Stirling. After working in the theatre for a number of years, he took up bookselling and became managing director, firstly of Sherratt and Hughes bookshops, and then of Waterstone's. He is known for his support for foreign literature, particularly from the Czech Republic. The idea for *uncovered editions* came while searching through the bookshelves of his late father-in-law, Air Commodore Patrick Cave, OBE. He is married to Bridget Cave, has two sons, and lives in London.

Tim Coates welcomes views and ideas on the *uncovered editions* series. He can be e-mailed at timcoates@theso.co.uk

CONTENTS

On November 22, 1963, President John F. Kennedy was assassinated while riding slowly through Dallas, Texas, in an open limousine. Lee Harvey Oswald, a 24-year-old citizen of Dallas, was accused of the murder, although he denied all charges made against him. Then, on November 24, less than 18 hours after his arrest, Oswald was fatally shot while in the custody of the police by Jack Ruby, a local nightclub owner. This killing was captured on film by national television cameramen.

After the shooting of Lee Harvey Oswald, it was no longer possible to obtain a complete story of the assassination through the normal judicial procedures. Therefore on November 29, a week after the assassination of President Kennedy, President Lyndon B. Johnson appointed a commission to investigate the circumstances surrounding his predecessor's death. The chairman of the commission was the chief justice of the United States, Earl Warren. The other members included two US senators, two members of the US House of Representatives and two private citizens.

This book is a collection of extracts from the Warren Commission's report, which was submitted in September 1964. As with other reports in the series, many of which have subsequently been questioned, the fascination lies partly with the findings, but as much with the views and the attitudes of the people at the time at which they were written.

The calibre of a weapon is the diameter of the interior of the barrel. The calibre of American weapons is expressed in inches; thus a .30-calibre weapon has a barrel which is thirty one-hundredths or three-tenths of an inch in diameter. The calibre of continental European weapons is measured in millimetres. A 6.5-millimetre calibre weapon corresponds to an American .257 weapon; that is, its barrel diameter is about a quarter or one-fourth inch.

Dealey Plaza, Dallas, November 22, 1963

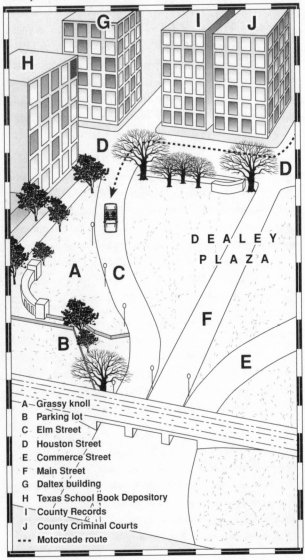

A — Grassy knoll
B — Parking lot
C — Elm Street
D — Houston Street
E — Commerce Street
F — Main Street
G — Daltex building
H — Texas School Book Depository
I — County Records
J — County Criminal Courts
- - - Motorcade route

A BRIEF HISTORY OF
PRESIDENTIAL PROTECTION

In the course of the history of the United States four presidents have been assassinated, within less than 100 years, beginning with Abraham Lincoln in 1865. Attempts were also made on the lives of two other presidents, one president-elect, and one ex-president. Still other presidents were the objects of plots that were never carried out. The actual attempts are set out in the table overleaf.

Attempts have thus been made on the lives of one of every five American presidents. One of every nine presidents has been killed. Since 1865, there have been attempts on the lives of one of every four presidents and the successful assassination of one of every five. During the last three decades, three attacks were made.

President	Date of assassination attempt	Outcome
Andrew Jackson	January 30, 1835	
Abraham Lincoln	April 14, 1865	Died April 15, 1865
James A. Garfield	July 2, 1881	Died September 19, 1881
William McKinley	September 6, 1901	Died September 14, 1901
Theodore Roosevelt	October 14, 1912	Wounded; recovered
Franklin D. Roosevelt	February 15, 1933	
Harry S. Truman	November 1, 1950	
John F. Kennedy	November 22, 1963	Died that day

It was only after William McKinley was shot that systematic and continuous protection of the president was instituted. Protection before McKinley was intermittent and spasmodic. The problem had existed from the days of the early presidents, but no action was taken until three tragic events had occurred. In considering the effectiveness of present day protection arrangements, it is worthwhile to examine the development of presidential protection over the years, to understand both the high degree of continuing danger and the anomalous reluctance to take the necessary precautions.

Before the Civil War
In the early days of the Republic, there was remarkably little concern about the safety of presidents and few measures were taken to protect them. They were at times the objects of abuse and the recipients of threatening letters as more recent presidents have been, but they did not take the threats seriously and moved about freely without protective escorts.

On his inauguration day, Thomas Jefferson walked from his boarding house to the Capitol, unaccompanied by any guard, to take the oath of office. There was no police authority in Washington itself until 1805, when the mayor appointed a high constable and 40 deputy constables.

John Quincy Adams received many threatening letters and on one occasion was threatened in person in the White House by a court-martialed Army sergeant. In spite of this incident, the president asked for no protection and continued to indulge his fondness for solitary walks and early morning swims in the Potomac.

Among pre-Civil War presidents, Andrew Jackson aroused particularly strong feelings. He received many threatening letters which, with a fine contempt, he would endorse and send to the *Washington Globe* for publication. On one occasion in May 1833, Jackson was assaulted by a former Navy lieutenant, Robert B. Randolph, but refused to prosecute him. This is not regarded as an attempt at assassination, since Randolph apparently did not intend serious injury.

Less than two years later, on the morning of January 10, 1835, as Jackson emerged from the east portico of the Capitol, he was accosted by a would-be assassin, Richard Lawrence, an English-born house painter. Lawrence fired his two pistols at the president, but they both misfired. Lawrence was quickly overpowered and held for trial. A jury found him not guilty by reason of insanity. He was confined in jails and mental hospitals for the rest of his life.

The attack on Jackson did not inspire any action to provide protection for the chief executive. Jackson's immediate successor, Martin Van Buren, often walked to church alone and rode horseback alone in the woods not far from the White House. In August 1842, after an intoxicated painter had thrown rocks at President John Tyler, who was walking on the grounds to the south of the White House, Congress passed an act to establish an auxiliary watch for the protection of public and private property in Washington. The force was to consist of a captain and 15 men. This act was apparently aimed more at the protection of the White House, which had been defaced on occasion, than of the president.

Lincoln

Even before he took the oath of office, Abraham Lincoln was thought to be the object of plots and conspiracies to kidnap or kill him. Extremist opponents apparently contemplated desperate measures to prevent his inauguration, and there is some evidence that they plotted to attack him while he was passing through Baltimore on his way to Washington.

For the inauguration, the Army took precautions unprecedented up to that time and perhaps more elaborate than any precautions taken since. Soldiers occupied strategic points throughout the city, along the procession route, and at the Capitol, while armed men in plain clothes mingled with the crowds. Lincoln himself, in a carriage with President Buchanan, was surrounded on all sides by such dense masses of soldiers that he was almost completely hidden from the view of the crowds. The precautions at the Capitol during the ceremony were almost as thorough and equally successful.

Lincoln lived in peril during all his years in office. The volume of threatening letters remained high throughout the war, but little attention was paid to them. The few letters that were investigated yielded no results. Lincoln was reluctant to surround himself with guards and often rejected protection or sought to slip away from it. This has been characteristic of almost all American presidents. They have regarded protection as a necessary affliction at best and contrary to their normal instincts for either personal privacy or freedom to meet the people. In Lincoln these instincts were especially strong, and he suffered with impatience the efforts of his friends, the police, and the military to safeguard him.

The protection of the president during the war varied greatly, depending on Lincoln's susceptibility to warnings. Frequently, military units were assigned to guard the White House and to accompany the president on his travels. Lincoln's friend, Ward H. Lamon, on becoming marshal of the District of Columbia in 1861, took personal charge of protecting the president and provided guards for the purpose, but he became so exasperated at the president's lack of cooperation that he tendered his resignation. Lincoln did not accept it. Finally, late in the war, in November 1864, four Washington policemen were detailed to the White House to act as personal bodyguards to the president. Lincoln tolerated them reluctantly and insisted they remain as inconspicuous as possible.

In the closing days of the war, rumors of attempts on Lincoln's life persisted. The well-known actor, John Wilkes Booth, a fanatical Confederate sympathizer, plotted with others for months to kidnap the president. The fall of the Confederacy apparently hardened his determination to kill Lincoln. Booth's opportunity came on Good Friday, April 14, 1865, when he learned that the president would be attending a play at Ford's Theater that night. The president's bodyguard for the evening was Patrolman John F. Parker of the Washington Police, a man who proved himself unfit for protective duty. He was supposed to remain on guard in the corridor outside the presidential box during the entire performance of the play, but he soon wandered off to watch the play and then even went outside the theater to have a drink at a nearby saloon. Parker's dereliction of duty left the president totally unprotected. Shortly after 10 o'clock on that evening, Booth found his way up to the presidential box and shot the president in the head. The president's wound was a mortal one; he died the next morning, April 15.

A detachment of troops captured Booth on April 26 at a farm near Bowling Green, Virginia; he received a bullet wound and died a few hours later. At a trial in June, a military tribunal sentenced four of Booth's associates to death and four others to terms of imprisonment.

Lincoln's assassination revealed the total inadequacy of presidential protection. A congressional committee conducted an extensive investigation of the assassination, but with traditional reluctance, called for no action to provide better protection for the president in the future. Nor did requests for protective measures come from the president or from Government departments. This lack of concern for the protection of the president may have derived also from the tendency of the time to regard Lincoln's assassination as part of a unique crisis that was not likely to happen to a future chief executive.

The need for protection further demonstrated

For a short time after the war, soldiers assigned by the War Department continued to protect the White House and its grounds. Metropolitan Washington policemen assisted on special occasions to maintain order and prevent the congregation of crowds. The permanent Metropolitan Police guard was reduced to three and assigned entirely to protection at the White House. There was no special group of trained officers to protect the person of the president. Presidents after Lincoln continued to move about in Washington virtually unattended, as their predecessors had done before the Civil War, and, as before, such protection as they got at the White House came from the doormen, who were not especially trained for guard duty.

This lack of personal protection for the president came again tragically to the attention of the country with the shooting of President James A. Garfield in 1881. The president's assassin, Charles J. Guiteau, was a self-styled "lawyer, theologian, and politician" who had convinced himself that his unsolicited efforts to help elect Garfield in 1880 entitled him to appointment as a consul in Europe. Bitterly disappointed that the president ignored his repeated written requests for appointment to office and obsessed with a kind of megalomania, he resolved to kill Garfield.

At that time Guiteau was 38 years old and had an unusually checkered career behind him. He had been an itinerant and generally unsuccessful lecturer and evangelist, a lawyer, and a would-be politician. While it is true he resented Garfield's failure to appoint him consul in Paris as a reward for his wholly illusory contribution to the Garfield campaign, and he verbally attacked Garfield for his lack of support for the so-called Stalwart wing of the Republican Party, these may not have supplied the total motivation for his crime. At his trial he testified that the "Deity" had commanded him to remove the president. There is no evidence that he confided his assassination plans to anyone or that he had any close friends or confidants. He made his attack on the president under circumstances where escape after the shooting was inconceivable.

There were some hereditary mental problems in his family and Guiteau apparently believed in divine inspiration. Guiteau later testified that he had three opportunities to attack the president prior to the actual shooting. On all of these occasions, within a brief period of three weeks, the president was unguarded. Guiteau finally realized his intent on the morning of July 2, 1881. As Garfield was walking to a train in the Baltimore and Potomac Railroad Station in Washington, Guiteau stepped up and shot him in the back. Garfield did not die from the effects of the wound until

September 19, 1881. Although there was evidence of serious abnormality in Guiteau, he was found guilty of murder and sentenced to be hanged. The execution took place on June 30, 1882.

At least one newspaper, the *New York Tribune*, predicted that the assault on Garfield would lead to the president becoming "the slave of his office, the prisoner of forms and restrictions," in sharp and unwelcome contrast to the splendidly simple life he had been able to live before:

> The bullet of the assassin who lurked in the Washington railway station to take the life of President Garfield shattered the simple Republican manner of life which the custom of nearly a century has prescribed for the Chief Magistrate of the United States. Our presidents have been the first citizens of the Republic, nothing more. With a measure of power in their hands far greater than is wielded by the ruler of any limited monarchy in Europe, they have never surrounded themselves with the forms and safeguards of courts. The White House has been a business office to everybody. Its occupant has always been more accessible than the heads of great commercial establishments. When the passions of the war were at fever heat, Mr Lincoln used to have a small guard of cavalry when he rode out to his summer residence at the Soldier's Home; but at no other time in our history has it been thought needful for a president to have any special protection against violence when inside or outside the White House. Presidents have driven about Washington like other people and traveled over the country as unguarded and unconstrained as any private citizen.

The prediction of the *Tribune* did not come to pass. Although the nation was shocked by this deed, its representatives took no steps to provide the president with personal protection. The president continued to move about Washington, sometimes completely alone, and to travel without special protection. There is a story that President Chester A. Arthur, Garfield's successor, once went to a ceremony at the Washington Navy Yard on a public conveyance that he hailed in front of the White House.

During Grover Cleveland's second administration (1893-97) the number of threatening letters addressed to the president increased markedly, and Mrs Cleveland persuaded the president to increase the number of White House policemen to 27 from the three who had constituted the force since the Civil War. In 1894, the Secret Service began to provide protection, on an informal basis.

The Secret Service was organized as a division of the Department of the Treasury in 1865, to deal with counterfeiting. Its jurisdiction was extended to other fiscal crimes against the United States in later Appropriations Acts but its early work in assisting in protecting the president was an unofficial, stopgap response to a need for a trained organization, with investigative capabilities, to perform this task. In 1894, while investigating a plot by a group of gamblers in Colorado to assassinate President Cleveland, the Secret Service assigned a small detail of operatives to the White House to help protect him. Secret Service men accompanied the president and his family to their vacation home in Massachusetts; special details protected the president in Washington, on trips, and at special functions. For a time, two agents rode in a buggy behind President Cleveland's carriage, but this practice attracted so much attention in the opposition newspapers that it was soon discontinued at the president's insistence. These initially informal and part-time arrangements eventually led to the organization of permanent systematic protection for the president and his family.

During the Spanish-American War the Secret Service stationed a detail at the White House to provide continuous protection for President McKinley. The special wartime protective measures were relaxed after the war, but Secret Service guards remained on duty at the White House at least part of the time.

Between 1894 and 1900, anarchists murdered the president of France, the premier of Spain, the empress of Austria, and the king of Italy. At the turn of the century the Secret Service thought that the strong police action taken against the anarchists in Europe was compelling them to flee and that many were coming to the United States. Concerned about the protection of the president, the Secret Service increased the number of guards and directed that a guard accompany him on all of his trips.

Unlike Lincoln and Garfield, President McKinley was being guarded when he was shot by Leon F. Czolgosz, an American-born 28-year-old factory worker and farmhand. On September 6, 1901, the president was holding a brief reception for the public in the Temple of Music at the Pan American Exposition in Buffalo. Long lines of people passed between two rows of policemen and soldiers to reach the president and shake his hand. In the immediate vicinity of the president were four Buffalo detectives, four soldiers, and three Secret Service agents. Two of the Secret Service men were facing the president at a distance of 3 feet. One of them stated later that it was normally his custom to stand at the side of the president on such occasions, but that he had been requested not to do so at this time in order to permit McKinley's secretary and the president of the exposition to stand on either side of McKinley. Czolgosz joined the line, concealed a pistol under a handkerchief, and when he stood in front of the president shot twice through the handkerchief. McKinley fell, critically wounded.

Czolgosz, a self-styled anarchist, did not believe in rulers of any kind. There is evidence that the organized anarchists in the USA did not accept or trust him. He was not admitted as a member to any of the secret anarchist societies. No co-plotters were ever discovered, and there is no evidence that he had confided in anyone. A calm inquiry, made by two eminent alienists [experts on the mental competence of a witness] about a year after Czolgosz was executed, found that Czolgosz had for some time been suffering from delusions. One was that he was an anarchist; another was that it was his duty to assassinate the president.

The assassin said he had no grudge against the president personally but did not believe in the republican form of government or in rulers of any kind. In his written confession he included the words, "I don't believe one man should have so much service and another man should have none." As he was strapped to the chair to be electrocuted, he said: "I killed the president because he was the enemy of the good people, the good working people. I am not sorry for my crime."

McKinley lingered on for eight days before he died of blood poisoning early on the morning of September 14. Czolgosz, who had been captured immediately, was swiftly tried, convicted, and condemned to death. Although it seemed to some contemporaries that Czolgosz was incompetent, the defense made no effort to plead insanity. Czolgosz was executed 45 days after the president's death. Investigations by the Buffalo police and the Secret Service revealed no accomplices and no plot of any kind.

Development of presidential protection

This third assassination of a president in a little more than a generation – it was only 36 years since Lincoln had been killed – shook the nation and aroused it to a greater awareness of the uniqueness of the presidency and the grim hazards that surrounded an incumbent of that office. The first congressional session after the assassination of McKinley gave more attention to legislation concerning attacks on the president than had any previous Congress, but did not pass any measures for the protection of the president. Nevertheless, the Secret Service, which was then the only Federal general investigative agency of any consequence, assumed full-time responsibility for the safety of the president. Protection of the president now became one of its major permanent functions, and it assigned two men to its original full-time White House detail. Additional agents were provided when the president traveled or went on vacation.

Theodore Roosevelt, who was the first president to experience the extensive system of protection that has surrounded the president ever since, voiced an opinion of presidential protection that was probably shared in part by most of his successors. In a letter to Senator Henry Cabot Lodge from his summer home, he wrote:

> The Secret Service men are a very small but very necessary thorn in the flesh. Of course, they would not be the least use preventing any assault upon my life. I do not believe there is any danger of such an assault, and if there were, as Lincoln said, "though it would be safer for a president to live in a cage, it would interfere with his business." But it is only the Secret Service men who render life endurable, as you would realize if you saw the procession of carriages that pass through the place, the procession of people on foot who try to get into the place, not to speak of the multitude of cranks and others who are stopped in the village.

Roosevelt, who had succeeded to the presidency because of an assassin's bullet, himself became the object of an assassination attempt a few years after he left office and when he was no longer under Secret Service protection. During the presidential campaign of 1900, just as he was about to make a political speech in Milwaukee on October 14, he was shot and wounded in the breast by John N.

Schrank, a 36-year-old German-born ex-tavern keeper. A folded manuscript of his long speech and the metal case for his eyeglasses in the breast pocket of Roosevelt's coat were all that prevented the assassination.

Schrank had a vision in 1901, induced possibly by McKinley's assassination, which took on meaning for him after Roosevelt, 11 years later, started to campaign for the presidency. In this vision the ghost of McKinley appeared to him and told him not to let a murderer (i.e. Roosevelt, who according to the vision had murdered McKinley) become president. It was then that he determined upon the assassination. At the bidding of McKinley's ghost, he felt he had no choice but to kill Theodore Roosevelt. After his attempt on Roosevelt, Schrank was found to be insane and was committed to mental hospitals in Wisconsin for the rest of his life.

The establishment and extension of the Secret Service authority for protection was a prolonged process. Although the Secret Service undertook to provide full-time protection for the president beginning in 1902, it received neither funds for the purpose nor sanction from the Congress until 1906 when the Sundry Civil Expenses Act for 1907 included funds for protection of the president by the Secret Service. Following the election of William Howard Taft in 1908, the Secret Service began providing protection for the president-elect. This practice received statutory authorization in 1913, and in the same year, Congress authorized permanent protection of the president. It remained necessary to renew the authority annually in the Appropriations Acts until 1951.

As in the Civil and Spanish-American Wars, the coming of war in 1917 caused increased concern for the safety of the president. Congress enacted a law, since referred to as the threat statute, making it a crime to threaten the president by mail or in any other manner. In 1917 Congress also authorized protection for the president's immediate family by the Secret Service.

As the scope of the presidency expanded during the 20th century, the Secret Service found the problems of protection becoming more numerous. In 1906, for the first time in history, a president traveled outside the United States while in office. When Theodore Roosevelt visited Panama in that year, he was accompanied and protected by Secret Service men. In 1918–19 Woodrow Wilson broadened the precedent of presidential foreign travel when he traveled to Europe with a Secret Service escort of 10 men to attend the Versailles Peace Conference.

The attempt on the life of President-elect Franklin D. Roosevelt in 1933 further demonstrated the broad scope and complexity of the protection problems facing the Secret Service. Giuseppe Zangara was a bricklayer and stonemason with a professed hatred of capitalists and presidents. He seemed to be obsessed with the desire to kill a president. After his arrest he confessed that he had first planned to go to Washington to kill President Herbert Hoover, but as the cold climate of the North was bad for his stomach trouble, he was loath to leave Miami, where he was staying. When he read in the paper that President-elect Roosevelt would be in Miami, he resolved to kill him.

On the night of February 15, 1933, at, a political rally in Miami's Bayfront Park, the president-elect sat on the top of the rear seat of his automobile with a small microphone in his hand as he made a short informal talk. Fortunately for him, however, he slid down into the seat just before Zangara could get near enough to take aim. The assassin's arm may have been jogged just as he shot; the five rounds he directed at Roosevelt went awry. However, he mortally wounded Mayor Anton Cermak, of Chicago, and hit four other persons; the president-elect, by a miracle, escaped. Zangara, of course, never had any chance of escaping.

Zangara was electrocuted on March 20, 1933, only 33 days after his attempt on Roosevelt. No evidence of accomplices or conspiracy came to light, but there was some sensational newspaper speculation, wholly undocumented, that Zangara may have been hired by Chicago gangsters to kill Cermak.

The force provided since the Civil War by the Washington Metropolitan Police for the protection of the White House had grown to 54 men by 1922. In that year Congress enacted legislation creating the White House Police Force as a separate organization under the direct control of the president. This force was actually supervised by the president's military aide until 1930, when Congress placed supervision under the Chief of the Secret Service. Although Congress transferred control and supervision of the force to the Secretary of the Treasury in 1962, the Secretary delegated supervision to the Chief of the Secret Service.

The White House detail of the Secret Service grew in size slowly from the original two men assigned in 1902. In 1914 it still numbered only five, but during World War I it was increased to 10 men. Additional men were added when the president traveled. After the war the size of the detail grew until it reached 16 agents and two supervisors by 1939. World War II created new and greater protection problems, especially those arising from the president's trips abroad to the Grand Strategy Conferences in such places as Casablanca, Quebec, Tehran, Cairo, and Yalta. To meet the increased demands, the White House detail was increased to 37 men early in the war.

The volume of mail received by the White House had always been large, but it reached huge proportions under Franklin D. Roosevelt. Presidents had always received threatening letters but never in such quantities. To deal with this growing problem, the Secret Service established in

1940 the Protective Research Section to analyze and make available to those charged with protecting the president, information from White House mail and other sources concerning people potentially capable of violence to the president. The Protective Research Section undoubtedly permitted the Secret Service to anticipate and forestall many incidents that might have been embarrassing or harmful to the president.

Although there was no advance warning of the attempt on Harry S. Truman's life on November 1, 1950, the protective measures taken by the Secret Service availed, and the assassins never succeeded in firing directly at the president. The assassins, Oscar Collazo and Griselio Torresola, Puerto Rican Nationalists living in New York, tried to force their way into Blair House, at the time the president's residence while the White House was being repaired. Blair House was guarded by White House policemen and Secret Service agents. In the ensuing gun battle, Torresola and one White House policeman were killed, and Collazo and two White House policemen were wounded. Had the assassins succeeded in entering the front door of Blair House, they would probably have been cut down immediately by another Secret Service agent inside, who kept the doorway covered with a submachine gun from his vantage point at the foot of the main stairs. In all, some 27 shots were fired in less than three minutes.

Collazo was brought to trial in 1951 and sentenced to death, but President Truman commuted the sentence to life imprisonment on July 24, 1952. Although there was a great deal of evidence linking Collazo and Torresola to the Nationalist Party of Puerto Rico and its leader, Pedro Albizu Campos, the Government could not establish that the attack on the president was part of a larger Nationalist conspiracy.

The attack on President Truman led to the enactment in 1951 of legislation that permanently authorized the Secret Service to protect the president, his immediate family, the president-elect, and the vice president, the last upon his request. Protection of the vice president by the Secret Service had begun in January 1945 when Harry S. Truman occupied the office.

In 1962 Congress further enlarged the list of Government officers to be safeguarded, authorizing protection of the vice president (or the officer next in order of succession to the presidency) without requiring his request therefor; of the vice president-elect; and of a former president, at his request, for a reasonable period after his departure from office. The Secret Service considered this "reasonable period" to be six months.

Amendments to the threat statute of 1917, passed in 1955 and 1962, made it a crime to threaten to harm the president-elect, the vice president or other officers next in succession to either office. The president's immediate family was not included in the threat statute.

Congressional concern regarding the uses to which the president might put the Secret Service, first under Theodore Roosevelt and subsequently under Woodrow Wilson, caused Congress to place tight restrictions on the functions of the Service and the uses of its funds. The restrictions probably prevented the Secret Service from developing into a general investigative agency, leaving the field open for some other agency when the need arose. The other agency proved to be the Federal Bureau of Investigation (FBI), established within the Department of Justice in 1908.

The FBI grew rapidly in the 1920s, and especially in the 1930s and after, establishing itself as the largest, best equipped, and best known of all US Government investigative agencies. In the appropriations of the FBI there recurred annually an item for the "protection of the person of the President of the United States," that had first appeared in the appropriation of the Department of Justice in 1910 under the heading "Miscellaneous Objects." But there is no evidence that the Justice Department ever exercised any direct responsibility for the protection of the president. Although it had no prescribed protection functions, according to its director, J. Edgar Hoover, the FBI did provide protection to Vice President Charles Curtis at his request, when he was serving under Herbert Hoover from 1929 to 1933. Over the years the FBI contribution to presidential protection was confined chiefly to the referral to the Secret Service of the names of people who might be potentially dangerous to the president.

In recent years the Secret Service has remained a small and specialized bureau, restricted to very limited functions prescribed by Congress. In 1949, a task force of the Commission on Organization of the Executive Branch of the Government (Hoover Commission) recommended non-fiscal functions be removed from the Treasury Department. The recommendation called for transfer of the White House detail, White House Police Force, and Treasury Guard Force from the Secret Service to the Department of Justice. The final report of the Commission on the Treasury Department omitted this recommendation, leaving the protective function with the Secret Service. At a meeting of the commission, ex-President Hoover, in a reference to the proposed transfer, expressed the opinion that "the President will object to having a 'private eye' looking after these fellows and would rather continue with the service."

In 1963 the Secret Service was one of several investigative agencies in the Treasury Department. Its major functions were to combat counterfeiting and to protect the president, his family, and other designated persons. The

Chief of the Secret Service administered its activities through four divisions: Investigation, Inspection, Administrative and Security, and 65 field offices throughout the country, each under a special agent in charge who reported directly to Washington. The Security Division supervised the White House detail, the White House Police, and the Treasury Guard Force. During fiscal year 1963 (July 1, 1962–June 30, 1963) the Secret Service had an average strength of 513, of whom 351 were special agents. Average strength of the White House Police during the year was 179.

[*Editor's note: since 1964 there was an unsuccessful assassination attempt on President Ronald Reagan on March 10, 1981.*]

A SUMMARY OF THE REPORT

The assassination of John Fitzgerald Kennedy on November 22, 1963, was a cruel and shocking act of violence directed against a man, a family, a nation, and against all mankind. A young and vigorous leader, whose years of public and private life stretched before him, was the victim of the fourth presidential assassination in the history of a country dedicated to the concepts of reasoned argument and peaceful political change. This Commission was created on November 29, 1963, in recognition of the right of people everywhere to full and truthful knowledge concerning these events. This report endeavors to fulfill that right and to appraise this tragedy by the light of reason and the standard of fairness. It has been prepared with a deep awareness of the Commission's responsibility to present to the American people an objective report of the facts relating to the assassination.

NARRATIVE OF EVENTS

At 11.40 am, CST [Central Standard Time] on Friday, November 22, 1963, President John F. Kennedy, Mrs Kennedy, and their party arrived at Love Field, Dallas, Texas. Behind them was the first day of a Texas trip planned five months before by the president, Vice President Lyndon B. Johnson, and John B. Connally, Jr, Governor of Texas. After leaving the White House on Thursday morning, the president had flown initially to San Antonio where Vice President Lyndon B. Johnson joined the party and the president dedicated new research facilities at the US Air Force School of Aerospace Medicine. Following a testimonial dinner in Houston for US Representative Albert Thomas, the president flew to Fort Worth where he spent the night and spoke at a large breakfast gathering on Friday.

Planned for later that day were a motorcade through downtown Dallas, a luncheon speech at the Trade Mart, and a flight to Austin where the president would attend a reception and speak at a Democratic fundraising dinner. From Austin he would proceed to the Texas ranch of the vice president. Evident on this trip were the varied roles which an American president performs: Head of State, Chief Executive, party leader, and, in this instance, prospective candidate for re-election.

The Dallas motorcade, it was hoped, would evoke a demonstration of the president's personal popularity in a city which he had lost in the 1960 election. Once it had been decided that the trip to Texas would span two days, those responsible for planning, primarily Governor Connally and Kenneth O'Donnell, a special assistant to the president, agreed that a motorcade through Dallas would be desirable. The Secret Service was told on November 8 that 45 minutes had been allotted to a motorcade procession from Love Field to the site of a luncheon planned by Dallas business and civic leaders in honor of the president. After considering the facilities and security problems of several buildings, the Trade Mart was chosen as the luncheon site. Given this selection, and in accordance with the customary practice of affording the greatest number of people an opportunity to see the president, the motorcade route selected was a natural one. The route was approved by the local host committee and White House representatives on November 18 and publicized in the local papers, starting on November 19. This advance publicity made it clear that the motorcade would leave Main Street and pass the intersection of Elm and Houston streets as it proceeded to the Trade Mart by way of the Stemmons Freeway.

By mid-morning of November 22, clearing skies in Dallas dispelled the threat of rain and the president greeted the crowds from his open limousine without the "bubble top", which was at that time a plastic shield furnishing protection only against inclement weather. To the left of the president in the rear seat was Mrs Kennedy. In the jump seats [collapsible seats] were Governor Connally, who was in front of the president, and Mrs Connally at the governor's left. Agent William R. Greer of the Secret Service was driving, and Agent Roy H. Kellerman was sitting to his right.

Directly behind the presidential limousine was an open "follow-up" car with eight Secret Service agents, two in the front seat, two in the rear, and two on each running board. These agents, in accordance with normal Secret Service procedures, were instructed to scan the crowds, the roofs, and windows of buildings, overpasses, and crossings for signs of trouble. Behind the "follow-up" car was the vice presidential car carrying the vice president and Mrs Johnson and Senator Ralph W. Yarborough. Next were a vice presidential "follow-up" car and several cars and buses for additional dignitaries, press representatives, and others.

The motorcade left Love Field shortly after 11.50 am, and proceeded through residential neighborhoods, stopping twice at the president's request to greet well-wishers among the friendly crowds. Each time the president's car halted, Secret Service agents from the "follow-up" car moved forward to assume a protective stance near the president and Mrs Kennedy. As the motorcade reached Main Street, a principal east-west artery in downtown Dallas, the welcome became tumultuous. At the extreme west end of Main Street the motorcade turned right on Houston Street and proceeded north for one block in order to make a left turn on Elm Street, the most direct and convenient approach to the Stemmons Freeway and the Trade Mart. As the president's car approached the intersection of Houston and Elm streets, there loomed directly ahead on the intersection's northwest corner a seven-story, orange brick warehouse and office building, the Texas School Book Depository. Riding in the vice president's car, Agent Rufus W. Youngblood of the Secret Service noticed that the clock atop the building indicated 12.30 pm, the scheduled arrival time at the Trade Mart.

The president's car, which had been going north, made a sharp turn toward the southwest onto Elm Street. At a speed of about 11 miles per hour, it started down the gradual descent toward a railroad overpass under which the motorcade would proceed before reaching the Stemmons Freeway. The front of the Texas School Book Depository was now on the president's right, and he waved to the crowd assembled there as he passed the building. Dealey Plaza – an open, landscaped area marking the western end of downtown Dallas – stretched out to the president's left. A Secret Service agent riding in the motorcade radioed the Trade Mart that the president would arrive in 5 minutes.

Seconds later shots resounded in rapid succession. The president's hands moved to his neck. He appeared to stiffen momentarily and lurch slightly forward in his seat. A bullet had entered the base of the back of his neck slightly to the right of the spine. It traveled downward and exited from the front of the neck, causing a nick in the left lower portion of the knot in the president's necktie. Before the shooting started, Governor Connally had been facing toward the crowd on the right. He started to turn toward the left and suddenly felt a blow on his back. The governor had been hit by a bullet which entered at the extreme right side of his back at a point below his right armpit. The bullet traveled through his chest in a downward and forward direction, exited below his right nipple, passed through his right wrist which had been in his lap, and then caused a wound to his left thigh. The force of the bullet's impact appeared to spin the governor to his right, and Mrs Connally pulled him down into her lap. Another bullet then struck President Kennedy in the rear portion of his head, causing a massive and fatal wound. The president fell to the left into Mrs Kennedy's lap.

Secret Service Agent Clinton J. Hill, riding on the left running board of the "follow-up" car, heard a noise which sounded like a firecracker and saw the president suddenly lean forward and to the left. Hill jumped off the car and raced toward the president's limousine. In the front seat of the vice presidential car, Agent Youngblood heard an explosion and noticed unusual movements in the crowd. He vaulted into the rear seat and sat on the vice president in order to protect him. At the same time Agent Kellerman in the front seat of the presidential limousine turned to observe the president. Seeing that the president was struck, Kellerman instructed the driver, "Let's get out of here; we are hit." He radioed ahead to the lead car, "Get us to the hospital immediately." Agent Greer immediately accelerated the presidential car. As it gained speed, Agent Hill managed to pull himself onto the back of the car where Mrs Kennedy had climbed. Hill pushed her back into the rear seat and shielded the stricken president and Mrs Kennedy as the president's car proceeded at high speed to Parkland Memorial Hospital, 4 miles away.

At Parkland, the president was immediately treated by a team of physicians who had been alerted for the president's arrival by the Dallas Police Department, as the result of a radio message from the motorcade after the shooting. The doctors noted irregular breathing movements and a possible heartbeat, although they could not detect a pulse beat. They observed the extensive wound in the president's head and a small wound approximately one-quarter inch in diameter in the lower third of his neck. In an effort to facilitate breathing, the physicians performed a tracheotomy by enlarging the throat wound and inserting a tube. Totally absorbed in the immediate task of trying to preserve the president's life, the attending doctors never turned the president over for an examination of his back. At 1 pm, after all heart activity ceased and the Last Rites were administered by a priest, President Kennedy was pronounced dead. Governor Connally underwent surgery and ultimately recovered from his serious wounds.

Upon learning of the president's death, Vice President Johnson left Parkland Hospital under close guard and proceeded to the presidential plane at Love Field. Mrs Kennedy, accompanying her husband's body, boarded the plane shortly thereafter. At 2.38 pm, in the central compartment of the plane, Lyndon B. Johnson was sworn in as the 36th president of the United States by Federal District Court Judge Sarah T. Hughes. The plane left immediately for Washington, DC, arriving at Andrews AFB [Air Force Base], Maryland, at 5.58 pm, EST [Eastern Standard Time]. The president's body was taken to the National Naval

Medical Center, Bethesda, Maryland, where it was given a complete pathological examination. The autopsy disclosed the large head wound observed at Parkland and the wound in the front of the neck which had been enlarged by the Parkland doctors when they performed the tracheotomy. Both of these wounds were described in the autopsy report as being "presumably of exit". In addition the autopsy revealed a small wound of entry in the rear of the president's skull and another wound of entry near the base of the back of the neck. The autopsy report stated the cause of death as "Gunshot wound, head" and the bullets which struck the president were described as having been fired "from a point behind and somewhat above the level of the deceased."

At the scene of the shooting, there was evident confusion at the outset concerning the point of origin of the shots. Witnesses differed in their accounts of the direction from which the sound of the shots emanated. Within a few minutes, however, attention centered on the Texas School Book Depository Building as the source of the shots. The building was occupied by a private corporation, the Texas School Book Depository Co., which distributed school textbooks of several publishers and leased space to representatives of the publishers. Most of the employees in the building worked for these publishers. The balance, including a 15-man warehousing crew, were employees of the Texas School Book Depository Co. itself.

Several eyewitnesses in front of the building reported that they saw a rifle being fired from the southeast corner window on the sixth floor of the Texas School Book Depository. One eyewitness, Howard L. Brennan, had been watching the parade from a point on Elm Street directly opposite and facing the building. He promptly told a policeman that he had seen a slender man, about 5 feet 10 inches, in his early thirties, take deliberate aim from the sixth-floor corner window and fire a rifle in the direction of the president's car. Brennan thought he might be able to identify the man since he had noticed him in the window a few minutes before the motorcade made the turn onto Elm Street. At 12.34 pm, the Dallas police radio mentioned the Depository Building as a possible source of the shots, and at 12.45 pm, the police radio broadcast a description of the suspected assassin based primarily on Brennan's observations.

When the shots were fired, a Dallas motorcycle patrolman, Marrion L. Baker, was riding in the motorcade at a point several cars behind the president. He had turned right from Main Street onto Houston Street and was about 200 feet south of Elm Street when he heard a shot. Baker, having recently returned from a week of deer hunting, was certain the shot came from a high-powered rifle. He looked up and saw pigeons scattering in the air from their perches on the Texas School Book Depository Building. He raced his motorcycle to the building, dismounted, scanned the area to the west and pushed his way through the spectators toward the entrance. There he encountered Roy Truly, the building superintendent, who offered Baker his help. They entered the building, and ran toward the two elevators in the rear. Finding that both elevators were on an upper floor, they dashed up the stairs. Not more than 2 minutes had elapsed since the shooting.

When they reached the second floor landing on their way up to the top of the building, Patrolman Baker thought he caught a glimpse of someone through the small glass window in the door separating the hall area near the stairs from the small vestibule leading into the lunchroom. Gun in hand, he rushed to the door and saw a man about 20 feet away walking toward the other end of the lunchroom. The man was empty-handed. At Baker's command, the man turned and approached him. Truly, who had started up the stairs to the third floor ahead of Baker, returned to see what had delayed the patrolman. Baker asked Truly whether he knew the man in the lunchroom. Truly replied that the man worked in the building, whereupon Baker turned from the man and proceeded, with Truly, up the stairs. The man they encountered had started working in the Texas School Book Depository Building on October 16, 1963. His fellow workers described him as a very quiet "loner." His name was Lee Harvey Oswald.

Within about 1 minute after his encounter with Baker and Truly, Oswald was seen passing through the second-floor offices. In his hand was a full Coke bottle which he had purchased from a vending machine in the lunchroom. He was walking toward the front of the building where a passenger elevator and a short flight of stairs provided access to the main entrance of the building on the first floor. Approximately 7 minutes later, at about 12.40 pm, Oswald boarded a bus at a point on Elm Street seven short blocks east of the Depository Building. The bus was traveling west toward the very building from which Oswald had come. Its route lay through the Oak Cliff section in southwest Dallas, where it would pass seven blocks east of the rooming house in which Oswald was living, at 1026 North Beckley Avenue. On the bus was Mrs Mary Bledsoe, one of Oswald's former landladies, who immediately recognized him. Oswald stayed on the bus approximately 3 or 4 minutes, during which time it proceeded only two blocks because of the traffic jam created by the motorcade and the assassination. Oswald then left the bus.

A few minutes later he entered a vacant taxi four blocks away and asked the driver to take him to a point on North Beckley Avenue several blocks beyond his rooming house. The trip required 5 or 6 minutes. At about 1 pm Oswald arrived at the rooming house. The housekeeper, Mrs Earlene Roberts, was surprised to see Oswald at midday and remarked to him that he seemed to be in quite a hurry. He made no reply. A few minutes later Oswald emerged from his room zipping up his jacket and rushed out of the house.

Approximately 14 minutes later, and just 45 minutes after the assassination, another violent shooting occurred in Dallas. The victim was Patrolman J. D. Tippit of the Dallas police, an officer with a good record during his more than 11 years with the police force. He was shot near the intersection of 10th Street and Patton Avenue, about nine-tenths of a mile from Oswald's rooming house. At the time of the assassination, Tippit was alone in his patrol car, the routine practice for most police patrol officers at this time of day. He had been ordered by radio at 12.45 pm to proceed to the central Oak Cliff area as part of a concentration of patrol car activity around the center of the city following the assassination. At 12.54 Tippit radioed that he had moved as directed and would be available for any emergency. By this time the police radio had broadcast several messages alerting the police to the suspect described by Brennan at the scene of the assassination – slender white male, about 30 years old, 5 feet 10 inches and weighing about 165 pounds.

At approximately 1.15 pm, Tippit was driving slowly in an easterly direction on East 10th Street in Oak Cliff. About 100 feet past the intersection of 10th Street and Patton Avenue, Tippit pulled up alongside a man walking in the same direction. The man met the general description of the suspect wanted in connection with the assassination. He walked over to Tippit's car, rested his arms on the door on the right-hand side of the car, and apparently exchanged words with Tippit through the window. Tippit opened the door on the left side and started to walk around the front of his car. As he reached the front wheel on the driver's side, the man on the sidewalk drew a revolver and fired several shots in rapid succession, hitting Tippit four times and killing him instantly. An automobile repairman, Domingo Benavides, heard the shots and stopped his pickup truck on the opposite side of the street about 25 feet in front of Tippit's car. He observed the gunman start back toward Patton Avenue, removing the empty cartridge cases from the gun as he went. Benavides rushed to Tippit's side. The patrolman, apparently dead, was lying on his revolver, which was out of its holster. Benavides promptly reported the shooting to police headquarters over the radio in Tippit's car. The message was received shortly after 1.16 pm.

As the gunman left the scene, he walked hurriedly back toward Patton Avenue and turned left, heading south. Standing on the northwest corner of 10th Street and Patton Avenue was Helen Markham, who had been walking south on Patton Avenue and had seen both the killer and Tippit cross the intersection in front of her as she waited on the curb for traffic to pass. She witnessed the shooting and then saw the man with a gun in his hand walk back toward the corner and cut across the lawn of the corner house as he started south on Patton Avenue.

In the corner house itself, Mrs Barbara Jeanette Davis and her sister-in-law, Mrs Virginia Davis, heard the shots and rushed to the door in time to see the man walk rapidly across the lawn shaking a revolver as if he were emptying it of cartridge cases. Later that day each woman found a cartridge case near the home. As the gunman turned the corner he passed alongside a taxicab which was parked on Patton Avenue, a few feet from 10th Street. The driver, William W. Scoggins, had seen the slaying and was now crouched behind his cab on the street side. As the gunman cut through the shrubbery on the lawn, Scoggins looked up and saw the man approximately 12 feet away. In his hand was a pistol and he muttered words which sounded to Scoggins like "poor dumb cop" or "poor damn cop."

After passing Scoggins, the gunman crossed to the west side of Patton Avenue and ran south toward Jefferson Boulevard, a main Oak Cliff thoroughfare. On the east side of Patton, between 10th Street and Jefferson Boulevard, Ted Callaway, a used car salesman, heard the shots and ran to the sidewalk. As the man with the gun rushed past, Callaway shouted "What's going on?" The man merely shrugged, ran on to Jefferson Boulevard and turned right. On the next corner was a gas station with a parking lot in the rear. The assailant ran into the lot, discarded his jacket and then continued his flight west on Jefferson.

In a shoe store a few blocks farther west on Jefferson, the manager, Johnny Calvin Brewer, heard the siren of a police car moments after the radio in his store announced the shooting of the police officer in Oak Cliff. Brewer saw a man step quickly into the entranceway of the store and stand there with his back toward the street. When the police car made a U-turn and headed back in the direction of the Tippit shooting, the man left and Brewer followed him. He saw the man enter the Texas Theater, a motion picture house about 60 feet away, without buying a ticket. Brewer pointed this out to the cashier, Mrs Julia Postal, who called the police. The time was shortly after 1.40 pm.

At 1.29 pm, the police radio had noted the similarity in the descriptions of the suspects in the Tippit shooting and the assassination. At 1.45 pm, in response to Mrs Postal's call, the police radio sounded the alarm: "Have information a suspect just went in the Texas Theater on West Jefferson." Within minutes the theater was surrounded. The house lights were then turned up. Patrolman M. N. McDonald and several other policemen approached the man, who had been pointed out to them by Brewer.

McDonald ordered the man to his feet and heard him say, "Well, it's all over now." The man drew a gun from his waist with one hand and struck the officer with the other.

McDonald struck out with his right hand and grabbed the gun with his left hand. After a brief struggle McDonald and several other police officers disarmed and handcuffed the suspect and drove him to police headquarters, arriving at approximately 2 pm. Following the assassination, police cars had rushed to the Texas School Book Depository in response to the many radio messages reporting that the shots had been fired from the Depository Building. Inspector J. Herbert Sawyer of the Dallas Police Department arrived at the scene shortly after hearing the first of these police radio messages at 12.34 pm. Some of the officers who had been assigned to the area of Elm and Houston streets for the motorcade were talking to witnesses and watching the building when Sawyer arrived. Sawyer entered the building and rode a passenger elevator to the fourth floor, which was the top floor for this elevator. He conducted a quick search, returned to the main floor and, between approximately 12.37 and 12.40 pm, ordered that no one be permitted to leave the building.

Shortly before 1 pm Captain J. Will Fritz, chief of the homicide and robbery bureau of the Dallas Police Department, arrived to take charge of the investigation. Searching the sixth floor, Deputy Sheriff Luke Mooney noticed a pile of cartons in the southeast corner. He squeezed through the boxes and realized immediately that he had discovered the point from which the shots had been fired. On the floor were three empty cartridge cases. A carton had apparently been placed on the floor at the side of the window so that a person sitting on the carton could look down Elm Street toward the overpass and scarcely be noticed from the outside. Between this carton and the half open window were three additional cartons arranged at such an angle that a rifle resting on the top carton would be aimed directly at the motorcade as it moved away from the building. The high stack of boxes, which first attracted

Mooney's attention, effectively screened a person at the window from the view of anyone else on the floor.

Mooney's discovery intensified the search for additional evidence on the sixth floor, and at 1.22 pm, approximately 10 minutes after the cartridge cases were found, Deputy Sheriff Eugene Boone turned his flashlight in the direction of two rows of boxes in the northwest corner near the staircase. Stuffed between the two rows was a bolt action rifle with a telescopic sight. The rifle was not touched until it could be photographed. When Lieutenant J. C. Day of the police identification bureau decided that the wooden stock and the metal knob at the end of the bolt contained no prints, he held the rifle by the stock while Captain Fritz ejected a live shell by operating the bolt. Lieutenant Day promptly noted that stamped on the rifle itself was the serial number "C2766" as well as the markings "1940", "MADE ITALY" and "CAL. 6.5." The rifle was about 40 inches long and when disassembled it could fit into a handmade paper sack which, after the assassination, was found in the southeast corner of the building within a few feet of the cartridge cases.

As Fritz and Day were completing their examination of this rifle on the sixth floor, Roy Truly, the building superintendent, approached with information which he felt should be brought to the attention of the police. Earlier, while the police were questioning the employees, Truly had observed that Lee Harvey Oswald, one of the 15 men who worked in the warehouse, was missing. After Truly provided Oswald's name, address, and general description, Fritz left for police headquarters. He arrived at headquarters shortly after 2 pm and asked two detectives to pick up the employee who was missing from the Texas School Book Depository. Standing nearby were the police officers who had just arrived with the man arrested in the Texas Theater. When Fritz mentioned the name of the missing employee, he learned that the man was already in the interrogation room. The missing School Book Depository employee and the suspect who had been apprehended in the Texas Theater were one and the same Lee Harvey Oswald.

The suspect Fritz was about to question in connection with the assassination of the president and the murder of a policeman was born in New Orleans on October 18, 1939, two months after the death of his father. His mother, Marguerite Claverie Oswald, had two older children. One, John Pic, was a half brother to Lee from an earlier marriage which had ended in divorce. The other was Robert Oswald, a full brother to Lee and five years older. When Lee Oswald was three, Mrs Oswald placed him in an orphanage where his brother and half brother were already living, primarily because she had to work.

In January 1944, when Lee was four, he was taken out of the orphanage, and shortly thereafter his mother moved with him to Dallas, Texas, where the older boys joined them at the end of the school year. In May of 1945 Marguerite Oswald married her third husband, Edwin A. Ekdahl. While the two older boys attended a military boarding school, Lee lived at home and developed a warm attachment to Ekdahl, occasionally accompanying his mother and stepfather on business trips around the country. Lee started school in Benbrook, Texas, but in the fall of 1946, after a separation from Ekdahl, Marguerite Oswald re-entered Lee in the first grade in Covington, Louisiana. In January 1947, while Lee was still in the first grade, the family moved to Fort Worth, Texas, as the result of an attempted reconciliation between Ekdahl and Lee's mother. A year and a half later, before Lee was nine, his mother was divorced from her third husband as the result of a divorce action instituted by Ekdahl. Lee's school record during the next five and a half years in Fort Worth was average, although generally it grew poorer each year. The comments of teachers and others who knew him at that time do not reveal any unusual personality traits or characteristics.

Another change for Lee Oswald occurred in August 1952, a few months after he completed the sixth grade. Marguerite Oswald and her 12-year-old son moved to New York City where Marguerite's oldest son, John Pic, was stationed with the Coast Guard. The ensuing year and a half in New York was marked by Lee's refusals to attend school and by emotional and psychological problems of a seemingly serious nature. Because he had become a chronic school truant, Lee underwent psychiatric study at Youth House, an institution in New York for juveniles who have had truancy problems or difficulties with the law, and who appear to require psychiatric observation, or other types of guidance. The social worker assigned to his case described him as "seriously detached" and "withdrawn" and noted "a rather pleasant, appealing quality about this emotionally starved, affectionless youngster." Lee expressed the feeling to the social worker that his mother did not care for him and regarded him as a burden. He experienced fantasies about being all-powerful and hurting people, but during his stay at Youth House his behavior was apparently not a problem. He appeared withdrawn and evasive, a boy who preferred to spend his time alone, reading and watching television. His tests indicated that he was above average in intelligence for his age group. The chief psychiatrist of Youth House diagnosed Lee's problem as a "personality pattern disturbance with schizoid features and passive aggressive tendencies." He concluded that the boy was "an emotionally, quite disturbed youngster" and recommended psychiatric treatment.

In May 1953, after having been at Youth House for three weeks, Lee Oswald returned to school where his attendance and grades temporarily improved. By the following fall, however, the probation officer reported that virtually every teacher complained about the boy's behavior. His mother insisted that he did not need psychiatric assistance. Although there was apparently some improvement in Lee's behavior during the next few months, the court recommended further treatment. In January 1954, while Lee's case was still pending, Marguerite and Lee left for New Orleans, the city of Lee's birth.

Upon his return to New Orleans, Lee maintained mediocre grades but had no obvious behavior problems. Neighbors and others who knew him outside of school remembered him as a quiet, solitary and introverted boy who read a great deal and whose vocabulary made him quite articulate. About one month after he started the 10th grade and 11 days before his 16th birthday in October 1955, he brought to school a note purportedly written by his mother, stating that the family was moving to California. The note was written by Lee. A few days later he dropped out of school and almost immediately tried to join the Marine Corps. Because he was only 16, he was rejected. After leaving school Lee worked for the next 10 months at several jobs in New Orleans as an office messenger or clerk. It was during this period that he started to read communist literature. Occasionally, in conversations with others, he praised communism and expressed to his fellow employees a desire to join the Communist Party. At about this time, when he was not yet 17, he wrote to the Socialist Party of America, professing his belief in Marxism.

Another move followed in July 1956 when Lee and his mother returned to Fort Worth. He re-entered high school but again dropped out after a few weeks and enlisted in the Marine Corps on October 1956, six days after his 17th birthday. On December 21, 1956, during boot camp in San Diego, Oswald fired a score of 212 for record with the M-1 rifle – two points over the minimum for a rating of "sharpshooter" on a marksman/sharpshooter/expert scale. After his basic training, Oswald received training in aviation fundamentals and then in radar scanning.

Most people who knew Oswald in the Marines described him as a "loner" who resented the exercise of authority by others. He spent much of his free time reading. He was court-martialed once for possessing an unregistered privately owned weapon and, on another occasion, for using provocative language to a non-commissioned officer. He was, however, generally able to comply with Marine discipline. Even though his experiences in the Marine Corps did not live up to his expectations, Oswald served 15 months overseas until November 1958, most of it in Japan. During his final year in the Marine Corps he was stationed for the most part in Santa Ana, California, where he showed marked interest in the Soviet Union and sometimes expressed politically radical views with dogmatic conviction. Oswald again fired the M-1 rifle for record on May 6, 1959, and this time he shot a score of 191 on a shorter course than before, only one point over the minimum required to be a "marksman". According to one of his fellow marines, Oswald was not particularly interested in his rifle performance, and his unit was not expected to exhibit the usual rifle proficiency. During this period he expressed strong admiration for Fidel Castro and an interest in joining the Cuban army. He tried to impress those around him as an intellectual, but his thinking appeared to some as shallow and rigid.

Oswald's Marine service terminated on September 11, 1959, when at his own request he was released from active service a few months ahead of his scheduled release. He offered as the reason for his release the ill health and economic plight of his mother. He returned to Fort Worth, remained with his mother only three days and left for New Orleans, telling his mother he planned to get work there in the shipping or import-export business. In New Orleans he booked passage on the freighter SS *Marion Lykes*, which sailed from New Orleans to Le Havre, France, on September 20, 1959.

Lee Harvey Oswald had presumably planned this step in his life for quite some time. In March of 1959 he had applied to the Albert Schweitzer College in Switzerland for admission to the Spring 1960 term. His letter of application contained many blatant falsehoods concerning his qualifications and background. A few weeks before his discharge he had applied for and obtained a passport, listing the Soviet Union as one of the countries which he planned to visit. During his service in the Marines he had saved a comparatively large sum of money, possibly as much as $1,500, which would appear to have been accomplished by considerable frugality and apparently for a specific purpose.

The purpose of the accumulated fund soon became known. On October 16, 1959, Oswald arrived in Moscow by train after crossing the border from Finland, where he had secured a visa for a six-day stay in the Soviet Union. He immediately applied for Soviet citizenship. On the afternoon of October 21, 1959, Oswald was ordered to leave the Soviet Union by 8 pm that evening. That same afternoon in his hotel room Oswald, in an apparent suicide attempt, slashed his left wrist. He was hospitalized immediately. On October 31, three days after his release from the hospital, Oswald appeared at the American Embassy, announced that he wished to renounce his US citizenship and become a Russian citizen, and handed the Embassy officer a written statement he had prepared for the occasion. When asked his reasons, Oswald replied, "I am a Marxist". Oswald never formally complied with the legal steps necessary to renounce his American citizenship. The Soviet Government did not grant his request for citizenship, but in January 1960 he was given permission to remain in the Soviet Union on a year-to-year basis. At the same time Oswald was sent to Minsk where he worked in a radio factory as an unskilled laborer. In January 1961 his permission to remain in the Soviet Union was extended for another year. A few weeks later, in February 1961, he wrote to the American Embassy in Moscow expressing a desire to return to the United States.

The following month Oswald met a 19-year-old Russian girl, Marina Nikolaevna Prusakova, a pharmacist, who had been brought up in Leningrad but was then living with an aunt and uncle in Minsk. They were married on April 30, 1961. Throughout the following year he carried on a correspondence with American and Soviet authorities seeking approval for the departure of himself and his wife to the United States. In the course of this effort, Oswald and his wife visited the US Embassy in Moscow in July of 1961. Primarily on the basis of an interview and questionnaire completed there, the embassy concluded that Oswald had not lost his citizenship, a decision subsequently ratified by the Department of State in Washington, DC. Upon their return to Minsk, Oswald and his wife filed with the Soviet authorities for permission to leave together. Their formal application was made in July 1961, and on December 25, 1961, Marina Oswald was advised it would be granted.

A daughter was born to the Oswalds in February 1962. In the months that followed they prepared for their return to the United States. On May 9, 1962 the US Immigration and Naturalization Service, at the request of the Department of State, agreed to waive a restriction under the law which would have prevented the issuance of a United States visa to Oswald's Russian wife until she had left the Soviet Union. They finally left Moscow on June 1, 1962, and were assisted in meeting their travel expenses by a loan of $435.71 from the US Department of State. Two weeks later they arrived in Fort Worth, Texas.

For a few weeks Oswald, his wife and child lived with Oswald's brother Robert. After a similar stay with Oswald's mother, they moved into their own apartment in early August. Oswald obtained a job on July 16 as a sheet metal worker. During this period in Fort Worth, Oswald was interviewed twice by agents of the FBI. The report of the first interview, which occurred on June 26, described him as arrogant and unwilling to discuss the reasons why he had gone to the Soviet Union. Oswald denied that he was involved in Soviet intelligence activities and promised to advise the FBI if Soviet representatives ever communicated with him. He was interviewed again on August 16, when he displayed a less belligerent attitude and once again agreed to inform the FBI of any attempt to enlist him in intelligence activities.

In early October 1962 Oswald quit his job at the sheet metal plant and moved to Dallas. While living in Forth Worth the Oswalds had been introduced to a group of Russian-speaking people in the Dallas Fort Worth area. Many of them assisted the Oswalds by providing small amounts of food, clothing, and household items. Oswald himself was disliked by almost all of this group, whose help to the family was prompted primarily by sympathy for Marina Oswald and the child. Despite the fact that he had left the Soviet Union, disillusioned with its government, Oswald seemed more firmly committed than ever to his concepts of Marxism. He showed disdain for democracy, capitalism, and American society in general. He was highly critical of the Russian-speaking group because they seemed devoted to American concepts of democracy and capitalism and were ambitious to improve themselves economically.

In February 1963 the Oswalds met Ruth Paine at a social gathering. Ruth Paine was temporarily separated from her husband and living with her two children in their home in Irving, Texas, a suburb of Dallas. Because of an interest in the Russian language and sympathy for Marina Oswald, who spoke no English and had little funds, Ruth Paine befriended Marina and, during the next two months, visited her on several occasions.

On April 6, 1963, Oswald lost his job with a photography firm. A few days later, on April 10, he attempted to kill Major General Edwin A. Walker (Resigned, US Army), using a rifle which he had ordered by mail one month previously under an assumed name. Marina Oswald learned of her husband's act when she confronted him with a note which he had left, giving her instructions in the event he did not return. That incident, and their general economic difficulties, impelled Marina Oswald to suggest that her husband leave Dallas and go to New Orleans to look for work.

Oswald left for New Orleans on April 24, 1963. Ruth Paine, who knew nothing of the Walker shooting, invited Marina Oswald and the baby to stay with her in the Paines' modest home while Oswald sought work in New Orleans. Early in May, upon receiving word from Oswald that he had found a job, Ruth Paine drove Marina Oswald and the baby to New Orleans to rejoin Oswald.

During the stay in New Orleans, Oswald formed a fictitious New Orleans Chapter of the Fair Play for Cuba Committee. He posed as secretary of this organization and represented that the president was A. J. Hidell. In reality, Hidell was a completely fictitious person created by Oswald, the organization's only member. Oswald was arrested on August 9 in connection with a scuffle which occurred while he was distributing pro-Castro leaflets. The next day, while at the police station, he was interviewed by an FBI agent after Oswald requested the police to arrange such an interview. Oswald gave the agent false information about his own background and was evasive in his replies concerning Fair Play for Cuba activities. During the next two weeks Oswald appeared on radio programs twice, claiming to be the spokesman for the Fair Play for Cuba Committee in New Orleans.

On July 19, 1963, Oswald lost his job as a greaser of coffee processing machinery. In September, after an exchange of correspondence with Marina Oswald, Ruth Paine drove to New Orleans and on September 23, transported Marina, the child, and the family belongings to Irving, Texas. Ruth Paine suggested that Marina Oswald, who was expecting her second child in October, live at the Paine house until after the baby was born. Oswald remained behind, ostensibly to find work either in Houston or some other city. Instead, he departed by bus for Mexico, arriving in Mexico City on September 27, where he promptly visited the Cuban and Russian Embassies. His stated objective was to obtain official permission to visit Cuba, on his way to the Soviet Union. The Cuban Government would not grant his visa unless the Soviet Government would also issue a visa permitting his entry into Russia. Oswald's efforts to secure these visas failed, and he left for Dallas, where he arrived on October 3, 1963.

When he saw his wife the next day, it was decided that Oswald would rent a room in Dallas and visit his family on weekends. For one week he rented a room from Mrs Bledsoe, the woman who later saw him on the bus shortly after the assassination. On October 14, 1963, he rented the Beckley Avenue room and listed his name as O. H. Lee. On the same day, at the suggestion of a neighbor, Mrs Paine phoned the Texas School Book Depository and was told that there was a job opening. She informed Oswald who was interviewed the following day at the Depository and started to work there on October 16, 1963.

On October 20 the Oswalds' second daughter was born. During October and November Oswald established a general pattern of weekend visits to Irving, arriving on

Friday afternoon and returning to Dallas Monday morning with a fellow employee, Buell Wesley Frazier, who lived near the Paines. On Friday, November 15, Oswald remained in Dallas at the suggestion of his wife who told him that the house would be crowded because of a birthday party for Ruth Paine's daughter. On Monday, November 18, Oswald and his wife quarreled bitterly during a telephone conversation, because she learned for the first time that he was living at the rooming-house under an assumed name. On Thursday, November 21, Oswald told Frazier that he would like to drive to Irving to pick up some curtain rods for an apartment in Dallas. His wife and Mrs Paine were quite surprised to see him since it was a Thursday night. They thought he had returned to make up after Monday's quarrel. He was conciliatory, but Marina Oswald was still angry.

Later that evening, when Mrs Paine had finished cleaning the kitchen, she went into the garage and noticed that the light was burning. She was certain that she had not left it on, although the incident appeared unimportant at the time. In the garage were most of the Oswalds' personal possessions. The following morning Oswald left while his wife was still in bed feeding the baby. She did not see him leave the house, nor did Ruth Paine. On the dresser in their room he left his wedding ring which he had never done before. His wallet, containing $170, was left intact in a dresser-drawer.

Oswald walked to Frazier's house about half a block away and placed a long bulky package, made out of wrapping paper and tape, into the rear seat of the car. He told Frazier that the package contained curtain rods. When they reached the Depository parking lot, Oswald walked quickly ahead. Frazier followed and saw Oswald enter the Depository Building carrying the long bulky package with him.

During the morning of November 22, Marina Oswald followed President Kennedy's activities on television. She and Ruth Paine cried when they heard that the president had been shot. Ruth Paine translated the news of the shooting to Marina Oswald as it came over the television, including the report that the shots were probably fired from the building where Oswald worked. When Marina Oswald heard this, she recalled the Walker episode and the fact that her husband still owned the rifle. She went quietly to the Paines' garage where the rifle had been concealed in a blanket among their other belongings. It appeared to her that the rifle was still there, although she did not actually open the blanket.

At about 3 pm the police arrived at the Paine house and asked Marina Oswald whether her husband owned a rifle. She said that he did and then led them into the garage and pointed to the rolled up blanket. As a police officer lifted it, the blanket hung limply over either side of his arm. The rifle was not there.

Meanwhile, at police headquarters Captain Fritz had begun questioning Oswald. Soon after the start of the first interrogation, agents of the FBI and the US Secret Service arrived and participated in the questioning. Oswald denied having anything to do with the assassination of President Kennedy or the murder of Patrolman Tippit. He claimed that he was eating lunch at the time of the assassination, and that he then spoke with his foreman for 5 to 10 minutes before going home. He denied that he owned a rifle and when confronted, in a subsequent interview, with a picture showing him holding a rifle and pistol, he claimed that his face had been superimposed on someone else's body. He refused to answer any questions about the presence in his wallet of a Selective Service card [notice of call-up for military service] with his picture and the name "Alek J. Hidell."

During the questioning of Oswald on the third floor of the police department, more than 100 representatives of the press, radio, and television were crowded into the hallway through which Oswald had to pass when being taken from his cell to Captain Fritz' office for interrogation. Reporters tried to interview Oswald during these trips. Between Friday afternoon and Sunday morning he appeared in the hallway at least 16 times. The generally confused conditions outside and inside Captain Fritz' office increased the difficulty of police questioning. Advised by the police that he could communicate with an attorney, Oswald made several telephone calls on Saturday in an effort to procure representation of his own choice and discussed the matter with the president of the local bar association, who offered to obtain counsel. Oswald declined the offer, saying that he would first try to obtain counsel by himself. By Sunday morning he had not engaged an attorney.

At 7.10 pm on November 22, 1963, Lee Harvey Oswald was formally advised that he had been charged with the murder of Patrolman J. D. Tippit. Several witnesses to the Tippit slaying and to the subsequent flight of the gunman had positively identified Oswald in police lineups. While positive firearm identification evidence was not available at the time, the revolver in Oswald's possession at the time of his arrest was of a type which could have fired the shots that killed Tippit.

The formal charge against Oswald for the assassination of President Kennedy was lodged shortly after 1.30 am on Saturday, November 23. By 10 pm of the day of the assassination, the FBI had traced the rifle found on the sixth floor of the Texas School Book Depository to a mail order house in Chicago, which had purchased it from a distributor in New York. Approximately six hours later the Chicago firm advised that this rifle had been ordered in March 1963 by an A. Hidell for shipment to Post Office Box 2915, in Dallas, Texas, a box rented by Oswald. Payment for the rifle was remitted by a money order signed by A. Hidell. By 6.45 pm on November 23, the FBI was able to advise the Dallas police that, as a result of handwriting analysis of the documents used to purchase the rifle, it had concluded that the rifle had been ordered by Lee Harvey Oswald.

Throughout Friday and Saturday, the Dallas police released to the public many of the details concerning the alleged evidence against Oswald. Police officials discussed important aspects of the case, usually in the course of impromptu and confused press conferences in the third-floor corridor. Some of the information divulged was erroneous. Efforts by the news media representatives to reconstruct the crime and promptly report details frequently led to erroneous and often conflicting reports. At the urgings of the newsmen, Chief of Police Jesse E. Curry brought Oswald to a press conference in the police assembly room shortly after midnight of the day Oswald was arrested. The assembly room was crowded with newsmen who had come to Dallas from all over the country. They shouted questions at Oswald and flashed cameras at him. Among this group was a 52-year-old Dallas nightclub operator – Jack Ruby.

On Sunday morning, November 24, arrangements were made for Oswald's transfer from the city jail to the Dallas County jail, about 1 mile away. The news media had been informed on Saturday night that the transfer of Oswald would not take place until after 10 am on Sunday. Earlier on Sunday, between 2.30 and 3 am, anonymous telephone calls threatening Oswald's life had been received by the Dallas office of the FBI and by the office of the county sheriff. Nevertheless, on Sunday morning, television, radio, and newspaper representatives crowded into the basement to record the transfer. As viewed through television cameras, Oswald would emerge from a door in front of the cameras and proceed to the transfer vehicle. To the right of the cameras was a "down" ramp from Main Street on the north. To the left was an "up" ramp leading to Commerce Street on the south.

The armored truck in which Oswald was to be transferred arrived shortly after 11 am. Police officials then decided, however, that an unmarked police car would be preferable for the trip because of its greater speed and maneuverability. At approximately 11.20 am Oswald emerged from the basement jail office flanked by detectives on either side and at his rear. He took a few steps toward the car and was in the glaring light of the television cameras when a man suddenly darted out from an area on the right of the cameras where newsmen had been assembled. The man was carrying a Colt .38 revolver in his right hand and, while millions watched on television, he moved quickly to within a few feet of Oswald and fired one shot into Oswald's abdomen. Oswald groaned with pain as he fell to the ground and quickly lost consciousness. Within 7 minutes Oswald was at Parkland Hospital where, without having regained consciousness, he was pronounced dead at 1.07 pm.

The man who killed Oswald was Jack Ruby. He was instantly arrested and, minutes later, confined in a cell on the fifth floor of the Dallas police jail. Under interrogation, he denied that the killing of Oswald was in any way connected with a conspiracy involving the assassination of President Kennedy. He maintained that he had killed Oswald in a temporary fit of depression and rage over the president's death. Ruby was transferred the following day to the county jail without notice to the press or to police officers not directly involved in the transfer. Indicted for the murder of Oswald by the State of Texas on November 26, 1963, Ruby was found guilty on March 14, 1964, and sentenced to death. As of September 1964, his case was pending on appeal.

CONCLUSIONS

(1) The shots which killed President Kennedy and wounded Governor Connally were fired from the sixth-floor window at the southeast corner of the Texas School Book Depository. This determination is based upon the following:

(a) Witnesses at the scene of the assassination saw a rifle being fired from the sixth-floor window of the Depository Building, and some witnesses saw a rifle in the window immediately after the shots were fired.

(b) The nearly whole bullet found on Governor Connally's stretcher at Parkland Memorial Hospital and the two bullet fragments found in the front seat of the presidential limousine were fired from the 6.5 millimeter Mannlicher Carcano rifle found on the sixth floor of the Depository Building to the exclusion of all other weapons.

(c) The three used cartridge cases found near the window on the sixth floor at the southeast corner of the building were fired from the same rifle which fired the above described bullet and fragments, to the exclusion of all other weapons.

(d) The windshield in the presidential limousine was struck by a bullet fragment on the inside surface of the glass, but was not penetrated.

(e) The nature of the bullet wounds suffered by President Kennedy and Governor Connally and the location of the car at the time of the shots establish that the bullets were fired from above and behind the presidential limousine, striking the president and the governor as follows:

(i) President Kennedy was first struck by a bullet which entered at the back of his neck and exited through the lower front portion of his neck, causing a wound which would not necessarily have been lethal. The president was struck a second time by a bullet which entered the right rear portion of his head, causing a massive and fatal wound.

(ii) Governor Connally was struck by a bullet which entered on the right side of his back and traveled downward through the right side of his chest, exiting below his right nipple. This bullet then passed through his right wrist and entered his left thigh where it caused a superficial wound.

(f) There is no credible evidence that the shots were fired from the Triple Underpass, ahead of the motorcade, or from any other location.

(2) The weight of the evidence indicates that there were three shots fired.

(3) Although it is not necessary to any essential findings of the Commission to determine just which shot hit Governor Connally, there is very persuasive evidence from the experts to indicate that the same bullet which pierced the president's throat also caused Governor Connally's wounds. However, Governor Connally's testimony and certain other factors have given rise to some difference of opinion as to this probability, but there is no question in the mind of any member of the Commission that all the shots which caused the president's and Governor Connally's wounds were fired from the sixth-floor window of the Texas School Book Depository.

(4) The shots which killed President Kennedy and wounded Governor Connally were fired by Lee Harvey Oswald. This conclusion is based upon the following:

(a) The Mannlicher-Carcano 6.5 millimeter Italian rifle from which the shots were fired was owned by and in the possession of Oswald.

(b) Oswald carried this rifle into the Depository Building on the morning of November 22, 1963.

(c) Oswald, at the time of the assassination, was present at the window from which the shots were fired.

(d) Shortly after the assassination, the Mannlicher-Carcano rifle belonging to Oswald was found partially hidden between some cartons on the sixth floor, and the improvised paper bag in which Oswald brought the rifle to the Depository was found close by the window from which the shots were fired.

(e) Based on the testimony of the experts and their analysis of films of the assassination, the Commission has concluded that a rifleman of Lee Harvey Oswald's capabilities could have fired the shots from the rifle used in the assassination within the elapsed time of the shooting. The Commission has concluded further that Oswald possessed the capability with a rifle which enabled him to commit the assassination.

(f) Oswald lied to the police after his arrest concerning important substantive matters.

(g) Oswald had attempted to kill Major General Edwin A. Walker (Resigned, US Army) on April 10, 1963, thereby demonstrating his disposition to take human life.

(5) Oswald killed Dallas Police Patrolman J. D. Tippit approximately 45 minutes after the assassination. This conclusion upholds the finding that Oswald fired the shots which killed President Kennedy and wounded Governor Connally, and is supported by the following:

(a) Two eyewitnesses saw the Tippit shooting and seven eyewitnesses heard the shots and saw the gunman leave the scene with revolver in hand. These nine eyewitnesses positively identified Lee Harvey Oswald as the man they saw.

(b) The cartridge cases found at the scene of the shooting were fired from the revolver in the possession of Oswald at the time of his arrest to the exclusion of all other weapons.

(c) The revolver in Oswald's possession at the time of his arrest was purchased by and belonged to Oswald.

(d) Oswald's jacket was found along the path of flight taken by the gunman as he fled from the scene of the killing.

(6) Within 80 minutes of the assassination and 35 minutes of the Tippit killing, Oswald resisted arrest at the theater by attempting to shoot another Dallas police officer.

(7) The Commission has reached the following conclusions concerning Oswald's interrogation and detention by the Dallas police:

(a) Except for the force required to effect his arrest, Oswald was not subjected to any physical coercion by any law enforcement officials. He was advised that he could not be compelled to give any information and that any statements made by him might be used against him in court. He was advised of his right to counsel. He was given the opportunity to obtain counsel of his own choice and was offered legal assistance by the Dallas Bar Association, which he rejected at that time.

(b) Newspaper, radio, and television reporters were allowed uninhibited access to the area through which Oswald had to pass when he was moved from his cell to the interrogation room and other sections of the building, thereby subjecting Oswald to harassment and creating chaotic conditions which were not conducive to orderly interrogation or the protection of the rights of the prisoner.

(c) The numerous statements, sometimes erroneous, made to the press by various local law enforcement officials during this period of confusion and disorder in the police station, would have presented serious obstacles to the obtaining of a fair trial for Oswald. To the extent that the information was erroneous or misleading, it helped to create doubts, speculations, and fears in the mind of the public which might otherwise not have arisen.

(8) The Commission has reached the following conclusions concerning the killing of Oswald by Jack Ruby on November 24, 1963:

(a) Ruby entered the basement of the Dallas Police Department shortly after 11.17 am and killed Lee Harvey Oswald at 11.21 am.

(b) Although the evidence on Ruby's means of entry is not conclusive, the weight of the evidence indicates that he walked down the ramp leading from Main Street to the basement of the police department.

(c) There is no evidence to support the rumor that Ruby may have been assisted by any members of the Dallas Police Department in the killing of Oswald.

(d) The Dallas Police Department's decision to transfer Oswald to the county jail in full public view was unsound.

(e) The arrangements made by the police department on Sunday morning, only a few hours before the attempted transfer, were inadequate. Of critical importance was the fact that news media representatives and others were not excluded from the basement even after the police were notified of threats to Oswald's life. These deficiencies contributed to the death of Lee Harvey Oswald.

(9) The Commission has found no evidence that either Lee Harvey Oswald or Jack Ruby was part of any conspiracy, domestic or foreign, to assassinate President Kennedy. The reasons for this conclusion are:

(a) The Commission has found no evidence that anyone assisted Oswald in planning or carrying out the assassination. In this connection it has thoroughly investigated, among other factors, the circumstances surrounding the planning of the motorcade route through Dallas, the hiring of Oswald by the Texas School Book Depository Co. on October 15, 1963, the method by which the rifle was brought into the building, the placing of cartons of books at the window, Oswald's escape from the building, and the testimony of eyewitnesses to the shooting.

(b) The Commission has found no evidence that Oswald was involved with any person or group in a conspiracy to assassinate the president, although it has thoroughly investigated, in addition to other possible leads, all facets of Oswald's associations, finances, and personal habits, particularly during the period following his return from the Soviet Union in June 1962.

(c) The Commission has found no evidence to show that Oswald was employed, persuaded, or encouraged by any foreign government to assassinate President Kennedy or that he was an agent of any foreign government, although the Commission has reviewed the circumstances surrounding Oswald's defection to the Soviet Union, his life there from October of 1959 to June of 1962 so far as it can be reconstructed, his known contacts with the Fair Play for Cuba Committee and his visits to the Cuban and Soviet Embassies in Mexico City during his trip to Mexico from September 26 to October 3, 1963, and his known contacts with the Soviet Embassy in the United States.

(d) The Commission has explored all attempts of Oswald to identify himself with various political groups, including the Communist Party, USA, the Fair Play for Cuba Committee, and the Socialist Workers Party, and has been unable to find any evidence that the contacts which he initiated were related to Oswald's subsequent assassination of the president.

(e) All of the evidence before the Commission established that there was nothing to support the speculation that Oswald was an agent, employee, or informant of the FBI, the CIA, or any other governmental agency. It has thoroughly investigated Oswald's relationships prior to the assassination with all agencies of the US Government. All contacts with Oswald by any of these agencies were made in the regular exercise of their different responsibilities.

(f) No direct or indirect relationship between Lee Harvey Oswald and Jack Ruby has been discovered by the Commission, nor has it been able to find any credible evidence that either knew the other, although a thorough investigation was made of the many rumors and speculations of such a relationship.

(g) The Commission has found no evidence that Jack Ruby acted with any other person in the killing of Lee Harvey Oswald.

(h) After careful investigation the Commission has found no credible evidence either that Ruby and Officer Tippit, who was killed by Oswald, knew each other or that Oswald and Tippit knew each other. Because of the difficulty of proving negatives to a certainty, the possibility of others being involved with either Oswald or Ruby cannot be established categorically, but if there is any such evidence it has been beyond the reach of all the investigative agencies and resources of the United States and has not come to the attention of this Commission.

(10) In its entire investigation the Commission has found no evidence of conspiracy, subversion, or disloyalty to the US Government by any Federal, State, or local official.

(11) On the basis of the evidence before the Commission it concludes that Oswald acted alone. Therefore, to determine the motives for the assassination of President Kennedy, one must look to the assassin himself. Clues to Oswald's motives can be found in his family history, his education or lack of it, his acts, his writings, and the recollections of those who had close contacts with him throughout his life. The Commission has presented with this report all of the background information bearing on motivation which it could discover. Thus, others may study Lee Oswald's life and arrive at their own conclusions as to his possible motives. The Commission could not make any definitive determination of Oswald's motives. It has endeavored to isolate factors which contributed to his character and which might have influenced his decision to assassinate President Kennedy. These factors were:

(a) His deep-rooted resentment of all authority which was expressed in a hostility toward every society in which he lived.

(b) His inability to enter into meaningful relationships with people, and a continuous pattern of rejecting his environment in favor of new surroundings.

(c) His urge to try to find a place in history and despair at times over failures in his various undertakings.

(d) His capacity for violence as evidenced by his attempt to kill General Walker.

(e) His avowed commitment to Marxism and communism, as he understood the terms and developed his own interpretation of them; this was expressed by his antagonism toward the United States, by his defection to the Soviet Union, by his failure to be reconciled with life in the United States even after his disenchantment with the Soviet Union, and by his efforts, though frustrated, to go to Cuba. Each of these contributed to his capacity to risk all in cruel and irresponsible actions.

(12) The Commission recognizes that the varied responsibilities of the president require that he make frequent trips to all parts of the United States and abroad. Consistent with their high responsibilities presidents can never be protected from every potential threat. The Secret Service's difficulty in meeting its protective responsibility varies with the activities and the nature of the occupant of the Office of President and his willingness to conform to plans for his safety. In appraising the performance of the Secret Service it should be understood that it has to do its work within such limitations. Nevertheless, the Commission believes that recommendations for improvements in presidential protection are compelled by the facts disclosed here.

(a) The complexities of the presidency have increased so rapidly in recent years that the Secret Service has not been able to develop or to secure adequate resources of personnel and facilities to fulfill its important assignment. This situation should be promptly remedied.

(b) The Commission has concluded that the criteria and procedures of the Secret Service designed to identify and protect against persons considered threats to the president were not adequate prior to the assassination.

   (i) The Protective Research Section of the Secret Service, which is responsible for its preventive work, lacked sufficient trained personnel and the mechanical and technical assistance needed to fulfill its responsibility.

   (ii) Prior to the assassination the Secret Service's criteria dealt with direct threats against the president. Although the Secret Service treated the direct threats against the president adequately, it failed to recognize the necessity of identifying other potential sources of danger to his security. The Secret Service did not develop adequate and specific criteria defining those persons or groups who might present a danger to the president. In effect, the Secret Service largely relied upon other Federal or State agencies to supply the information necessary for it to fulfill its preventive responsibilities, although it did ask for information about direct threats to the president.

(c) The Commission has concluded that there was insufficient liaison and coordination of information between the Secret Service and other Federal agencies necessarily concerned with presidential protection. Although the FBI, in the normal exercise of its responsibility, had secured considerable information about Lee Harvey Oswald, it had no official responsibility, under the Secret Service criteria existing at the time of the president's trip to Dallas, to refer to the Secret Service the information it had about Oswald. The Commission has concluded, however, that the FBI took an unduly restrictive view of its role in preventive intelligence work prior to the assassination. A more carefully coordinated treatment of the Oswald case by the FBI might well have resulted in bringing Oswald's activities to the attention of the Secret Service.

(d) The Commission has concluded that some of the advance preparations in Dallas made by the Secret Service, such as the detailed security measures taken at Love Field and the Trade Mart, were thorough and well executed. In other respects, however, the Commission has concluded that the advance preparations for the president's trip were deficient.

    (i) Although the Secret Service is compelled to rely to a great extent on local law enforcement officials, its procedures at the time of the Dallas trip did not call for well defined instructions as to the respective responsibilities of the police officials and others assisting in the protection of the president.

    (ii) The procedures relied upon by the Secret Service for detecting the presence of an assassin located in a building along a motorcade route were inadequate. At the time of the trip to Dallas, the Secret Service as a matter of practice did not investigate, or cause to be checked, any building located along the motorcade route to be taken by the president. The responsibility for observing windows in these buildings during the motorcade was divided between local police personnel stationed on the streets to regulate crowds and Secret Service agents riding in the motorcade. Based on its investigation the Commission has concluded that these arrangements during the trip to Dallas were clearly not sufficient.

(e) The configuration of the presidential car and the seating arrangements of the Secret Service agents in the car did not afford the Secret Service agents the opportunity they should have had to be of immediate assistance to the president at the first sign of danger.

(f) Within these limitations, however, the Commission finds that the agents most immediately responsible for the president's safety reacted promptly at the time the shots were fired from the Texas School Book Depository Building.

RECOMMENDATIONS

Prompted by the assassination of President Kennedy, the Secret Service has initiated a comprehensive and critical review of its total operations. As a result of studies conducted during the past several months, and in cooperation with this Commission, the Secret Service has prepared a planning document dated August 27, 1964, which recommends various programs considered necessary by the service to improve its techniques and enlarge its resources. The Commission is encouraged by the efforts taken by the Secret Service since the assassination and suggests the following recommendations.

A committee of Cabinet members including the Secretary of the Treasury and the Attorney General, or the National Security Council, should be assigned the responsibility of reviewing and overseeing the protective activities of the Secret Service and the other Federal agencies that assist in safeguarding the president. Once given this responsibility, such a committee would insure that the maximum resources of the Federal Government are fully engaged in the task of protecting the president, and would provide guidance in defining the general nature of domestic and foreign dangers to presidential security.

Suggestions have been advanced to the Commission for the transfer of all or parts of the presidential protective responsibilities of the Secret Service to some other department or agency. The Commission believes that if there is to be any determination of whether or not to relocate these responsibilities and functions, it ought to be made by the Executive and the Congress, perhaps upon recommendations based on studies by the previously suggested committee.

Meanwhile, in order to improve daily supervision of the Secret Service within the Department of the Treasury, the Commission recommends that the Secretary of the Treasury appoint a special assistant with the responsibility of supervising the Secret Service. This special assistant should have sufficient stature and experience in law enforcement, intelligence, and allied fields to provide effective continuing supervision, and to keep the secretary fully informed regarding the performance of the Secret Service. One of the initial assignments of this special assistant should be the supervision of the current effort by the Secret Service to revise and modernize its basic operating procedures.

The Commission recommends that the Secret Service completely overhaul its facilities devoted to the advance detection of potential threats against the president. The Commission suggests the following measures:

(1) The Secret Service should develop as quickly as possible more useful and precise criteria defining those potential threats to the president which should be brought to its attention by other agencies. The criteria should, among other additions, provide for prompt notice to the Secret Service of all returned defectors.

(2) The Secret Service should expedite its current plans to utilize the most efficient data processing techniques.

(3) Once the Secret Service has formulated new criteria delineating the information it desires, it should enter into agreements with each Federal agency to insure its receipt of such information.

(4) The Commission recommends that the Secret Service improve the protective measures followed in the planning and conducting of presidential motorcades. In particular the Secret Service should continue its current efforts to increase the precautionary attention given to buildings along the motorcade route.

(5) The Commission recommends that the Secret Service continue its recent efforts to improve and formalize its relationships with local police departments in areas to be visited by the president.

(6) The Commission believes that when the new criteria and procedures are established, the Secret Service will not have sufficient personnel or adequate facilities. The Commission recommends that the Secret Service be provided with the personnel and resources which the service and the Department of the Treasury may be able to demonstrate are needed to fulfill its important mission.

(7) Even with an increase in Secret Service personnel, the protection of the president will continue to require the resources and cooperation of many Federal agencies. The Commission recommends that these agencies, specifically the FBI, continue the practice as

it has developed, particularly since the assassination, of assisting the Secret Service upon request by providing personnel or other aid, and that there be a closer association and liaison between the Secret Service and all Federal agencies.

(8) The Commission recommends that the president's physician always accompany him during his travels and occupy a position near the president where he can be immediately available in case of any emergency.

(9) The Commission recommends to Congress that it adopt legislation which would make the assassination of the president and vice president a Federal crime. A state of affairs where US authorities have no clearly defined jurisdiction to investigate the assassination of a president is anomalous.

(10) The Commission has examined the Department of State's handling of the Oswald matters and finds that it followed the law throughout. However, the Commission believes that the department, in accordance with its own regulations, should in all cases exercise great care in the return to this country of defectors who have evidenced disloyalty or hostility to this country or who have expressed a desire to renounce their American citizenship and that when such persons are so returned, procedures should be adopted for the better dissemination of information concerning them to the intelligence agencies of the government.

(11) The Commission recommends that the representatives of the bar, law enforcement associations, and the news media work together to establish ethical standards concerning the collection and presentation of information to the public, so that there will be no interference with pending criminal investigations, court proceedings, or the right of individuals to a fair trial.

THE ASSASSINATION

This chapter describes President Kennedy's trip to Dallas, from its origin through to its tragic conclusion. The narrative of these events is based largely on the recollections of the participants, although in many instances documentary or other evidence has also been used by the Commission. Beginning with the advance plans and Secret Service preparations for the trip, this chapter reviews the motorcade through Dallas, the fleeting moments of the assassination, the activities at Parkland Memorial Hospital, and the return of the presidential party to Washington.

PLANNING THE TEXAS TRIP

President Kennedy's visit to Texas in November 1963 had been under consideration for almost a year before it occurred.

He had made only a few brief visits to the state since the 1960 presidential campaign and in 1962 he began to consider a formal visit. During 1963, the reasons for making the trip became more persuasive. As a political leader, the president wished to resolve the factional controversy within the Democratic Party in Texas before the election of 1964. The party itself saw an opportunity to raise funds by having the president speak at a political dinner, eventually planned for Austin. As Chief of State, the president always welcomed the opportunity to learn, first-hand, about the problems which concerned the American people. Moreover, he looked forward to the public appearances which he personally enjoyed.

The basic decision on the November trip to Texas was made at a meeting of President Kennedy, Vice President Johnson, and Governor Connally on June 5, 1963, at the Cortez Hotel in El Paso, Texas. The president had spoken earlier that day at the Air Force Academy in Colorado Springs, Colorado, and had stopped in El Paso to discuss the proposed visit and other matters with the vice president and the governor. The three agreed that the president would come to Texas in late November 1963. The original plan called for the president to spend only one day in the state, making whirlwind visits to Dallas, Fort Worth, San Antonio, and Houston. In September, the White House decided to permit further visits by the president and extended the trip to run from the afternoon of November 21 through the evening of Friday, November 22. When Governor Connally called at the White House on October 4 to discuss the details of the visit, it was agreed that the planning of events in Texas would be left largely to the governor. At the White House, Kenneth O'Donnell, special assistant to the president, acted as coordinator for the trip.

Everyone agreed that, if there was sufficient time, a motorcade through downtown Dallas would be the best way for the people to see their president. When the trip was planned for only one day, Governor Connally had opposed the motorcade because there was not enough time. The Governor stated, however, that "once we got San Antonio moved from Friday to Thursday afternoon, where that was his initial stop in Texas, then we had the time, and I withdrew my objections to a motorcade." According to O'Donnell, "we had a motorcade wherever we went," particularly in large cities where the purpose was to let the president be seen by as many people as possible. In his experience, "it would be automatic" for the Secret Service to arrange a route which would, within the time allotted, bring the president "through an area which exposes him to the greatest number of people."

Advance preparations for the Dallas trip

Advance preparations for President Kennedy's visit to Dallas were primarily the responsibility of two Secret Service agents: Special Agent Winston G. Lawson, a member of the White House detail who acted as the advance agent, and Forrest V. Sorrels, special agent in charge of the Dallas office. Both agents were advised of the trip on November 4. Lawson received a tentative schedule of the Texas trip on November 8 from Roy H. Kellerman, assistant special agent in charge of the White House detail, who was the Secret Service official responsible for the entire Texas journey. As advance agent working closely with Sorrels, Lawson had responsibility for arranging the timetable for the president's visit to Dallas and coordinating local activities with the White House staff, the organizations directly concerned with the visit, and local law enforcement officials. Lawson's most important responsibilities were to take preventive action against anyone in Dallas considered a threat to the president, to select the luncheon site and motorcade route, and to plan security measures for the luncheon and the motorcade.

Preventive intelligence activities

The Protective Research Section (PRS) of the Secret Service maintains records of people who have threatened the president or so conducted themselves as to be deemed a potential danger to him. On November 8, 1963, after undertaking the responsibility for advance preparations for the visit to Dallas, Agent Lawson went to the PRS offices in Washington. A check of the geographic indexes there revealed no listing for any individual deemed to be a potential danger to the president in the territory of the Secret Service regional office which includes Dallas and Fort Worth.

To supplement the PRS files, the Secret Service depends largely on local police departments and local offices of other Federal agencies which advise it of potential threats immediately before the visit of the president to their community. Upon his arrival in Dallas on November 12, Lawson conferred with the local police and the local office of the Federal Bureau of Investigation about potential dangers to the president. Although there was no mention in PRS files of the demonstration in Dallas against Ambassador Adlai Stevenson on October 24, 1963, Lawson inquired about the incident and obtained through the local police photographs of some of the persons involved. On November 22 a Secret Service agent stood at the entrance to the Trade Mart, where the president was scheduled to speak, with copies of these photographs. Dallas detectives in the lobby of the Trade Mart and in the luncheon area also had copies of these photographs. A number of people who resembled some of those in the photographs were placed under surveillance at the Trade Mart.

The FBI office in Dallas gave the local Secret Service representatives the name of a possibly dangerous individual in the Dallas area who was investigated. It also advised the Secret Service of the circulation on November 21 of a handbill sharply critical of President Kennedy. Shortly before, the Dallas police had reported to the Secret Service that the handbill had appeared on the streets of Dallas. Neither the Dallas police nor the FBI had yet learned the source of the handbill. No one else was identified to the Secret Service through local inquiry as potentially dangerous, nor did PRS develop any additional information between November 12, when Lawson left Washington, and November 22.

The luncheon site

An important purpose of the president's visit to Dallas was to speak at a luncheon given by business and civic leaders. The White House staff informed the Secret Service that the president would arrive and depart from Dallas Love Field; that a motorcade through the downtown area of Dallas to the luncheon site should be arranged; and that following the luncheon the president would return to the airport by the most direct route. Accordingly, it was important to determine the luncheon site as quickly as possible, so that security could be established at the site and the motorcade route selected.

On November 4, Gerald A. Behn, agent in charge of the White House detail, asked Sorrels to examine three potential sites for the luncheon. One building, Market Hall, was unavailable for November 22. The second, the Women's Building at the State Fair Grounds, was a one-story building with few entrances and easy to make secure, but it lacked necessary food-handling facilities and had certain unattractive features, including a low ceiling with exposed conduits and beams. The third possibility, the Trade Mart, a handsome new building with all the necessary facilities, presented security problems. It had numerous entrances, several tiers of balconies surrounding the central court where the luncheon would be held, and several catwalks crossing the court at each level. On November 4, Sorrels told Behn he believed security difficulties at the Trade Mart could be overcome by special precautions. Lawson also evaluated the security hazards at the Trade Mart on November 13. Kenneth O'Donnell made the final decision to hold the luncheon at the Trade Mart; Behn so notified Lawson on November 14.

Once the Trade Mart had been selected, Sorrels and Lawson worked out detailed arrangements for security at the building. In addition to the preventive measures already mentioned, they provided for controlling access to the building, closing off and policing areas around it, securing the roof and insuring the presence of numerous police officers inside and around the building. Ultimately more than 200 law enforcement officers, mainly Dallas police but including eight Secret Service agents, were deployed in and around the Trade Mart.

THE MOTORCADE ROUTE

On November 8, when Lawson was briefed on the itinerary for the trip to Dallas, he was told that 45 minutes had been allotted for a motorcade procession from Love Field to the luncheon site. Lawson was not specifically instructed to select the parade route, but he understood that this was one of his functions. Even before the Trade Mart had been definitely selected, Lawson and Sorrels began to consider the best motorcade route from Love Field to the Trade Mart. On November 14, Lawson and Sorrels attended a meeting at Love Field and on their return to Dallas drove over the route which Sorrels believed best suited for the proposed motorcade. This route, eventually selected for the motorcade from the airport to the Trade Mart, measured 10 miles and could be driven easily within the allotted 45 minutes. From Love Field the route passed through a portion of suburban Dallas, through the downtown area along Main Street and then to the Trade Mart via Stemmons Freeway. For the president's return to Love Field following the luncheon, the agents selected the most direct route, which was approximately 4 miles.

After the selection of the Trade Mart as the luncheon site, Lawson and Sorrels met with Dallas Chief of Police Jesse E. Curry, Assistant Chief Charles Batchelor, Deputy Chief N. T. Fisher, and several other command officers to discuss details of the motorcade and possible routes. The route was further reviewed by Lawson and Sorrels with Assistant Chief Batchelor and members of the local host committee on November 15. The police officials agreed that the route recommended by Sorrels was the proper one and did not express a belief that any other route might be better. On November 18, Sorrels and Lawson drove over the selected route with Batchelor and other police officers, verifying that it could be traversed within 45 minutes. Representatives of the local host committee and the White House staff were advised by the Secret Service of the actual route on the afternoon of November 18.

The route impressed the agents as a natural and desirable one. Sorrels, who had participated in presidential protection assignments in Dallas since a visit by President Franklin D. Roosevelt in 1936, testified that the traditional parade route in Dallas was along Main Street, since the tall buildings along the street gave more people an opportunity to participate. The route chosen from the airport to Main Street was the normal one, except where Harwood Street was selected as the means of access to Main Street in preference to a short stretch of the Central Expressway, which presented a minor safety hazard and could not accommodate spectators as conveniently as Harwood Street. According to Lawson, the chosen route seemed to be the best:

It afforded us wide streets most of the way, because of the buses that were in the motorcade. It afforded us a chance to have alternative routes if something happened on the motorcade route. It was the type of suburban area a good part of the way where the crowds would be able to be controlled for a great distance, and we figured that the largest crowds would be downtown, which they were, and that the wide streets that we would use downtown would be of sufficient width to keep the public out of our way.

Elm Street, parallel to Main Street and one block north, was not used for the main portion of the downtown part of the motorcade because Main Street offered better vantage points for spectators.

To reach the Trade Mart from Main Street the agents decided to use the Stemmons Freeway (Route No. 77), the most direct route. The only practical way for westbound traffic on Main Street to reach the northbound lanes of the Stemmons Freeway is via Elm Street, which Route No. 77 traffic is instructed to follow in this part of the city. Elm Street was to be reached from Main by turning right at Houston, going one block north and then turning left onto Elm. On this last portion of the journey, only 5 minutes from the Trade Mart, the president's motorcade would pass the Texas School Book Depository Building on the north-west corner of Houston and Elm Streets. The building overlooks Dealey Plaza, an attractively landscaped triangle of three acres. From Houston Street, which forms the base of the triangle, three streets – Commerce, Main, and Elm – trisect the plaza, converging at the apex of the triangle to form a triple underpass beneath a multiple railroad bridge almost 500 feet from Houston Street. Elm Street, the northernmost of the three, after intersecting Houston curves in a southwesterly arc through the underpass and leads into an access road, which branches off to the right and is used by traffic going to the Stemmons Freeway and the Dallas–Fort Worth Turnpike.

The Elm Street approach to the Stemmons Freeway is necessary in order to avoid the traffic hazards which would otherwise exist if right turns were permitted from both Main and Elm into the freeway. To create this traffic pattern, a concrete barrier between Main and Elm streets presents an obstacle to a right turn from Main across Elm to the access road to Stemmons Freeway and the Dallas–Fort Worth Turnpike. This concrete barrier extends far enough beyond the access road to make it impracticable for vehicles to turn right from Main directly to the access road. A sign located on this barrier instructs Main Street traffic not to make any turns. In conformity with these arrangements, traffic proceeding west on Main is directed to turn right at Houston in order to reach the Dallas–Fort Worth Turnpike, which has the same access road from Elm Street as does the Stemmons Freeway.

The planning for the motorcade also included advance preparations for security arrangements along the route. Sorrels and Lawson reviewed the route in cooperation with Assistant Chief Batchelor and other Dallas police officials, who took notes on the requirements for controlling the crowds and traffic, watching the overpasses, and providing motorcycle escort. To control traffic, arrangements were made for the deployment of foot patrolmen and motorcycle police at various positions along the route. Police were assigned to each overpass on the route and instructed to keep them clear of unauthorized persons. No arrangements were made for police or building custodians to inspect buildings along the motorcade route since the Secret Service did not normally request or make such a check. Under standard procedures, the responsibility for watching the windows of buildings was shared by local police stationed along the route and Secret Service agents riding in the motorcade.

As the date for the president's visit approached, the two Dallas newspapers carried several reports of his motorcade route. The selection of the Trade Mart as the possible site for the luncheon first appeared in the Dallas *Times-Herald* on November 15, 1963. The following day, the newspaper reported that the presidential party "apparently will loop through the downtown area, probably on Main Street, en route from Dallas Love Field" on its way to the Trade Mart. On November 19, the *Times-Herald* afternoon paper detailed the precise route:

> From the airport, the president's party will proceed to Mockingbird Lane to Lemmon and then to Turtle Creek, turning south to Cedar Springs. The motorcade will then pass through downtown on Harwood and then west on Main, turning back to Elm at Houston and then out Stemmons Freeway to the Trade Mart.

Also on November 19, the *Morning News* reported that the president's motorcade would travel from Love Field along specified streets, then "Harwood to Main, Main to Houston, Houston to Elm, Elm under the Triple Underpass to Stemmons Freeway, and on to the Trade Mart." On November 20 a front-page story reported that the streets on which the presidential motorcade would travel included "Main and Stemmons Freeway." On the morning of the president's arrival, the *Morning News* noted that the motorcade would travel through downtown Dallas on to the Stemmons Freeway, and reported that "the motorcade will move slowly so that crowds can 'get a good view' of President Kennedy and his wife."

Dallas before the visit

The president's intention to pay a visit to Texas in the fall of 1963 aroused interest throughout the state. The two Dallas newspapers provided their readers with a steady stream of information and speculation about the trip, beginning on September 13, when the *Times-Herald* announced in a front page article that President Kennedy was planning a brief one-day tour of four Texas cities: Dallas, Fort Worth, San Antonio, and Houston. Both Dallas papers cited White House sources on September 26 as confirming the president's intention to visit Texas on November 21 and 22, with Dallas scheduled as one of the stops.

Articles, editorials, and letters to the editor in the Dallas *Morning News* and the Dallas *Times-Herald* after September 13 reflected the feeling in the community toward the forthcoming presidential visit. Although there were critical editorials and letters to the editors, the news stories reflected the desire of Dallas officials to welcome the president with dignity and courtesy. An editorial in the *Times-Herald* of September 17 called on the people of Dallas to be "congenial hosts" even though "Dallas didn't vote for Mr Kennedy in 1960, may not endorse him in '64." On October 3 the Dallas *Morning News* quoted US Representative Joe Pool's hope that President Kennedy would receive a "good welcome" and would not face demonstrations like those encountered by Vice President Johnson during the 1960 campaign.

Increased concern about the president's visit was aroused by the incident involving the US Ambassador to the United Nations, Adlai E. Stevenson. On the evening of October 24, 1963, after addressing a meeting in Dallas, Stevenson was jeered, jostled, and spat upon by hostile demonstrators outside the Dallas Memorial Auditorium Theater. The local, national, and international reaction to this incident evoked from Dallas officials and newspapers strong condemnations of the demonstrators. Mayor Earle Cabell called on the city to redeem itself during President Kennedy's visit. He asserted that Dallas had shed its reputation of the twenties as the

"Southwest hate capital of Dixie." On October 26 the press reported Chief of Police Curry's plans to call in 100 extra off-duty officers to help protect President Kennedy. Any thought that the president might cancel his visit to Dallas was ended when Governor Connally confirmed on November 8 that the president would come to Texas on November 21–22, and that he would visit San Antonio, Houston, Fort Worth, Dallas, and Austin.

During November the Dallas papers reported frequently on the plans for protecting the president, stressing the thoroughness of the preparations. They conveyed the pleas of Dallas leaders that citizens not demonstrate or create disturbances during the president's visit. On November 18 the Dallas City Council adopted a new city ordinance [regulation] prohibiting interference with attendance at lawful assemblies. Two days before the president's arrival Chief Curry warned that the Dallas police would not permit improper conduct during the president's visit.

Meanwhile, on November 17 the president of the Dallas Chamber of Commerce referred to the city's reputation for being the friendliest town in America and asserted that citizens would "greet the president of the United States with the warmth and pride that keep the Dallas spirit famous the world over." Two days later, a local Republican leader called for a "civilized non-partisan" welcome for President Kennedy, stating that "in many respects Dallas County has isolated itself from the mainstream of life in the world in this decade." Another reaction to the impending visit, hostile to the president, came to a head shortly before his arrival. On November 21 there appeared on the streets of Dallas the anonymous handbill mentioned at the start of the chapter. It was fashioned after the "wanted" circulars issued by law enforcement agencies. Beneath two photographs of President Kennedy, one full-face and one profile, appeared the caption, "Wanted for

Treason," followed by a scurrilous bill of particulars that constituted a vilification of the president. And on the morning of the president's arrival, there appeared in the *Morning News* a full page, black-bordered advertisement headed "Welcome Mr Kennedy to Dallas", sponsored by the American Factfinding Committee, which the sponsor later testified was an *ad hoc* committee "formed strictly for the purpose of having a name to put in the paper." The "welcome" consisted of a series of statements and questions critical of the president and his administration.

Visits to other Texas cities

The trip to Texas began with the departure of President and Mrs Kennedy from the White House by helicopter at 10.45 am, EST, on November 21, 1963, for Andrews AFB. They took off in the presidential plane, *Air Force One*, at 11 am, arriving at San Antonio at 1.30 pm, CST. They were greeted by Vice President Johnson and Governor Connally, who joined the presidential party in a motorcade through San Antonio. During the afternoon, President Kennedy dedicated the US Air Force School of Aerospace Medicine at Brooks AFB. Late in the afternoon he flew to Houston where he rode through the city in a motorcade, spoke at the Rice University Stadium, and attended a dinner in honor of US Representative Albert Thomas.

At Rice Stadium a very large, enthusiastic crowd greeted the president. In Houston, as elsewhere during the trip, the crowds showed much interest in Mrs Kennedy. David F. Powers of the president's staff later stated that when the president asked for his assessment of the day's activities, Powers replied "that the crowd was about the same as the one which came to see him before but there were 100,000 extra people on hand who came to see Mrs Kennedy." Late in the evening, the presidential party flew to Fort Worth where they spent the night at the Texas Hotel.

On the morning of November 22, President Kennedy attended a breakfast at the hotel and afterward addressed a crowd at an open parking lot. The president liked outdoor appearances because more people could see and hear him. Before leaving the hotel, the president, Mrs Kennedy, and Kenneth O'Donnell talked about the risks inherent in presidential public appearances. According to O'Donnell, the president commented that "if anybody really wanted to shoot the President of the United States, it was not a very difficult job, all one had to do was get a high building someday with a telescopic rifle, and there was nothing anybody could do to defend against such an attempt." Upon concluding the conversation, the president prepared to depart for Dallas.

ARRIVAL AT LOVE FIELD

In Dallas the rain had stopped, and by mid-morning a gloomy overcast sky had given way to the bright sunshine that greeted the presidential party when *Air Force One* touched down at Love Field at 11.40 am, CST. Governor and Mrs Connally and Senator Ralph W. Yarborough had come with the president from Fort Worth. Vice President Johnson's airplane, *Air Force Two*, had arrived at Love Field at approximately 11.35 am, and the vice president and Mrs Johnson were in the receiving line to greet President and Mrs Kennedy.

After a welcome from the Dallas reception committee, President and Mrs Kennedy walked along a chain-link fence at the reception area, greeting a large crowd of spectators that had gathered behind it. Secret Service agents formed a cordon to keep the press and photographers from impeding their passage and scanned the crowd for threatening movements. Dallas police stood at intervals along the fence and Dallas plainclothesmen mixed in the crowd.

Vice President and Mrs Johnson followed along the fence, guarded by four members of the vice presidential detail. Approximately 10 minutes after the arrival at Love Field, the president and Mrs Kennedy went to the presidential automobile to begin the motorcade.

Organization of the motorcade

Secret Service arrangements for presidential trips, which were followed in the Dallas motorcade, are designed to provide protection while permitting large numbers of people to see the president. Every effort is made to prevent unscheduled stops, although the president may, and in Dallas did, order stops in order to greet the public. When the motorcade slows or stops, agents take positions between the president and the crowd.

The order of vehicles in the motorcade was as follows:

Motorcycles
Dallas police motorcycles preceded the pilot car.

The pilot car
Manned by officers of the Dallas Police Department, this automobile preceded the main party by approximately quarter of a mile. Its function was to alert police along the route that the motorcade was approaching and to check for signs of trouble.

Motorcycles
Next came four to six motorcycle policemen whose main purpose was to keep the crowd back.

The lead car
Described as a "rolling command car", this was an unmarked Dallas police car, driven by Chief of Police Curry and occupied by Secret Service Agents Sorrels and

Lawson and by Dallas County Sheriff J. E. Decker. The occupants scanned the crowd and the buildings along the route. Their main function was to spot trouble in advance and to direct any necessary steps to meet the trouble. Following normal practice, the lead automobile stayed approximately four to five car-lengths ahead of the president's limousine.

The presidential limousine

The president's automobile was a specially designed 1961 Lincoln convertible with two collapsible jump seats between the front and rear seats. It was outfitted with a clear plastic bubble top which was neither bulletproof nor bullet resistant. Because the skies had cleared in Dallas, Lawson directed that the top not be used for the day's activities. He acted on instructions he had received earlier from Assistant Special Agent in Charge Roy H. Kellerman, who was in Fort Worth with the president. Kellerman had discussed the matter with O'Donnell, whose instructions were, "If the weather is clear and it is not raining, have that bubble top off." Elevated approximately 15 inches above the back of the front seat was a metallic frame with four handholds that riders in the car could grip while standing in the rear seat during parades. At the rear on each side of the automobile were small running boards, each designed to hold a Secret Service agent, with a metallic handle for the rider to grasp. The president had frequently stated that he did not want agents to ride on these steps during a motorcade except when necessary. He had repeated this wish only a few days before, during his visit to Tampa, Florida.

President Kennedy rode on the right-hand side of the rear seat with Mrs Kennedy on his left. Governor Connally occupied the right jump seat, Mrs Connally the left. Driving the presidential limousine was Special Agent

William R. Greer of the Secret Service; on his right sat Kellerman. Kellerman's responsibilities included maintaining radio communications with the lead and follow-up cars, scanning the route, and getting out and standing near the president when the cars stopped.

Motorcycles

Four motorcycles, two on each side, flanked the rear of the presidential car. They provided some cover for the president, but their main purpose was to keep back the crowd. On previous occasions, the president had requested that, to the extent possible, these flanking motorcycles keep back from the sides of his car.

Presidential follow-up car

This vehicle, a 1955 Cadillac eight-passenger convertible especially outfitted for the Secret Service, followed closely behind the president's automobile. It carried eight Secret Service agents, two in the front seat, two in the rear, and two on each of the right and left running boards. Each agent carried a .38-caliber pistol, and a shotgun and automatic rifle were also available. Presidential Assistants David F. Powers and Kenneth O'Donnell sat in the right and left jump seats, respectively.

The agents in this car, under established procedure, had instructions to watch the route for signs of trouble, scanning not only the crowds but the windows and roofs of buildings, overpasses, and crossings. They were instructed to watch particularly for thrown objects, sudden actions in the crowd, and any movements toward the presidential car. The agents on the front of the running boards had directions to move immediately to positions just to the rear of the president and Mrs Kennedy when the president's car slowed to a walking pace or stopped, or when the press of the crowd made it impossible for the escort motorcycles to stay in position on the car's rear flanks. The two agents on the rear of the running boards were to advance toward the front of the president's car whenever it stopped or slowed down sufficiently for them to do so.

Vice presidential car
The vice presidential automobile, a four-door Lincoln convertible obtained locally for use in the motorcade, proceeded approximately two to three car lengths behind the president's follow-up car. This distance was maintained so that spectators would normally turn their gaze from the president's automobile by the time the vice president came into view. Vice President Johnson sat on the right-hand side of the rear seat, Mrs Johnson in the center, and Senator Yarborough on the left. Rufus W. Youngblood, special agent in charge of the vice president's detail, occupied the right-hand side of the front seat, and Hurchel Jacks of the Texas State Highway patrol was the driver.

Vice presidential follow-up car
Driven by an officer of the Dallas Police Department, this vehicle was occupied by three Secret Service agents and Clifton C. Garter, assistant to the vice president. These agents performed for the vice president the same functions that the agents in the presidential follow-up car performed for the president.

Remainder of motorcade
The remainder of the motorcade consisted of five cars for other dignitaries, including the mayor of Dallas and Texas Congressmen, telephone and Western Union vehicles, a White House communications car, three cars for press photographers, an official party bus for White House staff members and others, and two press buses. Admiral George G. Burkley, physician to the president, was in a car following those "containing the local and national representatives."

Police car and motorcycles
A Dallas police car and several motorcycles at the rear kept the motorcade together and prevented unauthorized vehicles from joining the motorcade.

Communications in the motorcade
A base station at a fixed location in Dallas operated a radio network which linked together the lead car, presidential car, presidential follow-up car, White House communications car, Trade Mart, Love Field, and the presidential and vice presidential airplanes. The vice presidential car and vice presidential follow-up car used portable sets with a separate frequency for their own car-to-car communication.

THE DRIVE THROUGH DALLAS

The motorcade left Love Field shortly after 11.50 am and drove at speeds up to 25 to 30 miles an hour through thinly populated areas on the outskirts of Dallas. At the president's direction, his automobile stopped twice, the first time to permit him to respond to a sign asking him to shake hands. During this brief stop, agents in the front positions on the running boards of the presidential follow-up car came forward and stood beside the president's car, looking out toward the crowd, and Special Agent Kellerman assumed his position next to the car. On the other occasion, the president halted the motorcade to speak to a Catholic nun and a group of small children.

In the downtown area, large crowds of spectators gave the president a tremendous reception. The crowds were so dense that Special Agent Clinton J. Hill had to leave the left front running board of the president's follow-up car four times to ride on the rear of the president's limousine. Several times Special Agent John D. Ready came forward from the right front running board of the presidential follow-up car to the right side of the president's car. Special Agent Glen A. Bennett once left his place inside the follow-up car to help keep the crowd away from the president's car. When a teenage boy ran toward the rear of the president's car, Ready left the running board to chase the boy back into the crowd. On several occasions when the vice president's car was slowed down by the throng, Special Agent Youngblood stepped out to hold the crowd back.

According to plan, the president's motorcade proceeded west through downtown Dallas on Main Street to the intersection of Houston Street, which marks the beginning of Dealey Plaza. From Main Street the motorcade turned right and went north on Houston Street, passing tall buildings on the right, and headed toward the Texas School Book Depository. The spectators were still thickly congregated in front of the buildings which lined the east side of Houston Street, but the crowd thinned abruptly along Elm Street, which curves in a southwesterly direction as it proceeds toward the Triple Underpass and the Stemmons Freeway.

As the motorcade approached the intersection of Houston and Elm streets, there was general gratification in the presidential party about the enthusiastic reception. Evaluating the political overtones, Kenneth O'Donnell was especially pleased because it convinced him that the average Dallas resident was like other American citizens in respecting and admiring the president. Mrs Connally, elated by the reception, turned to President Kennedy and said, "Mr President, you can't say Dallas doesn't love you." The president replied, "That is very obvious."

THE ASSASSINATION

At 12.30 pm, CST, as the president's open limousine proceeded at approximately 11 miles per hour along Elm Street toward the Triple Underpass, shots fired from a rifle mortally wounded President Kennedy and seriously injured Governor Connally. One bullet passed through the president's neck; a subsequent bullet, which was lethal, shattered the right side of his skull. Governor Connally sustained bullet wounds in his back, the right side of his chest, right wrist, and left thigh.

The time

The exact time of the assassination was fixed by the testimony of four witnesses. Special Agent Rufus W. Youngblood observed that the large electric sign clock atop the Texas School Book Depository Building showed the numerals "12.30" as the vice-presidential automobile proceeded north on Houston Street, a few seconds before the shots were fired. Just prior to the shooting, David F. Powers, riding in the Secret Service follow-up car, remarked to Kenneth O'Donnell that it was 12.30 pm, the time they were due at the Trade Mart. Seconds after the shooting, Roy Kellerman, riding in the front seat of the presidential limousine, looked at his watch and said "12.30" to the driver, Special Agent Greer. The Dallas police radio log reflects that Chief of Police Curry reported the shooting of the president and issued his initial orders at 12.30 pm.

Speed of the limousine

William Greer, operator of the presidential limousine, estimated the car's speed at the time of the first shot as 12 to 15 miles per hour. Other witnesses in the motorcade estimated the speed of the president's limousine from 7 to 22 miles per hour. A more precise determination has been made from motion pictures taken on the scene by an amateur photographer, Abraham Zapruder. Based on these films, the speed of the president's automobile is computed at an average speed of 11.2 miles per hour. The car maintained this average speed over a distance of approximately

186 feet immediately preceding the shot which struck the president in the head. While the car traveled this distance, the Zapruder camera ran 152 frames. Since the camera operates at a speed of 18.3 frames per second, it was calculated that the car required 8.3 seconds to cover the 136 feet. This represents a speed of 11.2 miles per hour.

In the presidential limousine

Mrs John F. Kennedy, on the left of the rear seat of the limousine, looked toward her left and waved to the crowds along the route. Soon after the motorcade turned onto Elm Street, she heard a sound similar to a motorcycle noise and a cry from Governor Connally, which caused her to look to her right. On turning she saw a quizzical look on her husband's face as he raised his left hand to his throat. Mrs Kennedy then heard a second shot and saw the president's skull torn open under the impact of the bullet. As she cradled her mortally wounded husband, Mrs Kennedy cried, "Oh, my God, they have shot my husband. I love you, Jack."

Governor Connally testified that he recognized the first noise as a rifle shot and the thought immediately crossed his mind that it was an assassination attempt. From his position in the right jump seat immediately in front of the president, he instinctively turned to his right because the shot appeared to come from over his right shoulder. Unable to see the president as he turned to the right, the governor started to look back over his left shoulder, but he never completed the turn because he felt something strike him in the back. In his testimony before the Commission, Governor Connally was certain that he was hit by the second shot, which he stated he did not hear.

Mrs Connally, too, heard a frightening noise from her right. Looking over her right shoulder, she saw that the president had both hands at his neck but she observed no blood and heard nothing. She watched as he slumped down with an empty expression on his face. Roy Kellerman, in the right front seat of the limousine, heard a report like a firecracker pop. Turning to his right in the direction of the noise, Kellerman heard the president say "My God, I am hit," and saw both of the president's hands move up toward his neck. As he told the driver, "Let's get out of here; we are hit," Kellerman grabbed his microphone and radioed ahead to the lead car, "We are hit. Get us to the hospital immediately." The driver, William Greer, heard a noise which he took to be a backfire from one of the motorcycles flanking the presidential car. When he heard the same noise again, Greer glanced over his shoulder and saw Governor Connally fall. At the sound of the second shot he realized that something was wrong, and he pressed down on the accelerator as Kellerman said, "Get out of here fast." As he issued his instructions to Greer and to the lead car, Kellerman heard a "flurry of shots" within 5 seconds of the first noise. According to Kellerman, Mrs Kennedy then cried out: "What are they doing to you!" Looking back from the front seat, Kellerman saw Governor Connally in his wife's lap and Special Agent Clinton J. Hill lying across the trunk of the car.

Mrs Connally heard a second shot fired and pulled her husband down into her lap. Observing his blood-covered chest as he was pulled into his wife's lap, Governor Connally believed himself mortally wounded. He cried out, "Oh, no, no, no. My God, they are going to kill us all." At first Mrs Connally thought that her husband had been killed, but then she noticed an almost imperceptible movement and knew that he was still alive. She said, "It's all right. Be still." The governor was lying with his head on his wife's lap when he heard a shot hit the president. At that point, both Governor and Mrs Connally observed brain tissue splattered over the interior of the car. According to Governor and Mrs

Connally, it was after this shot that Kellerman issued his emergency instructions and the car accelerated.

Reaction by Secret Service agents

From the left front running-board of the president's follow-up car, Special Agent Hill was scanning the few people standing on the south side of Elm Street after the motorcade had turned off Houston Street. He estimated that the motorcade had slowed down to approximately 9 or 10 miles per hour on the turn at the intersection of Houston and Elm streets and then proceeded at a rate of 12 to 15 miles per hour with the follow-up car trailing the president's automobile by approximately 5 feet. Hill heard a noise, which seemed to be a firecracker, coming from his right rear. He immediately looked to his right, "and, in so doing, my eyes had to cross the presidential limousine and I saw President Kennedy grab at himself and lurch forward and to the left." Hill jumped from the follow-up car and ran to the president's automobile. At about the time he reached the president's automobile, Hill heard a second shot, approximately 5 seconds after the first, which removed a portion of the president's head.

At the instant that Hill stepped onto the left rear step of the president's automobile and grasped the handhold, the car lurched forward, causing him to lose his footing. He ran three or four steps, regained his position and mounted the car. Between the time he originally seized the handhold and the time he mounted the car, Hill recalled:

> Mrs Kennedy had jumped up from the seat and was, it appeared to me, reaching for something coming off the right rear bumper of the car, the right rear tail, when she noticed that I was trying to climb on the car. She turned toward me and I grabbed her and put her back in the back seat, crawled up on top of the back seat and lay there.

David Powers, who witnessed the scene from the president's follow-up car, stated that Mrs Kennedy would probably have fallen off the rear end of the car and been killed if Hill had not pushed her back into the presidential automobile. Mrs Kennedy had no recollection of climbing onto the back of the car.

Special Agent Ready, on the right front running-board of the presidential follow-up car, heard noises that sounded like firecrackers and ran toward the president's limousine. But he was immediately called back by Special Agent Emory P. Roberts, in charge of the follow-up car, who did not believe that he could reach the president's car at the speed it was then traveling. Special Agent George W. Hickey, Jr, in the rear seat of the presidential follow-up car, picked up and cocked an automatic rifle as he heard the last shot. At this point the cars were speeding through the underpass and had left the scene of the shooting, but Hickey kept the automatic weapon ready as the car raced to the hospital. Most of the other Secret Service agents in the motorcade had drawn their sidearms. Roberts noticed that the vice president's car was approximately one-half block behind the presidential follow-up car at the time of the shooting and signaled for it to move in closer.

Directing the security detail for the vice president from the right front seat of the vice presidential car, Special Agent Youngblood recalled:

> As we were beginning to go down this incline, all of a sudden there was an explosive noise. I quickly observed unnatural movement of crowds, like ducking or scattering, and quick movements in the presidential follow-up car. So I turned around and hit the vice president on the shoulder and hollered, get down, and then looked around again and saw more of this movement, and so I proceeded to go to the back seat and get on top of him.

Youngblood was not positive that he was in the rear seat before the second shot, but thought it probable because of President Johnson's statement to that effect immediately after the assassination. President Johnson emphasised Youngblood's instantaneous reaction after the first shot:

> I was startled by the sharp report or explosion, but I had no time to speculate as to its origin because Agent Youngblood turned in a flash, immediately after the first explosion, hitting me on the shoulder, and shouted to all of us in the back seat to get down. I was pushed down by Agent Youngblood. Almost in the same moment in which he hit or pushed me, he vaulted over the back seat and sat on me. I was bent over under the weight of Agent Youngblood's body, toward Mrs Johnson and Senator Yarborough.

Clifton C. Carter, riding in the vice president's follow-up car a short distance behind, reported that Youngblood was in the rear seat using his body to shield the vice president before the second and third shots were fired.

Other Secret Service agents assigned to the motorcade remained at their posts during the race to the hospital. None stayed at the scene of the shooting, and none entered the Texas School Book Depository Building at or immediately after the shooting. Secret Service procedure requires that each agent stay with the person being protected and not be diverted unless it is necessary to accomplish the protective assignment. Forrest V. Sorrels, special agent in charge of the Dallas office, was the first Secret Service agent to return to the scene of the assassination, approximately 20 or 25 minutes after the shots were fired.

PARKLAND MEMORIAL HOSPITAL

The race to the hospital

In the final instant of the assassination, the presidential motorcade began a race to Parkland Memorial Hospital, approximately four miles from the Texas School Book Depository Building. On receipt of the radio message from Kellerman to the lead car that the president had been hit, Chief of Police Curry and police motorcyclists at the head of the motorcade led the way to the hospital. Meanwhile, Chief Curry ordered the police base station to notify Parkland Hospital that the wounded president was en route. The radio log of the Dallas Police Department shows that at 12.30 pm on November 22 Chief Curry radioed, "Go to the hospital, Parkland Hospital. Have them stand by." A moment later Curry added, "Looks like the president has been hit. Have Parkland stand by." The base station replied, "They have been notified." Traveling at speeds estimated at times to be up to 70 or 80 miles per hour down the Stemmons Freeway and Harry Hines Boulevard, the presidential limousine arrived at the emergency entrance of the Parkland Hospital at about 12.35 pm. Arriving almost simultaneously were the president's follow-up car, the vice president's automobile, and the vice president's follow-up car. Admiral Burkley, the president's physician, arrived at the hospital "between three and five minutes following the arrival of the president," since the riders in his car "were not exactly aware what had happened" and the car went on to the Trade Mart first.

When Parkland Hospital received the notification, the staff in the emergency area was alerted and trauma rooms 1 and 2 were prepared. These rooms were for the emergency treatment of acutely ill or injured patients. Although the first message mentioned an injury only to President Kennedy, two rooms were prepared. As the president's limousine sped toward the hospital, 12 doctors rushed to the emergency area: surgeons, Drs Malcolm O. Perry, Charles R. Baxter, Robert N. McClelland, Ronald C. Jones; the chief neurologist, Dr William Kemp Clark; four anesthesiologists, Drs Marion T. Jenkins, Adolph H. Giesecke, Jr,

Jackie H. Hunt, Gene C. Akin; urological surgeon, Dr Paul C. Peters; an oral surgeon, Dr Don T. Curtis; and a heart specialist, Dr Fouad A. Bashour.

Upon arriving at Parkland Hospital, Lawson jumped from the lead car and rushed into the emergency entrance, where he was met by hospital staff members wheeling stretchers out to the automobile. Special Agent Hill removed his suit jacket and covered the president's head and upper chest to prevent the taking of photographs. Governor Connally, who had lost consciousness on the ride to the hospital, regained consciousness when the limousine stopped abruptly at the emergency entrance. Despite his serious wounds, Governor Connally tried to get out of the way so that medical help could reach the president. Although he was reclining in his wife's arms, he lurched forward in an effort to stand upright and get out of the car, but he collapsed again. Then he experienced his first sensation of pain, which became excruciating. The Governor was lifted onto a stretcher and taken into trauma room 2. For a moment, Mrs Kennedy refused to release the president, whom she held in her lap, but then Kellerman, Greer, and Lawson lifted the president onto a stretcher and pushed it into trauma room 1.

Treatment of President Kennedy

The first physician to see the president at Parkland Hospital was Dr Charles J. Carrico, a resident in general surgery.

Dr Carrico was in the emergency area, examining another patient, when he was notified that President Kennedy was en route to the hospital. Approximately two minutes later, Dr Carrico saw the president on his back, being wheeled into the emergency area. He noted that the president was blue-white or ashen in color; had slow, spasmodic, agonal respiration without any coordination; made no voluntary movements; had his eyes open with the pupils dilated without any reaction to light; evidenced no palpable pulse; and had a few chest sounds which were thought to be heart beats. On the basis of these findings, Dr Carrico concluded that President Kennedy was still alive.

Dr Carrico noted two wounds: a small bullet wound in the front lower neck, and an extensive wound in the president's head where a sizable portion of the skull was missing. He observed shredded brain tissue and "considerable slow oozing" from the latter wound, followed by "more profuse bleeding" after some circulation was established. Dr Carrico felt the president's back and determined that there was no large wound there which would be an immediate threat to life. Observing the serious problems presented by the head wound and inadequate respiration, Dr Carrico directed his attention to improving the president's breathing. He noted contusions, hematoma to the right of the larynx, which was deviated slightly to the left, and also ragged tissue which indicated a tracheal injury. Dr Carrico inserted a cuffed endotracheal tube past the injury, inflated the cuff, and connected it to a Bennett machine to assist in respiration.

At that point, direction of the president's treatment was undertaken by Dr Malcolm O. Perry, who arrived at trauma room 1 a few moments after the president. Dr Perry noted the president's back brace as he felt for a femoral pulse, which he did not find. Observing that an effective airway had to be established if treatment was to be effective, Dr Perry performed a tracheotomy, which required 3 to 5 minutes. While Dr Perry was performing the tracheotomy, Drs Carrico and Ronald Jones made cut-downs on the president's right leg and left arm, respectively, to infuse blood and fluids into the circulatory system. Dr Carrico treated the president's known adrenal insufficiency by administering hydrocortisone. Dr Robert N. McClelland entered at that point and assisted Dr Perry with the tracheotomy.

Dr Fouad Bashour, chief of cardiology, Dr M. T. Jenkins, chief of anesthesiology, and Dr A. H. Giesecke, Jr, then joined in the effort to revive the president. When Dr Perry noted free air and blood in the president's chest cavity, he asked that chest tubes be inserted to allow for drainage of blood and air. Drs Paul C. Peters and Charles R. Baxter initiated these procedures. As a result of the infusion of liquids through the cut-downs, the cardiac massage, and the airway, the doctors were able to maintain peripheral circulation as monitored at the neck (carotid) artery and at the wrist (radial) pulse. A femoral pulse was also detected in the president's leg. While these medical efforts were in progress, Dr Clark noted some electrical activity on the cardiotachyscope attached to monitor the president's heart responses. Dr Clark, who most closely observed the head wound, described a large, gaping wound in the right rear part of the head, with substantial damage and exposure of brain tissue, and a considerable loss of blood. Dr Clark did not see any other hole or wound on the president's head. According to Dr Clark, the small bullet hole on the right rear of the president's head discovered during the subsequent autopsy "could have easily been hidden in the blood and hair."

In the absence of any neurological, muscular, or heart response, the doctors concluded that efforts to revive the president were hopeless. This was verified by Admiral Burkley, the president's physician, who arrived at the hospital after emergency treatment was under way and concluded that "my direct services to him at that moment would have interfered with the action of the team which was in progress." At approximately 1 pm, after last rites were administered to the president by Father Oscar L. Huber, Dr Clark pronounced the president dead. He made the official determination because the ultimate cause of death, the severe head injury, was within his sphere of specialization.

The time was fixed at 1 pm, as an approximation, since it was impossible to determine the precise moment when life left the president. President Kennedy could have survived the neck injury, but the head wound was fatal. From a medical viewpoint, President Kennedy was alive when he arrived at Parkland Hospital; the doctors observed that he had a heart beat and was making some respiratory efforts. But his condition was hopeless, and the extraordinary efforts of the doctors to save him could not help but to have been unavailing. Since the Dallas doctors directed all their efforts to controlling the massive bleeding caused by the head wound, and to reconstructing an airway to his lungs, the president remained on his back throughout his medical treatment at Parkland.

When asked why he did not turn the president over, Dr Carrico testified as follows:

A: This man was in obvious extreme distress and any more thorough inspection would have involved several minutes, well, several, considerable time which at this juncture was not available. A thorough inspection would have involved washing and cleansing the back, and this is not practical in treating an acutely injured patient. You have to determine which things, which are immediately life threatening and cope with them, before attempting to evaluate the full extent of the injuries.

Q: Did you ever have occasion to look at the president's back?

A: No, sir. Before, well, in trying to treat an acutely injured patient, you have to establish an airway, adequate ventilation and you have to establish adequate circulation. Before this was accomplished the president's cardiac activity had ceased and closed cardiac massage was instituted, which made it impossible to inspect his back.

Q: Was any effort made to inspect the president's back after he had expired?

A: No, sir.

Q: And why was no effort made at that time to inspect his back ?
A: I suppose nobody really had the heart to do it.

Moreover, the Parkland doctors took no further action after the president had expired because they concluded that it was beyond the scope of their permissible duties.

Treatment of Governor Connally

While one medical team tried to revive President Kennedy, a second performed a series of operations on the bullet wounds sustained by Governor Connally. Governor Connally was originally seen by Dr Carrico and Dr Richard Dulany. While Dr Carrico went on to attend the president, Dr Dulany stayed with the governor and was soon joined by several other doctors. At approximately 12.45 pm, Dr Robert Shaw, chief of thoracic surgery, arrived at trauma room 2, to take charge of the care of Governor Connally, whose major wound fell within Dr Shaw's area of specialization.

Governor Connally had a large sucking wound in the front of the right chest which caused extreme pain and difficulty in breathing. Rubber tubes were inserted between the second and third ribs to re-expand the right lung, which had collapsed because of the opening in the chest wall. At 1.35 pm, after Governor Connally had been moved to the operating room, Dr Shaw started the first operation by cutting away the edges of the wound on the front of the governor's chest and suturing the damaged lung and lacerated muscles. The elliptical wound in the governor's back, located slightly to the left of the governor's right armpit approximately $\frac{5}{8}$ inch (a centimeter and a half) in its greatest diameter, was treated by cutting away the damaged skin and suturing the back muscle and skin. This operation was concluded at 3.20 pm.

Two additional operations were performed on Governor Connally for wounds which he had not realized he had sustained until he regained consciousness the following day. From approximately 4 pm to 4.50 pm on November 22, Dr Charles F. Gregory, chief of orthopedic surgery, operated on the wounds of Governor Connally's right wrist, assisted by Drs William Osborne and John Parker. The wound on the back of the wrist was left partially open for draining, and the wound on the palm side was enlarged, cleansed, and closed. The fracture was set, and a cast was applied with some traction utilized. While the second operation was in progress, Dr George T. Shires, assisted by Drs Robert McClelland, Charles Baxter, and Ralph Don Patman, treated the gunshot wound in the left thigh. This punctuate missile wound, about $\frac{2}{5}$ inch in diameter (1 centimeter) and located approximately 5 inches above the left knee, was cleansed and closed with sutures; but a small metallic fragment remained in the governor's leg.

Vice President Johnson at Parkland

As President Kennedy and Governor Connally were being removed from the limousine onto stretchers, a protective circle of Secret Service agents surrounded Vice President and Mrs Johnson and escorted them into Parkland Hospital through the emergency entrance. The agents moved a nurse and patient out of a nearby room, lowered the shades, and took emergency security measures to protect the vice president. Two men from the president's follow-up car were detailed to help protect the vice president. An agent was stationed at the entrance to stop anyone who was not a member of the presidential party. US Representatives Henry B. Gonzalez, Jack Brooks, Homer Thornberry, and Albert Thomas joined Clifton C. Carter and the group of special agents protecting the vice president. On one occasion Mrs Johnson, accompanied by two Secret Service agents, left the room to see Mrs Kennedy and Mrs Connally.

Concern that the vice president might also be a target for assassination prompted the Secret Service agents to urge him to leave the hospital and return to Washington immediately. The vice president decided to wait until he received definitive word of the president's condition. At approximately 1.20 pm, Vice President Johnson was notified by O'Donnell that President Kennedy was dead. Special Agent Youngblood learned from Mrs Johnson the location of her two daughters and made arrangements through Secret Service headquarters in Washington to provide them with protection immediately.

When consulted by the vice president, O'Donnell advised him to go to the airfield immediately and return to Washington. It was decided that the vice president should return on the presidential plane rather than on the vice presidential plane because it had better communication equipment. The vice president conferred with White House Assistant Press Secretary Malcolm Kilduff and decided that there would be no release of the news of the president's death until the vice president had left the hospital. When told that Mrs Kennedy refused to leave without the president's body, the vice president said that he would not leave Dallas without her. On the recommendation of the Secret Service agents, Vice President Johnson decided to board the presidential airplane, *Air Force One*, and wait for Mrs Kennedy and the president's body.

Secret Service emergency security arrangements

Immediately after President Kennedy's stretcher was wheeled into trauma room 1, Secret Service agents took positions at the door of the small emergency room. A nurse was asked to identify hospital personnel and to tell everyone, except necessary medical staff members, to leave the emergency room. Other Secret Service agents posted themselves in the corridors and other areas near the emergency room. Special Agent Lawson made certain that the Dallas police kept the public and press away from the immediate area of the hospital. Agents Kellerman and Hill telephoned the head of the White House detail, Gerald A. Behn, to advise him of the assassination. The telephone line to Washington was kept open throughout the remainder of the stay at the hospital.

Secret Service agents stationed at later stops on the president's itinerary of November 22 were redeployed. Men at the Trade Mart were driven to Parkland Hospital in Dallas police cars. The Secret Service group awaiting the president in Austin were instructed to return to Washington. Meanwhile, the Secret Service agents in charge of security at Love Field started to make arrangements for departure. As soon as one of the agents learned of the shooting, he asked the officer in charge of the police detail at the airport to institute strict security measures for the presidential aircraft, the airport terminal, and the surrounding area. The police were cautioned to prevent picture-taking. Secret Service agents working with police cleared the areas adjacent to the aircraft, including warehouses, other terminal buildings and the neighboring parking lots, of all people. The agents decided not to shift the presidential aircraft to the far side of the airport because the original landing area was secure and a move would require new measures.

When security arrangements at the airport were complete, the Secret Service made the necessary arrangements for the vice president to leave the hospital. Unmarked police cars took the vice president and Mrs Johnson from Parkland Hospital to Love Field. Chief Curry drove one automobile occupied by Vice President Johnson, US Representatives Thomas and Thornberry, and Special Agent Youngblood. In another car Mrs Johnson was driven to the airport accompanied by Secret Service agents and Representative Brooks. Motorcade policemen who escorted the automobiles were requested by the vice president and Agent Youngblood not to use sirens. During the drive Vice President Johnson, at Youngblood's instruction, kept below window level.

Removal of the president's body

While the team of doctors at Parkland Hospital tried desperately to save the life of President Kennedy, Mrs Kennedy alternated between watching them and waiting outside. After the president was pronounced dead, O'Donnell tried to persuade Mrs Kennedy to leave the area, but she refused. She said that she intended to stay with her husband. A casket was obtained and the president's body was prepared for removal. Before the body could be taken from the hospital, two Dallas officials informed members of the president's staff that the body could not be removed from the city until an autopsy was performed. Despite the protests of these officials, the casket was wheeled out of the hospital, placed in an ambulance, and transported to the airport shortly after 2 pm. At approximately 2.15 pm the casket was loaded, with some difficulty because of the narrow airplane door, onto the rear of the presidential plane where seats had been removed to make room. Concerned that the local officials might try to prevent the plane's departure, O'Donnell asked that the pilot take off immediately. He was informed that take-off would be delayed until Vice President Johnson was sworn in.

THE END OF THE TRIP

Swearing in of the new president

From the presidential airplane, the vice president telephoned Attorney General Robert F. Kennedy, who advised that Mr Johnson take the presidential oath of office before the plane left Dallas. Federal Judge Sarah T. Hughes hastened to the plane to administer the oath. Members of the presidential and vice-presidential parties filled the central compartment of the plane to witness the swearing in. At 2.38 pm,CST, Lyndon Baines Johnson took the oath of office as the 36th President of the United States. Mrs Kennedy and Mrs Johnson stood at the side of the new president as he took the oath of office. Nine minutes later, the presidential airplane departed for Washington, DC.

Return to Washington, DC

On the return flight, Mrs Kennedy sat with David Powers, Kenneth O'Donnell, and Lawrence O'Brien. At 5.58 pm, EST, *Air Force One* landed at Andrews AFB, where President Kennedy had begun his last trip only 31 hours before. Detailed security arrangements had been made by radio from the president's plane on the return flight. The public had been excluded from the base, and only government officials and the press were permitted near the landing area.

Upon arrival, President Johnson made a brief statement over television and radio. President and Mrs Johnson were flown by helicopter to the White House, from where Mrs Johnson was driven to her residence under Secret Service escort. The president then walked to the Executive Office Building, where he worked until 9 pm.

The autopsy

Given a choice between the National Naval Medical Center at Bethesda, Maryland, and the Army's Walter Reed Hospital, Mrs Kennedy chose the hospital in Bethesda for the autopsy because the president had served in the Navy. Mrs Kennedy and the Attorney General, with three Secret Service agents, accompanied President Kennedy's body on the 45-minute automobile trip from Andrews AFB to the hospital. On the 17th floor of the hospital, Mrs Kennedy and the Attorney General joined other members of the Kennedy family to await the conclusion of the autopsy. Mrs Kennedy was guarded by Secret Service agents in quarters assigned to her in the naval hospital. The Secret Service established a communication system with the White House and screened all telephone calls and visitors.

The hospital received the president's body for autopsy at approximately 7.35 pm. X-rays and photographs were taken preliminarily and the pathological examination began at about 8 pm. The autopsy report noted that President Kennedy was 46 years of age, $72\frac{1}{2}$ inches tall, weighed 170 pounds, had blue eyes and reddish-brown hair. The body was muscular and well developed with no gross skeletal abnormalities except for those caused by the gunshot wounds. Under "Pathological Diagnosis" the cause of death was set forth as "Gunshot wound, head."

The autopsy examination revealed two wounds in the president's head. One wound, approximately $\frac{1}{4}$ inch by $\frac{5}{8}$ inch (6 by 15 millimeters), was located about an inch (2.5 centimeters) to the right and slightly above the large bony protrusion (external occipital protuberance) which juts out at the center of the lower part of the back of the skull. The second head wound measured approximately 5 inches (13 centimeters) in its greatest diameter, but it was difficult to measure accurately because multiple crisscross fractures radiated from the large defect. During the autopsy examination, Federal agents brought the surgeons three pieces of bone recovered from Elm Street and the presidential automobile. When put together, these fragments accounted for approximately three-quarters of the missing portion of the skull. The surgeons observed, through X-ray analysis, 30 or 40 tiny dust like fragments of metal running in a line from the wound in the rear of the president's head toward the front part of the skull, with a sizable metal fragment lying just above the right eye. From this head wound two small irregularly shaped fragments of metal were recovered and turned over to the FBI.

The autopsy also disclosed a wound near the base of the back of President Kennedy's neck, slightly to the right of his spine. The doctors traced the course of the bullet through the body and, as information was received from Parkland Hospital, concluded that the bullet had emerged from the front portion of the president's neck that had been cut away by the tracheotomy at Parkland. After the autopsy was concluded at approximately 11 pm, the president's body was prepared for burial. This was finished at approximately 4 am. Shortly thereafter, the president's wife, family and aides left Bethesda Naval Hospital. The president's body was taken to the East Room of the White House where it was placed under ceremonial military guard.

THE SHOTS FROM THE TEXAS
SCHOOL BOOK DEPOSITORY

In this chapter the Commission analyzes the evidence and sets forth its conclusions concerning the source, effect, number and timing of the shots that killed President Kennedy and wounded Governor Connally. In that connection the Commission has evaluated:

(1) the testimony of eyewitnesses present at the scene of the assassination
(2) the damage to the presidential limousine
(3) the examination by qualified experts of the rifle and cartridge cases found on the sixth floor of the Texas School Book Depository and the bullet fragments found in the presidential limousine and at Parkland Hospital

(4) the wounds suffered by President Kennedy and Governor Connally

(5) wound ballistics tests

(6) the examination by qualified experts of the clothing worn by President Kennedy and Governor Connally

(7) motion-picture films and still photographs taken at the time of the assassination.

THE WITNESSES

As reflected in the previous chapter, passengers in the first few cars of the motorcade had the impression that the shots came from the rear and from the right, the general direction of the Texas School Book Depository Building, although none of these passengers saw anyone fire the shots. Some spectators at Houston and Elm streets, however, did see a rifle being fired in the direction of the president's car from the easternmost window of the sixth floor on the south side of the building. Other witnesses saw a rifle in this window immediately after the assassination. Three employees of the Depository, observing the parade from the fifth floor, heard the shots fired from the floor immediately above them. No credible evidence suggests that the shots were fired from the railroad bridge over the Triple Underpass, the nearby railroad yards or any place other than the Texas School Book Depository Building.

Near the Depository

Eyewitnesses testified that they saw a man fire a weapon from the sixth-floor window. Howard L. Brennan, a 45-year-old steam fitter, watched the motorcade from a concrete retaining wall at the southwest corner of Elm and Houston, where he had a clear view of the south side of the Depository Building. He was approximately 107 feet from the Depository entrance and 120 feet from the southeast corner window of the sixth floor. Brennan's presence and vantage point are corroborated by a motion picture of the motorcade taken by amateur photographer Abraham Zapruder, which shows Brennan, wearing gray khaki work clothes and a gray work helmet, seated on the retaining wall. Brennan later identified himself in the Zapruder movie. While waiting about seven minutes for the president to arrive, he observed the crowd on the street and the people at the windows of the Depository Building. He noticed a man at the southeast corner window of the sixth floor, and observed him leave the window "a couple of times". Brennan watched the president's car as it turned the corner at Houston and Elm and moved down the incline toward the Triple Underpass. Soon after the president's car passed, he heard an explosion like the backfire of a motorcycle.

Brennan recalled:

> Well, then something, just right after this explosion, made me think that it was a firecracker being thrown from the Texas Book Store. And I glanced up. And this man that I saw previous was aiming for his last shot.
>
> Well, as it appeared to me he was standing up and resting against the left window sill, with gun shouldered to his right shoulder, holding the gun with his left hand and taking positive aim and fired his last shot. As I calculate a couple of seconds. He drew the gun back from the window as though he was drawing it back to his side and maybe paused for another second as though to assure hisself that he hit his mark, and then he disappeared.

Brennan stated that he saw 70 to 85 per cent of the gun when it was fired and the body of the man from the waist up. The rifle was aimed southwesterly down Elm Street toward the underpass. Brennan saw the man fire one shot and he remembered hearing a total of only two shots.

When questioned about the number of shots, Brennan testified:

> I don't know what made me think that there was fire-crackers thrown out of the Book Store unless I did hear the second shot, because I positively thought the first shot was a backfire, and subconsciously I must have heard a second shot, but I do not recall it. I could not swear to it.

Brennan quickly reported his observations to police officers. Brennan's description of the man he saw is discussed on pp. 191–195.

Amos Lee Euins, a 15-year-old ninth grade student, stated that he was facing the Depository as the motorcade turned the corner at Elm and Houston. He recalled:

> Then I was standing here, and as the motorcade turned the corner, I was facing, looking dead at the building. And so I seen this pipe thing sticking out the window. I wasn't paying too much attention to it. Then when the first shot was fired, I started looking around, thinking it was a backfire. Everybody else started looking around. Then I looked up at the window, and he shot again.

After witnessing the first shots, Euins hid behind a fountain bench and saw the man shoot again from the window in the southeast corner of the Depository's sixth floor. According to Euins, the man had one hand on the barrel and the other on the trigger. Euins believed that there were four shots. Immediately after the assassination, he reported his observations to Sergeant D. V. Harkness of the Dallas Police Department and also to James Underwood of station KRLD-TV of Dallas. Sergeant Harkness testified that Euins told him that the shots came from the last window of the floor "under the ledge" on the side of the building they were facing. Based on Euins' statements, Harkness radioed to headquarters at 12.36 pm that "I have a witness that says that it came from the fifth floor of the Texas Book Depository Store." Euins accurately described the sixth floor as the floor "under the ledge." Harkness testified that the error in the radio message was due to his own "hasty count of the floors."

Other witnesses saw a rifle in the window after the shots were fired. Robert H. Jackson, staff photographer, Dallas *Times-Herald*, was in a press car in the presidential motorcade, eight or nine cars from the front. On Houston Street about halfway between Main and Elm, Jackson heard the first shot. As someone in the car commented that it sounded like a firecracker, Jackson heard two more shots. He testified:

> Then we realized or we thought that it was gunfire, and then we could not at that point see the president's car. We were still moving slowly, and after the third shot the second two shots seemed much closer together than the first shot, than they were to the first shot. Then after the last shot, I guess all of us were just looking all around and I just looked straight up ahead of me which would have been looking at the School Book Depository and I noticed two Negro men in a window straining to see directly above them, and my eyes followed right on up to the window above them and I saw the rifle or what looked like a rifle, approximately half of the weapon, I guess I saw, and just as I looked at it, it was drawn fairly slowly back into the building, and I saw no one in the window with it. I didn't even see a form in the window.

In the car with Jackson were James Underwood, television station KRLD-TV; Thomas Dillard, chief photographer, Dallas *Morning News*; Malcolm O. Couch and James Darnell, television newsreel cameramen. Dillard,

Underwood, and the driver were in the front seat, Couch and Darnell were sitting on top of the back seat of the convertible with Jackson. Dillard, Couch, and Underwood confirmed that Jackson spontaneously exclaimed that he saw a rifle in the window. According to Dillard, at the time the shots were fired he and his fellow passengers "had an absolutely perfect view of the School Depository from our position in the open car." Dillard immediately took two pictures of the building: one of the east two-thirds of the south side and the other of the southeast corner, particularly the fifth- and sixth-floor windows. These pictures show three Negro men in windows on the fifth floor and the partially open window on the sixth floor directly above them. Couch also saw the rifle in the window, and testified:

> And after the third shot, Bob Jackson, who was, as I recall, on my right, yelled something like, "Look up in the window! There's the rifle!" And I remember glancing up to a window on the far right, which at the time impressed me as the sixth or seventh floor, and seeing about a foot of a rifle being the barrel brought into the window.

Couch testified he saw people standing in other windows on the third or fourth floor in the middle of the south side, one of them being a Negro in a white T-shirt leaning out to look up at the windows above him.

Mayor and Mrs Earle Cabell rode in the motorcade immediately behind the vice-presidential follow-up car. Mrs Cabell was seated in the back seat behind the driver and was facing US Representative Ray Roberts on her right as the car made the turn at Elm and Houston. In this position Mrs Cabell "was actually facing" the seven-story Depository when the first shot rang out. She "jerked" her head up immediately and saw a "projection" in the first group of windows on a floor which she described both as the sixth floor and the top floor. According to Mrs Cabell, the object was "rather long looking", but she was unable to determine whether it was a mechanical object or a person's arm. She turned away from the window to tell her husband that the noise was a shot, and "just as I got the words out . . . the second two shots rang out." Mrs Cabell did not look at the sixth-floor window when the second and third shots were fired.

James N. Crawford and Mary Ann Mitchell, two deputy district clerks for Dallas County, watched the motorcade at the southeast corner of Elm and Houston. After the president's car turned the corner, Crawford heard a loud report which he thought was backfire coming from the direction of the Triple Underpass. He heard a second shot seconds later, followed quickly by a third. At the third shot, he looked up and saw a "movement" in the far east corner of the sixth floor of the Depository, the only open window on that floor. He told Miss Mitchell "that if those were shots they came from that window." When asked to describe the movement more exactly, he said:

> . . . I would say that it was a profile, somewhat from the waist up, but it was a very quick movement and rather indistinct and it was very light colored . . . When I saw it, I automatically in my mind came to the conclusion that it was a person having moved out of the window . . .

He could not state whether the person was a man or a woman. Miss Mitchell confirmed that after the third shot Crawford told her, "Those shots came from that building." She saw Crawford pointing at a window but was not sure at which window he was pointing.

On the fifth floor

Three Depository employees shown in the picture taken by Dillard were on the fifth floor of the building when the shots were fired: James Jarman, Jr, age 34, a wrapper in the shipping department; Bonnie Ray Williams, age 20, a warehouseman temporarily assigned to laying a plywood floor on the sixth floor; and Harold Norman, age 26, an "order filler." Norman and Jarman decided to watch the parade during the lunch hour from the fifth-floor windows. From the ground floor they took the west elevator, which operates with push-button controls, to the fifth floor. Meanwhile, Williams had gone up to the sixth floor where he had been working and ate his lunch on the south side of that floor. Since he saw no one around when he finished his lunch, he started down on the east elevator, looking for company. He left behind his paper lunch sack, chicken bones and an empty pop bottle. Williams went down to the fifth floor, where he joined Norman and Jarman at approximately 12.20 pm.

Harold Norman was in the fifth-floor window in the southeast corner, directly under the window where witnesses saw the rifle. He could see light through the ceiling cracks between the fifth and sixth floors. As the motorcade went by, Norman thought that the president was saluting with his right arm,

> ... and I can't remember what the exact time was but I know I heard a shot, and then after I heard the shot, well, it seems as though the president, you know, slumped or something, and then another shot and I believe Jarman or someone told me, he said, "I believe someone is shooting at the president," and I think I made a statement, "It is someone shooting at the president, and I believe it came from up above us." Well, I couldn't see at all during the time but I know I heard a third shot fired, and I could also hear something sounded like the shell hulls hitting the floor and the ejecting of the rifle ...

Williams said that he "really did not pay any attention" to the first shot:

> A: . . . because I did not know what was happening. The second shot, it sounded like it was right in the building, the second and third shot. And it sounded, it even shook the building, the side we were on. Cement fell on my head.
>
> Q: You say cement fell on your head?
>
> A: Cement, gravel, dirt, or something, from the old building, because it shook the windows and everything.
> Harold was sitting next to me, and he said it came right from over our head.

Williams testified Norman said "I can even hear the shell being ejected from the gun hitting the floor." When Jarman heard the first sound, he thought that it was either a backfire,

> . . . or an officer giving a salute to the president. And then at that time I didn't, you know, think too much about it. . .
> Well, after the third shot was fired, I think I got up and I run over to Harold Norman and Bonnie Ray Williams, and told them, I said, I told them that it wasn't a backfire or anything, that somebody was shooting at the president.

Jarman testified that Norman said "that he thought the shots had come from above us, and I noticed that Bonnie Ray had a few debris in his head. It was sort of white stuff, or something." Jarman stated that Norman said "that he was sure that the shot came from inside the building because he had been used to guns and all that, and he said it didn't sound like it was too far off anyway." The three men ran to the west side of the building, where they could look toward the Triple Underpass to see what had happened to the motorcade.

After the men had gone to the window on the west side of the building, Jarman "got to thinking about all the debris on Bonnie Ray's head" and said, "That shot probably did come from upstairs, up over us." He testified that Norman said, "I know it did, because I could hear the action of the bolt, and I could hear the cartridges drop on the floor." After pausing for a few minutes, the three men ran downstairs. Norman and Jarman ran out of the front entrance of the building, where they saw Brennan, the construction worker who had seen the man in the window firing the gun, talking to a police officer, and they then reported their own experience.

On March 20, 1964, preceding their appearance before the Commission, these witnesses were interviewed in Dallas. At that time members of the Commission's legal staff conducted an experiment. Norman, Williams, and Jarman placed themselves at the windows of the fifth floor as they had been on November 22. A Secret Service agent operated the bolt of a rifle directly above them at the southeast corner window of the sixth floor. At the same time, three cartridge shells were dropped to the floor at intervals of about three seconds. According to Norman, the noise outside was less on the day of the assassination than on the day of the test. He testified, "Well, I heard the same sound, the sound similar. I heard three something that he dropped on the floor and then I could hear the rifle or whatever he had up there." The experiment with the shells and rifle was repeated for members of the Commission on May 9, 1964, on June 7, 1964, and again on September 6, 1964. All seven of the Commissioners clearly heard the shells drop to the floor.

At the Triple Underpass

In contrast to the testimony of the witnesses who heard and observed shots fired from the Depository, the Commission's investigation has disclosed no credible evidence that any shots were fired from anywhere else. When the shots were fired, many people near the Depository believed that the shots came from the railroad bridge over the Triple Underpass or from the area to the west of the Depository. In the hectic moments after the assassination, many spectators ran in the general direction of the Triple Underpass or the railroad yards northwest of the building. Some were running toward the place from which the sound of the rifle fire appeared to come, others were fleeing the scene of the shooting. None of these people saw anyone with a rifle, and the Commission's inquiry has yielded no evidence that shots were fired from the bridge over the Triple Underpass or from the railroad yards.

On the day of the motorcade, Patrolman J. W. Foster stood on the east side of the railroad bridge over the Triple Underpass and Patrolman J. C. White stood on the west side. Patrolman Joe E. Murphy was standing over Elm Street on the Stemmons Freeway overpass, west of the railroad bridge farther away from the Depository. Two other officers were stationed on Stemmons Freeway to control traffic as the motorcade entered the Freeway. Under the advance preparations worked out between the Secret Service and the Dallas Police Department, the policemen were under instructions to keep "unauthorized" people away from these locations. When the motorcade reached the intersection of Elm and Houston streets, there were no spectators on Stemmons Freeway where Patrolman Murphy was stationed. Patrolman Foster estimated that there were 10 or 11 people on the railroad bridge where he was assigned; another witness testified that there were between 14 and 18 people there as the motorcade came into view. Investigation has disclosed 15 persons who were on the railroad bridge at this time, including two policemen, two employees of the Texas-Louisiana Freight Bureau and 11 employees of the

Union Terminal Co. In the absence of any explicit definition of "unauthorized" persons, the policemen permitted these employees to remain on the railroad bridge to watch the motorcade. At the request of the policemen, S. M. Holland, signal supervisor for Union Terminal Co., came to the railroad bridge at about 11.45 am and remained to identify those persons who were railroad employees. In addition, Patrolman Foster checked credentials to determine if persons seeking access to the bridge were railroad employees. Persons who were not railroad employees were ordered away, including one news photographer who wished only to take a picture of the motorcade.

Another employee of the Union Terminal Co., Lee E. Bowers, Jr, was at work in a railroad tower about 14 feet above the tracks to the north of the railroad bridge and northwest of the corner of Elm and Houston, approximately 50 yards from the back of the Depository. From the tower he could view people moving in the railroad yards and at the rear of the Depository. According to Bowers, "Since approximately 10 o'clock in the morning traffic had been cut off into the area so that anyone moving around could actually be observed." During the 20 minutes prior to the arrival of the motorcade, Bowers noticed three automobiles which entered his immediate area; two left without discharging any passengers and the third was apparently on its way out when last observed by Bowers. Bowers observed only three or four people in the general area, as well as a few bystanders on the railroad bridge over the Triple Underpass.

As the motorcade proceeded toward the Triple Underpass, the spectators were clustered together along the east concrete wall of the railroad bridge facing the oncoming procession. Patrolman Foster stood immediately behind them and could observe all of them. Secret Service agents in the lead car of the motorcade observed the bystanders and the police officer on the bridge. Special Agent

Winston G. Lawson motioned through the windshield in an unsuccessful attempt to instruct Patrolman Foster to move the people away from their position directly over the path of the motorcade. Some distance away, on the Stemmons Freeway overpass above Elm Street, Patrolman Murphy also had the group on the railroad bridge within view. When he heard the shots, Foster rushed to the wall of the railroad bridge over the Triple Underpass and looked toward the street. After the third shot, Foster ran toward the Depository and shortly thereafter informed Inspector Herbert J. Sawyer of the Dallas Police Department that he thought the shots came from the vicinity of Elm and Houston.

Other witnesses on the railroad bridge had varying views concerning the source and number of the shots. Austin L. Miller, employed by the Texas-Louisiana Freight Bureau, heard three shots and thought that they came from the area of the presidential limousine itself. One of his co-workers, Royce G. Skelton, thought he heard four shots, but could not tell their exact source. Frank E. Reilly, an electrician at Union Terminal, heard three shots which seemed to come from the trees, "on the north side of Elm Street at the corner up there." According to S. M. Holland, there were four shots which sounded as though they came from the trees on the north side of Elm Street where he saw a puff of smoke. Thomas J. Murphy, a mail foreman at Union Terminal Co, heard two shots and said that they came from a spot just west of the Depository. In the railroad tower, Bowers heard three shots, which sounded as though they came either from the Depository Building or near the mouth of the Triple Underpass. Prior to November 22, 1963, Bowers had noted the similarity of the sounds coming from the vicinity of the Depository and those from the Triple Underpass, which he attributed to "a reverberation which takes place from either location." Immediately after the shots were fired, neither the policemen nor the spectators on the railroad bridge over the Triple Underpass saw anything suspicious on the bridge in their vicinity. No one saw anyone with a rifle. As he ran around through the railroad yards to the Depository, Patrolman Foster saw no suspicious activity. The same was true of the other bystanders, many of whom made an effort after the shooting to observe any unusual activity. Holland, for example, immediately after the shots, ran off the overpass to see if there was anyone behind the picket fence on the north side of Elm Street, but he did not see anyone among the parked cars. Miller did not see anyone running across the railroad tracks or on the plaza west of the Depository. Bowers and others saw a motorcycle officer dismount hurriedly and come running up the incline on the north side of Elm Street. The motorcycle officer, Clyde A. Haygood, saw no one running from the railroad yards.

THE PRESIDENTIAL AUTOMOBILE

After the presidential car was returned to Washington on November 22, 1963, Secret Service agents found two bullet fragments in the front seat. One fragment, found on the seat beside the driver, weighed 44.6 grains[*] and consisted of the nose portion of a bullet. The other fragment, found along the right side of the front seat, weighed 21.0 grains and consisted of the base portion of a bullet. During the course of an examination on November 23, agents of the Federal Bureau of Investigation found three small lead particles, weighing between $\frac{7}{10}$ and $\frac{9}{10}$ of a grain each, on the rug underneath the left jump seat which had been occupied by Mrs Connally. During this examination, the Bureau agents noted a small residue of lead on the inside surface of

[*] A grain is a US unit of weight, equivalent to 0.002285 ounce/0.065 gram.

the laminated windshield and a very small pattern of cracks on the outer layer of the windshield immediately behind the lead residue. There was a minute particle of glass missing from the outside surface, but no penetration. The inside layer of glass was not broken. The agents also observed a dent in the strip of chrome across the top of the windshield, located to the left of the rear view mirror support.

The lead residue on the inside of the windshield was compared under spectrographic analysis by FBI experts with the bullet fragments found on and alongside the front seat and with the fragments under the left jump seat. It was also compared with bullet fragments found at Parkland Hospital. All these bullet fragments were found to be similar in metallic composition, but it was not possible to determine whether two or more of the fragments came from the same bullet. It is possible for the fragments from the front seat to have been a part of the same bullet as the three fragments found near the left jump seat, since a whole bullet of this type weighs 160–161 grains. The physical characteristics of the windshield after the assassination demonstrate that the windshield was struck on the inside surface. The windshield is composed of two layers of glass with a very thin layer of plastic in the middle "which bonds them together in the form of safety glass." According to Robert A. Frazier, FBI firearms expert, the fact that cracks were present on the outer layer showed that the glass had been struck from the inside. He testified that the windshield:

> ... could not have been struck on the outside surface because of the manner in which the glass broke and further because of the lead residue on the inside surface. The cracks appear in the outer layer of the glass because the glass is bent outward at the time of impact which stretches the outer layer of the glass to the point where these small radial or wagon spoke, wagon wheel spoke-type cracks appear on the outer surface.

Although there is some uncertainty whether the dent in the chrome on the windshield was present prior to the assassination, Frazier testified that the dent "had been caused by some projectile which struck the chrome on the inside surface." If it was caused by a shot during the assassination, Frazier stated that it would not have been caused by a bullet traveling at full velocity, but rather by a fragment traveling at "fairly high velocity." It could have been caused by either fragment found in the front seat of the limousine.

EXPERT EXAMINATION OF RIFLE, CARTRIDGE CASES, AND BULLET FRAGMENTS

On the sixth floor of the Depository Building, the Dallas police found three spent cartridges and a rifle. A nearly whole bullet was discovered on the stretcher used to carry Governor Connally at Parkland Hospital. As described above, five bullet fragments were found in the president's limousine. The cartridge cases, the nearly whole bullet and the bullet fragments were all subjected to firearms identification analysis by qualified experts. It was the unanimous opinion of the experts that the nearly whole bullet, the two largest bullet fragments and the three cartridge cases were definitely fired in the rifle found on the sixth floor of the Depository Building to the exclusion of all other weapons.

Discovery of cartridge cases and rifle

Shortly after the assassination, police officers arrived at the Depository Building and began a search for the assassin and evidence. Around 1 pm Deputy Sheriff Luke Mooney noticed a pile of cartons in front of the window in the southeast corner of the sixth floor. Searching that area he found at approximately 1.12 pm three empty cartridge cases on the floor near the window. When he was notified of Mooney's discovery, Captain J. W. Fritz, chief of the homicide bureau of the Dallas Police Department, issued instructions that nothing be moved or touched until technicians from the police crime laboratory could take photographs and check for fingerprints. Mooney stood guard to see that nothing was disturbed. A few minutes later, Lieutenant J. C. Day of the Dallas Police Department arrived and took photographs of the cartridge cases before anything had been moved.

At 1.22 pm Deputy Sheriff Eugene Boone and Deputy Constable Seymour Weitzman found a bolt-action rifle with a telescopic sight between two rows of boxes in the northwest corner near the staircase on the sixth floor. No one touched the weapon or otherwise disturbed the scene until Captain Fritz and Lieutenant Day arrived and the weapon was photographed as it lay on the floor. After Lieutenant Day determined that there were no fingerprints on the knob of the bolt and that the wooden stock was too rough to take fingerprints, he picked the rifle up by the stock and held it that way while Captain Fritz opened the bolt and ejected a live round. Lieutenant Day retained possession of the weapon and took it back to the police department for examination. Neither Boone nor Weitzman handled the rifle.

Discovery of bullet at Parkland Hospital

A nearly whole bullet was found on Governor Connally's stretcher at Parkland Hospital after the assassination. After his arrival at the hospital the governor was brought into trauma room 2 on a stretcher, removed from the room on that stretcher a short time later, and taken on an elevator to the second-floor operating room. On the second floor he was transferred from the stretcher to an operating table which was then moved into the operating room, and a hospital attendant wheeled the empty stretcher into an elevator. Shortly afterward, Darrell C. Tomlinson, the hospital's senior engineer, removed this stretcher from the elevator and placed it in the corridor on the ground floor, alongside another stretcher wholly unconnected with the care of Governor Connally. A few minutes later, he bumped one of the stretchers against the wall and a bullet rolled out.

Although Tomlinson was not certain whether the bullet came from the Connally stretcher or the adjacent one, the Commission has concluded that the bullet came from the governor's stretcher. That conclusion is buttressed by evidence which eliminated President Kennedy's stretcher as a source of the bullet. President Kennedy remained on the stretcher on which he was carried into the hospital while the doctors tried to save his life. He was never removed from the stretcher from the time he was taken into the emergency room until his body was placed in a casket in that same room. After the president's body was removed from that stretcher, the linen was taken off and placed in a hamper and the stretcher was pushed into trauma room 2, a completely different location from the site where the nearly whole bullet was found.

Description of rifle

The bolt-action, clip-fed rifle found on the sixth floor of the Depository is inscribed with various markings, including "MADE ITALY", "CAL. 6.5", "1940" and the number C2766. These markings have been explained as follows: "MADE ITALY" refers to its origin; "CAL. 6.5" refers to the rifle's caliber; "1940" refers to the year of manufacture; and the number C2766 is the serial number. This rifle is the only one of its type bearing that serial number. After review of standard reference works and the markings on the rifle, it was identified by the FBI as a 6.5-millimeter model 91/38 Mannlicher-Carcano rifle. Experts from the FBI made an independent determination of the caliber by inserting a Mannlicher-Carcano 6.5-millimeter cartridge into the weapon for fit, and by making a sulfur cast of the inside of the weapon's barrel and measuring the cast with a micrometer. From outward appearance, the weapon would appear to be a 7.35-millimeter rifle, but its mechanism had been re-barreled with a 6.5-millimeter barrel. Constable Deputy Sheriff Weitzman, who only saw the rifle at a glance and did not handle it, thought the weapon looked like a 7.65 Mauser bolt-action rifle.

The rifle is 40.2 inches long and weighs 8 pounds. The minimum length broken down is 34.8 inches, the length of the wooden stock. Attached to the weapon is an inexpensive four-power telescopic sight, stamped "OPTICS ORDNANCE INC./HOLLYWOOD CALIFORNIA," and "MADE IN JAPAN." The weapon also bears a sling consisting of two leather straps. The sling is not a standard rifle sling but appears to be a musical instrument strap or a sling from a carrying case or camera bag.

Expert testimony

Four experts in the field of firearms identification analyzed the nearly whole bullet, the two largest fragments and the three cartridge cases to determine whether they had been fired from the C2766 Mannlicher-Carcano rifle found on the sixth floor of the Depository. Two of these experts testified before the Commission. One was Robert A. Frazier, a special agent of the FBI assigned to the FBI Laboratory in Washington, DC. Frazier has worked generally in the field of firearms identification for 23 years, examining firearms of various types for the purpose of identifying the caliber and other characteristics of the weapons and making comparisons of bullets and cartridge cases for the purpose of determining whether or not they were fired in a particular weapon. He estimated that he has made "in the neighborhood of 50,000 to 60,000" firearms comparisons and has testified in court on about 400 occasions. The second witness who testified on this subject was Joseph D. Nicol, superintendent of the bureau of criminal identification and investigation for the State of Illinois. Nicol also has had long and substantial experience since 1941 in firearms identification, and estimated that he has made thousands of bullet and cartridge case examinations.

In examining the bullet fragments and cartridge cases, these experts applied the general principles accepted in the field of firearms identification. In brief, a determination that a particular bullet or cartridge case has been fired in a particular weapon is based upon a comparison of the bullet or case under examination with one or more bullets or cases known to have been fired in that weapon. When a bullet is fired in any given weapon, it is engraved with the characteristics of the weapon. In addition to the rifling characteristics of the barrel which are common to all weapons of a given make and model, every weapon bears distinctive microscopic markings on its barrel, firing pin and bolt face. These markings arise initially during manufacture, since the action of the manufacturing tools differs microscopically from weapon to weapon and since, in addition, the tools change microscopically while being used. As a weapon is used further distinctive markings are introduced. Under microscopic examination a qualified expert may be able to determine whether the markings on a bullet known to have been fired in a particular weapon and the markings on a suspect bullet are the same and, therefore, whether both bullets were fired in the same weapon to the exclusion of all other weapons. Similarly, firearms identification experts are able to compare the markings left upon the base of cartridge cases and thereby determine whether both cartridges were fired by the same weapon to the exclusion of all other weapons. According to Frazier, such an identification "is made on the presence of sufficient individual microscopic characteristics so that a very definite pattern is formed and visualized on the two surfaces." Under some circumstances, as where the bullet or cartridge case is seriously mutilated, there are not sufficient individual characteristics to enable the expert to make a firm identification.

After making independent examinations, both Frazier and Nicol positively identified the nearly whole bullet from the stretcher and the two larger bullet fragments found in the presidential limousine as having been fired in the C2766 Mannlicher-Carcano rifle found in the Depository to the exclusion of all other weapons. Each of the two bullet fragments had sufficient unmutilated area to provide the basis for an identification. However, it was not possible to determine whether the two bullet fragments were from the same bullet or from two different bullets. With regard to the other bullet fragments discovered in the limousine and in the course of treating President Kennedy and Governor Connally, however, expert examination could demonstrate only that the fragments were "similar in metallic composition" to each other, to the two larger fragments and to the nearly whole bullet. After examination of the three cartridge cases found on the sixth floor of the Depository, Frazier and Nicol concluded that they had been fired in the C2766 Mannlicher-Carcano rifle to the exclusion of all other weapons. Two other experts from the Federal Bureau of Investigation, who made independent examinations of the nearly whole bullet, bullet fragments and cartridge cases, reached identical conclusions.

THE BULLET WOUNDS

In considering the question of the source of the shots fired at President Kennedy and Governor Connally, the Commission has also evaluated the expert medical testimony of the doctors who observed the wounds during the emergency treatment at Parkland Hospital and during the autopsy at Bethesda Naval Hospital. It paid particular attention to any wound characteristics which would be of assistance in identifying a wound as the entrance or exit point of a missile. Additional information regarding the source and nature of the injuries was obtained by expert examination of the clothes worn by the two men, particularly those worn by President Kennedy, and from the results of special wound ballistics tests conducted at the Commission's request, using the C2766 Mannlicher-Carcano rifle with ammunition of the same type as that used and found on November 22, 1963.

The president's head wounds

The detailed autopsy of President Kennedy performed on the night of November 22 at the Bethesda Naval Hospital led the three examining pathologists to conclude that the smaller hole in the rear of the president's skull was the point of entry and that the large opening on the right side of his head was the wound of exit. The smaller hole on the back of the president's head measured $\frac{1}{4}$ inch by $\frac{5}{8}$ inch (6 by 15 millimeters). The dimensions of that wound were consistent with having been caused by a 6.5-millimeter bullet fired from behind and above which struck at a tangent or an angle causing a 15-millimeter cut. The cut reflected a larger dimension of entry than the bullet's diameter of 6.5 millimeters, since the missile, in effect, sliced along the skull for a fractional distance until it entered. The dimension of 6 millimeters, somewhat smaller than the diameter of a 6.5-millimeter bullet, was caused by the elastic recoil of the skull which shrinks the size of an opening after a missile passes through it.

Lieutenant-Colonel Pierre A. Finck, Chief of the Wound Ballistics Pathology Branch of the Armed Forces

Institute of Pathology, who has had extensive experience with bullet wounds, illustrated the characteristics which led to his conclusions about the head wound by a chart prepared by him. This chart, based on Colonel Finck's studies of more than 400 cases, depicted the effect of a perforating missile wound on the human skull. When a bullet enters the skull (cranial vault) at one point and exits at another, it causes a beveling or cratering effect where the diameter of the hole is smaller on the impact side than on the exit side. Based on his observations of that beveling effect on the president's skull, Colonel Finck testified: "President Kennedy was, in my opinion, shot from the rear. The bullet entered in the back of the head and went out on the right side of his skull ... he was shot from above and behind."

Commander James J. Humes, senior pathologist and director of laboratories at the Bethesda Naval Hospital, who acted as chief autopsy surgeon, concurred in Colonel Finck's analysis. He compared the beveling or coning effect to that caused by a BB shot [lead pellet] which strikes a pane of glass, causing a round or oval defect on the side of the glass where the missile strikes and a belled-out or coned-out surface on the opposite side of the glass. Referring to the bullet hole on the back of President Kennedy's head, Commander Humes testified: "The wound on the inner table, however, was larger and had what in the field of wound ballistics is described as a shelving or coning effect." After studying the other hole in the president's skull, Commander Humes stated: "... we concluded that the large defect to the upper right side of the skull, in fact, would represent a wound of exit." Those characteristics led Commander Humes and Commander J. Thornton Boswell, chief of pathology at Bethesda Naval Hospital, who assisted in the autopsy, to conclude that the bullet penetrated the rear of the president's head and exited through a large wound on the right side of his head.

Ballistics experiments showed that the rifle and bullets identified above were capable of producing the president's head wound. The Wound Ballistics Branch of the US Army laboratories at Edgewood Arsenal, Maryland, conducted an extensive series of experiments to test the effect of Western Cartridge Co. 6.5-millimeter bullets, the type found on Governor Connally's stretcher and in the presidential limousine, fired from the C2766 Mannlicher-Carcano rifle found in the Depository. The Edgewood Arsenal tests were performed under the immediate supervision of Alfred G. Olivier, a doctor who had spent seven years in wounds ballistics research for the US Army.

One series of tests, performed on reconstructed inert human skulls, demonstrated that the president's head wound could have been caused by the rifle and bullets fired by the assassin from the sixth-floor window. The results of this series were illustrated by the findings on one skull which was struck at a point closely approximating the wound of entry on President Kennedy's head. That bullet blew out the right side of the reconstructed skull in a manner very similar to the head wound of the president. As a result of these tests, Dr Olivier concluded that a Western Cartridge Co 6.5 bullet fired from the C2766 Mannlicher-Carcano rifle at a distance of 90 yards would make the same type of wound as that found on the president's head. Referring to the series of tests, Dr Olivier testified:

> It disclosed that the type of head wounds that the president received could be done by this type of bullet. This surprised me very much, because this type of stable bullet I didn't think would cause a massive head wound, I thought it would go through making a small entrance and exit, but the bones of the skull are enough to deform the end of this bullet causing it to expend a lot of energy and blowing out the side of the skull or blowing out fragments of the skull.

After examining the fragments of the bullet which struck the reconstructed skull, Dr Olivier stated that:

> ... the recovered fragments were very similar to the ones recovered on the front seat and on the floor of the car. This, to me, indicates that those fragments did come from the bullet that wounded the president in the head.

The president's neck wounds

During the autopsy at Bethesda Naval Hospital another bullet wound was observed near the base of the back of President Kennedy's neck slightly to the right of his spine which provides further enlightenment as to the source of the shots. The hole was located approximately $5\frac{1}{2}$ inches (14 centimeters) from the tip of the right shoulder joint and approximately the same distance below the tip of the right mastoid process, the bony point immediately behind the ear. The wound was approximately $\frac{1}{4}$ inch by $\frac{1}{7}$ inch (7 by 4 millimeters), had clean edges, was sharply delineated, and had margins similar in all respects to those of the entry wound in the skull. Commanders Humes and Boswell agreed with Colonel Finck's testimony that this hole:

> ... is a wound of entrance ... The basis for that conclusion is that this wound was relatively small with clean edges. It was not a jagged wound, and that is what we see in wounds of entrance at a long range.

The autopsy examination further disclosed that, after entering the president, the bullet passed between two large muscles, produced a contusion on the upper part of the pleural cavity (without penetrating that cavity), bruised the top portion of the right lung and ripped the windpipe (trachea) in its path through the president's neck. The examining surgeons concluded that the wounds were caused by the bullet rather than the tracheotomy performed at Parkland Hospital. The nature of the bruises indicated that the president's heart and lungs were functioning when the bruises were caused, whereas there was very little circulation in the president's body when incisions on the president's chest were made to insert tubes during the tracheotomy. No bone was struck by the bullet which passed through the president's body. By projecting from a point of entry on the rear of the neck and proceeding at a slight downward angle through the bruised interior portions, the doctors concluded that the bullet exited from the front portion of the president's neck that had been cut away by the tracheotomy.

Concluding that a bullet passed through the president's neck, the doctors at Bethesda Naval Hospital rejected a theory that the bullet lodged in the large muscles in the back of his neck and fell out through the point of entry when external heart massage was applied at Parkland Hospital. In the earlier stages of the autopsy, the surgeons were unable to find a path into any large muscle in the back of the neck. At that time they did not know that there had been a bullet hole in the front of the president's neck when he arrived at Parkland Hospital because the tracheotomy incision had completely eliminated that evidence. While the autopsy was being performed, surgeons learned that a whole bullet had been found at Parkland Hospital on a stretcher which, at that time, was thought to be the stretcher occupied by the president. This led to speculation that the bullet might have penetrated a short distance into the back of the neck and then dropped out onto the stretcher as a result of the external heart massage.

Further exploration during the autopsy disproved that theory. The surgeons determined that the bullet had passed between two large strap muscles and bruised them without leaving any channel, since the bullet merely passed between them. Commander Humes, who believed that a tracheotomy had been performed from his observations at the autopsy, talked by telephone with Dr Perry early on the morning of November 23, and learned that his assumption was correct and that Dr Perry had used the missile wound in the neck as the point to make the incision. This confirmed the Bethesda surgeons' conclusion that the bullet had exited from the front part of the neck.

The findings of the doctors who conducted the autopsy were consistent with the observations of the doctors who treated the president at Parkland Hospital. Dr Charles S. Carrico, a resident surgeon at Parkland, noted a small wound approximately $\frac{1}{4}$ inch in diameter (5 to 8 millimeters) in the lower third of the neck below the Adam's apple. Dr Malcolm O. Perry, who performed the tracheotomy, described the wound as approximately $\frac{1}{5}$ inch in diameter (5 millimeters) and exuding blood which partially hid edges that were "neither clean-cut, that is, punched out, nor were they very ragged." Dr Carrico testified as follows:

Q: Based on your observations on the neck wound alone, did you have a sufficient basis to form an opinion as to whether it was an entrance or an exit wound?

A: No, sir; we did not. Not having completely evaluated all the wounds, traced out the course of the bullets, this wound would have been compatible with either entrance or exit wound depending upon the size, the velocity, the tissue structure and so forth.

The same response was made by Dr Perry to a similar query:

Q: Based on the appearance of the neck wound alone, could it have been either an entrance or an exit wound?

A: It could have been either.

Then each doctor was asked to take into account the other known facts, such as the autopsy findings, the approximate distance the bullet traveled and tested muzzle velocity of the assassination weapon. With these additional factors, the doctors commented on the wound on the front of the president's neck as follows:

> *Dr Carrico*: With those facts and the fact as I understand it, no other bullet was found, this would be, this was, I believe, was an exit wound.
> *Dr Perry*: A full jacketed bullet without deformation passing through skin would leave a similar wound for an exit and entrance wound and with the facts which you have made available and with these assumptions, I believe that it was an exit wound.

Other doctors at Parkland Hospital who observed the wound prior to the tracheotomy agreed with the observations of Drs Perry and Carrico. The bullet wound in the neck could be seen for only a short time, since Dr Perry eliminated evidence of it when he performed the tracheotomy. He selected that spot since it was the point where such an operation was customarily performed, and it was one of the safest and easiest spots from which to reach the trachea. In addition, there was possibly an underlying wound to the muscles in the neck, the carotid artery or the jugular vein, and Dr Perry concluded that the incision, therefore, had to be low in order to maintain respiration.

Considerable confusion has arisen because of comments attributed to Dr Perry concerning the nature of the neck wound. Immediately after the assassination, many people reached erroneous conclusions about the source of the shots because of Dr Perry's observations to the press. On the afternoon of November 22, a press conference was organized at Parkland Hospital by members of the White House press staff and a hospital administrator. Newsmen with microphones and cameras were crowded into a room to hear statements by Drs Perry and William Kemp Clark, chief neurosurgeon at Parkland, who had attended to President Kennedy's head injury. Dr Perry described the situation as "bedlam". The confusion was compounded by the fact that some questions were only partially answered before other questions were asked.

At the news conference, Dr Perry answered a series of hypothetical questions and stated to the press that a variety of possibilities could account for the president's wounds. He stated that a single bullet could have caused the president's wounds by entering through the throat, striking the spine, and being deflected upward with the point of exit being through the head. This would have accounted for the two wounds he observed, the hole in the front of the neck and the large opening in the skull. At that time, Dr Perry did not know about either the wound on the back of the president's neck or the small bullet-hole wound in the back of the head. As described on pp.90–94, the president was lying on his back during his entire time at Parkland. The small hole in the head was also hidden from view by the large quantity of blood which covered the president's head. Dr Perry said his answers at the press conference were intended to convey his theory about what could have happened, based on his limited knowledge at the time, rather than his professional opinion about what did happen. Commenting on his answers at the press conference, Dr Perry testified before the Commission:

> I expressed it [his answers] as a matter of speculation that this was conceivable. But, again, Dr Clark [who also answered questions at the conference] and I emphasized that we had no way of knowing.

Dr Perry's recollection of his comments is corroborated by some of the news stories after the press conference. The *New York Herald Tribune* on November 23, 1963, reported as follows:

> Dr Malcolm Perry, 34, attendant surgeon at Parkland Hospital who attended the president, said he saw two wounds, one below the Adam's apple, the other at the back of the head. He said he did not know if two bullets were involved. It is possible, he said, that the neck wound was the entrance and the other the exit of the missile.

According to this report, Dr Perry stated merely that it was "possible" that the neck wound was a wound of entrance. This conforms with his testimony before the Commission, where he stated that by themselves the characteristics of the neck wound were consistent with being either a point of entry or exit.

Wound ballistics tests
Experiments performed by the Army Wound Ballistics experts at Edgewood Arsenal, Maryland, showed that under simulated conditions entry and exit wounds are very similar in appearance. After reviewing the path of the bullet through the president's neck, as disclosed in the autopsy report, the experts simulated the neck by using comparable material with a thickness of approximately $5\frac{1}{2}$ inches ($13\frac{1}{2}$ to $14\frac{1}{2}$ centimeters), which was the distance traversed by the bullet. Animal skin was placed on each side, and Western Cartridge Co. 6.5 bullets were fired from the C2766 Mannlicher-Carcano rifle from a distance of 180 feet. The animal skin on the entry side showed holes which were regular and round. On the exit side two holes were only slightly elongated, indicating that the bullet had become only a little unstable at the point of exit. A third exit hole was round, although not

quite as regular as the entry holes. The exit holes, especially the one most nearly round, appeared similar to the descriptions given by Drs Perry and Carrico of the hole in the front of the president's neck.

The autopsy disclosed that the bullet which entered the back of the president's neck hit no bony structure and proceeded in a slightly downward angle. The markings on the president's clothing indicate that the bullet moved in a slight right-to-left lateral direction as it passed through the president's body. After the examining doctors expressed the thought that a bullet would have lost very little velocity in passing through the soft tissue of the neck, wound ballistics experts conducted tests to measure the exit velocity of the bullet. The tests were the same as those used to create entry and exit holes, supplemented by the use of break-type screens which measured the velocity of bullets. The entrance velocity of the bullet fired from the rifle averaged 1,904 feet per second after it traveled 180 feet. The exit velocity averaged 1,772 to 1,798 feet per second, depending upon the substance through which the bullet passed. A photograph of the path of the bullet traveling through the simulated neck showed that it proceeded in a straight line and was stable.

Examination of clothing

The clothing worn by President Kennedy on November 22 had holes and tears which showed that a missile entered the back of his clothing in the vicinity of his lower neck and exited through the front of his shirt immediately behind his tie, nicking the knot of his tie in its forward flight. Although the caliber of the bullet could not be determined and some of the clothing items precluded a positive determination that some tears were made by a bullet, all the defects could have been caused by a 6.5-millimeter bullet entering the back of the president's lower neck and exiting in the area of the knot of his tie.

An examination of the suit jacket worn by the president by FBI Agent Frazier revealed a roughly circular hole approximately $\frac{1}{4}$ inch in diameter on the rear of the coat, $5\frac{3}{8}$ inches below the top of the collar and $1\frac{3}{4}$ inches to the right of the center back seam of the coat. The hole was visible on the upper rear of the coat slightly to the right of center. Traces of copper were found in the margins of the hole and the cloth fibers around the margins were pushed inward. Those characteristics established that the hole was caused by an entering bullet. Although the precise size of the bullet could not be determined from the hole, it was consistent with having been made by a 6.5-millimeter bullet.

The shirt worn by the president contained a hole on the back side $5\frac{3}{4}$ inches below the top of the collar and $1\frac{1}{8}$ inches to the right of the middle of the back of the shirt. The hole on the rear of the shirt was approximately circular in shape and about $\frac{1}{4}$ inch in diameter, with the fibers pressed inward. These factors established it as a bullet entrance hole. The relative position of the hole in the back of the suit jacket to the hole in the back of the shirt indicated that both were caused by the same penetrating missile.

On the front of the shirt, examination revealed a hole $\frac{7}{8}$ inch below the collar button and a similar opening $\frac{7}{8}$ inch below the buttonhole. These two holes fell into alignment on overlapping positions when the shirt was buttoned. Each hole was a vertical, ragged slit approximately $\frac{1}{2}$ inch in height, with the cloth fibers protruding outward. Although the characteristics of the slit established that the missile had exited to the front, the irregular nature of the slit precluded a positive determination that it was a bullet hole. However, the hole could have been caused by a round bullet although the characteristics were not sufficiently clear to enable the examining expert to render a conclusive opinion.

When the president's clothing was removed at Parkland Hospital, his tie was cut off by severing the loop immediately to the wearer's left of the knot, leaving the knot in its original condition. The tie had a nick on the left side of the knot. The nick was elongated horizontally, indicating that the tear was made by some object moving horizontally, but the fibers were not affected in a manner which would shed light on the direction or the nature of the missile.

The governor's wounds

While riding in the right jump seat of the presidential limousine on November 22, Governor Connally sustained wounds of the back, chest, right wrist and left thigh. Because of the small size and clean-cut edges of the wound on the governor's back, Dr Robert Shaw concluded that it was an entry wound. The bullet traversed the governor's chest in a downward angle, shattering his fifth rib, and exited below the right nipple. The ragged edges of the 2-inch (5 centimeters) opening on the front of the chest led Dr Shaw to conclude that it was the exit point of the bullet. When Governor Connally testified before the Commission five months after the assassination, on April 21, 1964, the Commission observed the governor's chest wounds, as well as the injuries to his wrist and thigh and watched Dr Shaw measure with a caliper an angle of declination of 25 from the point of entry on the back to the point of exit on the front of the governor's chest.

At the time of the shooting, Governor Connally was unaware that he had sustained any injuries other than his chest wounds. On the back of his arm, about 2 inches (5 centimeters) above the wrist joint on the thumb side, Dr Charles F. Gregory observed a linear perforating wound approximately $\frac{1}{5}$ inch ($\frac{1}{2}$ centimeter) wide and 1 inch ($2\frac{1}{2}$ centimeters) long. During his operation on this injury, the doctor concluded that this ragged wound was the point of entry because thread and cloth had been carried into the wound to the region of the bone. Dr Gregory's conclusions were also based upon the location in the governor's wrist, as revealed by X-ray, of small fragments of metal shed by the missile upon striking the firm surface of the bone. Evidence of different amounts of air in the tissues of the wrist gave further indication that the bullet passed from the back to the front of the wrist. An examination of the palm surface of the wrist showed a wound approximately $\frac{1}{5}$ inch ($\frac{1}{2}$ centimeter) long and approximately $\frac{3}{4}$ inch (2 centimeters) above the crease of the right wrist. Dr Shaw had initially believed that the missile entered on the palm side of the governor's wrist and exited on the back side. After reviewing the factors considered by Dr Gregory, however, Dr Shaw withdrew his earlier opinion. He deferred to the judgment of Dr Gregory, who had more closely examined that wound during the wrist operation.

In addition, Governor Connally suffered a puncture wound in the left thigh that was approximately $\frac{2}{5}$ inch (1 centimeter) in diameter and located approximately 5 or 6 inches above the governor's left knee. On the governor's leg, very little soft-tissue damage was noted, which indicated a tangential wound or the penetration of a larger missile entering at low velocity and stopping after entering the skin. X-ray examination disclosed a tiny metallic fragment embedded in the governor's leg. The surgeons who attended the governor concluded that the thigh wound was not caused by the small fragment in the thigh but resulted from the impact of a larger missile.

Examination of clothing
The clothing worn by Governor Connally on November 22, 1963, contained holes which matched his wounds. On the back of the governor's coat, a hole was found $1\frac{1}{8}$ inches

from the seam where the right sleeve attached to the coat
and inches to the right of the midline. This hole was elongated in a horizontal direction approximately $\frac{5}{8}$ inch in
length and $\frac{1}{4}$ inch in height. The front side of the
Governor's coat contained a circular hole $\frac{3}{8}$ inch in diameter, located 5 inches to the right of the front right edge of
the coat slightly above the top button. A rough hole
approximately $\frac{5}{8}$ inch in length and $\frac{3}{8}$ inch in width was
found near the end of the right sleeve. Each of these holes
could have been caused by a bullet, but a positive determination of this fact or the direction of the missile was not
possible because the garment had been cleaned and pressed
prior to any opportunity for a scientific examination.

An examination of the governor's shirt disclosed a very
ragged tear $\frac{5}{8}$ inch long horizontally and $\frac{1}{2}$ inch vertically
on the back of the shirt near the right sleeve, 2 inches from
the line where the sleeve attaches. Immediately to the right
was another small tear, approximately $\frac{3}{16}$ inch long. The two
holes corresponded in position to the hole in the back of
the governor's coat. A very irregular tear in the form of an
"H" was observed on the front side of the governor's shirt,
approximately $1\frac{1}{2}$ inches high, with a crossbar tear approximately 1 inch wide, located 5 inches from the right side
seam and 9 inches from the top of the right sleeve. Because
the shirt had been laundered, there were insufficient characteristics for the expert examiner to form a conclusive
opinion on the direction or nature of the object causing the
holes. The rear hole could have been caused by the
entrance of a 6.5-millimeter bullet and the front hole by
the exit of such a bullet.

On the French cuff of the right sleeve of the governor's
shirt was a ragged, irregularly shaped hole located $1\frac{1}{2}$ inches
from the end of the sleeve and $5\frac{1}{2}$ inches from the outside
cuff-link hole. The characteristics after laundering did not
permit positive conclusions but these holes could have

been caused by a bullet passing through the governor's right wrist from the back to the front sides. The governor's trousers contained a hole approximately $\frac{1}{4}$ inch in diameter in the region of the left knee. The roughly circular shape of the hole and the slight tearing away from the edges gave the hole the general appearance of a bullet hole but it was not possible to determine the direction of the missile which caused the hole.

Course of bullet

Ballistics experiments and medical findings established that the missile which passed through the governor's wrist and penetrated his thigh had first traversed his chest. The Army Wound Ballistics experts conducted tests which proved that the governor's wrist wound was not caused by a pristine bullet. A bullet is pristine immediately on exiting from a rifle muzzle when it moves in a straight line with a spinning motion and maintains its uniform trajectory, with but a minimum of nose surface striking the air through which it passes. When the straight line of flight of a bullet is deflected by striking some object, it starts to wobble or become irregular in flight, a condition called yaw. A bullet with yaw has a greater surface exposed to the striking material or air, since the target or air is struck not only by the nose of the bullet, its smallest striking surface, but also by the bullet's sides.

The ballistics experts learned the exact nature of the governor's wrist wound by examining Parkland Hospital records and X-rays and conferring with Dr Gregory. The C2766 Mannlicher-Carcano rifle found in the Depository was fired with bullets of the same type as the bullet found on the governor's stretcher and the fragments found in the presidential limousine. Shots were fired from a distance of 70 yards at comparable flesh and bone protected by material similar to the clothing worn by the governor. One of the test shots wounded the comparable flesh and bone structure in virtually the same place and from the same angle as the wound inflicted on Governor Connally's wrist. An X-ray and photograph of the simulated wrist confirmed the similarity. The bullet which inflicted that injury during the tests had a nose which was substantially flattened from striking the material. The striking velocity at 70 yards of seven shots fired during the tests averaged 1,858 feet per second; the average exit velocity of five shots was 1,776 feet per second.

The conclusion that the governor's wrist was not struck by a pristine bullet was based upon the following:

(1) greater damage was inflicted on the test material than on the governor's wrist

(2) the test material had a smaller entry wound and a larger exit wound, characteristic of a pristine bullet, while the governor's wrist had a larger entry wound as compared with its exit wound, indicating a bullet which was tumbling

(3) cloth was carried into the wrist wound, which is characteristic of an irregular missile

(4) the partial cutting of a radial nerve and tendon leading to the governor's thumb further suggested that the bullet which struck him was not pristine, since such a bullet would merely push aside a tendon and nerve rather than catch and tear them

(5) the bullet found on the governor's stretcher probably did not pass through the wrist as a pristine bullet because its nose was not considerably flattened, as was the case with the pristine bullet which struck the simulated wrist

(6) the bullet which caused the governor's thigh injury and then fell out of the wound had a "very low velocity", whereas the pristine bullets fired during the tests possessed a very high exit velocity.

All the evidence indicated that the bullet found on the governor's stretcher could have caused all his wounds. The weight of the whole bullet prior to firing was approximately 160–161 grains and that of the recovered bullet was 158 grains. An X-ray of the governor's wrist showed very minute metallic fragments, and two or three of these fragments were removed from his wrist. All these fragments were sufficiently small and light so that the nearly whole bullet found on the stretcher could have deposited those pieces of metal as it tumbled through his wrist. In their testimony, the three doctors who attended Governor Connally at Parkland Hospital expressed independently their opinion that a single bullet had passed through his chest; tumbled through his wrist with very little exit velocity, leaving small metallic fragments from the rear portion of the bullet; punctured his left thigh after the bullet had lost virtually all of its velocity; and had fallen out of the thigh wound.

Governor Connally himself thought it likely that all his wounds were caused by a single bullet. In his testimony before the Commission, he re-positioned himself as he recalled his position on the jump seat, with his right palm on his left thigh, and said:

> I ... wound up the next day realizing I was hit in three places, and I was not conscious of having been hit but by one bullet, so I tried to reconstruct how I could have been hit in three places by the same bullet, and I merely, I know it penetrated from the back through the chest first. I assumed that I had turned as I described a moment ago, placing my right hand on my left leg, that it hit my wrist, went out the center of the wrist, the underside, and then into my leg, but it might not have happened that way at all.

The governor's posture explained how a single missile through his body would cause all his wounds. His doctors at Parkland Hospital had recreated his position, also, but they placed his right arm somewhat higher than his left thigh although in the same alignment. The wound ballistics experts concurred in the opinion that a single bullet caused all the governor's wounds.

THE TRAJECTORY

The cumulative evidence of eyewitnesses, firearms and ballistic experts and medical authorities demonstrated that the shots were fired from above and behind President Kennedy and Governor Connally, more particularly, from the sixth floor of the Texas School Book Depository Building. In order to determine the facts with as much precision as possible and to insure that all data were consistent with the shots having been fired from the sixth floor window, the Commission requested additional investigation, including the analysis of motion picture films of the assassination and on-site tests. The facts developed through this investigation by the FBI and Secret Service confirmed the conclusions reached by the Commission regarding the source and trajectory of the shots which hit the president and the governor. Moreover, these facts enabled the Commission to make certain approximations regarding the locations of the presidential limousine at the time of the shots and the relevant time intervals.

Films and tests
When the shots rang out the presidential limousine was moving beyond the Texas School Book Depository Building in a southwesterly direction on Elm Street between Houston Street and the Triple Underpass. The general location of the car was described and marked on maps by eyewitnesses as precisely as their observations and recollections permitted. More exact information was pro-

vided by motion pictures taken by Abraham Zapruder, Orville O. Nix and Mary Muchmore, who were spectators at the scene. Substantial light has been shed on the assassination sequence by viewing these motion pictures, particularly the Zapruder film, which was the most complete and from which individual 35-millimeter slides were made of each motion picture frame.

Examination of the Zapruder motion picture camera by the FBI established that 18.3 pictures or frames were taken each second, and therefore, the timing of certain events could be calculated by allowing 1/18.3 seconds for the action depicted from one frame to the next. The films and slides made from individual frames were viewed by Governor and Mrs Connally, the governor's doctors, the autopsy surgeons, and the Army wound ballistics scientists in order to apply the knowledge of each to determine the precise course of events. Tests of the assassin's rifle disclosed that at least 2 seconds were required between shots. In evaluating the films in the light of these timing guides, it was kept in mind that a victim of a bullet wound may not react immediately and, in some situations, according to experts, the victim may not even know where he has been hit, or when.

On May 24, 1964, agents of the FBI and Secret Service conducted a series of tests to determine as precisely as possible what happened on November 22, 1963. Since the presidential limousine was being remodeled and was therefore unavailable, it was simulated by using the Secret Service follow-up car, which is similar in design. Any differences were taken into account. Two Bureau agents with approximately the same physical characteristics sat in the car in the same relative positions as President Kennedy and Governor Connally had occupied. The back of the stand-in for the president was marked with chalk at the point where the bullet entered. The governor's model had on the same coat worn by Governor Connally when he was shot, with the hole in the back circled in chalk.

To simulate the conditions which existed at the assassination scene on November 22, the lower part of the sixth-floor window at the southeast corner of the Depository Building was raised halfway, the cardboard boxes were re-positioned, the C2766 Mannlicher-Carcano rifle found on the sixth floor of the Depository was used, and mounted on that rifle was a camera which recorded the view as was seen by the assassin. In addition, the Zapruder, Nix, and Muchmore cameras were on hand so that photographs taken by these cameras from the same locations where they were used on November 22, 1963, could be compared with the films of that date. The agents ascertained that the foliage of an oak tree that came between the gunman and his target along the motorcade route on Elm Street was approximately the same as on the day of the assassination.

The first bullet that hit

The position of President Kennedy's car when he was struck in the neck was determined with substantial precision from the films and on-site tests. The pictures or frames in the Zapruder film were marked by the agents, with the number "1" given to the first frame where the motorcycles leading the motorcade came into view on Houston Street. The numbers continue in sequence as Zapruder filmed the presidential limousine as it came around the corner and proceeded down Elm. The president was in clear view of the assassin as he rode up Houston Street and for 100 feet as he proceeded down Elm Street, until he came to a point denoted as frame 166 on the Zapruder film. These facts were determined in the test by placing the car and men on Elm Street in the exact spot where they were when each frame of the Zapruder film was photographed. To pinpoint their locations, a man stood at Zapruder's position and directed the automobile and both models to the positions shown on each frame, after which a Bureau photographer crouched at the sixth-floor window and looked through a camera whose lens recorded the view through the telescopic sight of the C2766 Mannlicher-Carcano rifle. Each position was measured to determine how far President Kennedy had gone down Elm from a point, which was designated as station C, on a line drawn along the west curbline of Houston Street.

Based on these calculations, the agents concluded that at frame 166 of the Zapruder film the president passed beneath the foliage of the large oak tree and the point of impact on the president's back disappeared from the gunman's view as seen through the telescopic lens. For a fleeting instant, the president came back into view in the telescopic lens at frame 186 as he appeared in an opening among the leaves. The test revealed that the next point at which the rifleman had a clear view through the telescopic sight of the point where the bullet entered the president's back was when the car emerged from behind the tree at frame 210. According to FBI Agent Lyndal L. Shaneyfelt, "There is no obstruction from the sixth-floor window from the time they leave the tree until they disappear down toward the triple overpass."

As the president rode along Elm Street for a distance of about 140 feet, he was waving to the crowd. Shaneyfelt testified that the waving is seen on the Zapruder movie until around frame 205, when a road sign blocked out most of the president's body from Zapruder's view through the lens of his camera. However, the assassin continued to have a clear view of the president as he proceeded down Elm. When President Kennedy again came fully into view in the Zapruder film at frame 225, he seemed to be reacting to his neck wound by raising his hands to his throat. According to

Shaneyfelt the reaction was "barely apparent in 225." It is probable that the president was not shot before frame 210, since it is unlikely that the assassin would deliberately have shot at him with a view obstructed by the oak tree when he was about to have a clear opportunity. It is also doubtful that even the most proficient marksman would have hit him through the oak tree. In addition, the president's reaction is "barely apparent" in frame 225, which is 15 frames or approximately $\frac{8}{10}$ second after frame 210, and a shot much before 210 would assume a longer reaction time than was recalled by eyewitnesses at the scene. Thus, the evidence indicated that the president was not hit until at least frame 210 and that he was probably hit by frame 225. The possibility of variations in reaction time in addition to the obstruction of Zapruder's view by the sign precluded a more specific determination than that the president was probably shot through the neck between frames 210 and 225, which marked his position between 138.9 and 153.8 feet west of station C.

According to Special Agent Robert A. Frazier, who occupied the position of the assassin in the sixth-floor window during the re-enactment, it is likely that the bullet which passed through the president's neck, as described previously, then struck the automobile or someone else in the automobile. The minute examination by the FBI inspection team, conducted in Washington between 14 and 16 hours after the assassination, revealed no damage indicating that a bullet struck any part of the interior of the presidential limousine, with the exception of the cracking of the windshield and the dent on the windshield chrome. Neither of these points of damage to the car could have been caused by the bullet which exited from the president's neck at a velocity of 1,772 to 1,779 feet per second. If the trajectory had permitted the bullet to strike the windshield, the bullet would have penetrated it and traveled a substantial distance down the road unless it struck some other object en route. Had that bullet struck the metal framing, which was dented, it would have torn a hole in the chrome and penetrated the framing, both inside and outside the car. At that exit velocity, the bullet would have penetrated any other metal or upholstery surface of the interior of the automobile.

The bullet that hit President Kennedy in the back and exited through his throat most likely could not have missed both the automobile and its occupants. Since it did not hit the automobile, Frazier testified that it probably struck Governor Connally. The relative positions of President Kennedy and Governor Connally at the time when the president was struck in the neck confirm that the same bullet probably passed through both men. Pictures taken of the president's limousine on November 22, 1963, showed that the governor sat immediately in front of the president. Even though the precise distance cannot be ascertained, it is apparent that President Kennedy was somewhat to the governor's right. The president sat on the extreme right, as noted in the films and by eyewitnesses, while the right edge of the jump seat in which the governor sat is 6 inches from the right door. The president wore a back brace which tended to make him sit up straight, and the governor also sat erect since the jump seat gave him little leg room.

Based on his observations during the re-enactment and the position of Governor Connally shown in the Zapruder film after the car emerged from behind the sign, Frazier testified that Governor Connally was in a position during the span from frame 207 to frame 225 to receive a bullet which would have caused the wounds he actually suffered. Governor Connally viewed the film and testified that he was hit between frames 231 and 234. According to Frazier, between frames 235 and 240 the governor turned sharply to his right, so that by frame 240 he was too far to the right to have received his injuries at that time. At some point between frames 235 and 240, therefore, is the last occasion when Governor Connally could have received his injuries, since in the frames following 240 he remained turned too far to his right. If Governor Connally was hit by a separate shot between frames 235 and 240 which followed the shot which hit the president's neck, it would follow that:

(1) the assassin's first shot, assuming a minimum firing time of 2.3 seconds (or 42 frames), was fired between frames 193 and 198 when his view was obscured by the oak tree

(2) President Kennedy continued waving to the crowd after he was hit and did not begin to react for about $1\frac{1}{2}$ seconds

(3) the first shot, although hitting no bones in the president's body, was deflected after its exit from the president's neck in such a way that it failed to hit either the automobile or any of the other occupants.

Viewed through the telescopic sight of the C2766 Mannlicher-Carcano rifle from the sixth-floor window during the test, the marks that simulated the entry wounds on the stand-ins for the president and the governor were generally in a straight line. That alignment became obvious to the viewer through the scope as the governor's model turned slightly to his right and assumed the position which Governor Connally had described as his position when he was struck. Viewing the stand-ins for the president and the governor in the sight of the C2766 Mannlicher-Carcano rifle at the location depicted in frames 207 and 210, Frazier testified: "They both are in direct alignment with the telescopic sight at the window. The governor is immediately behind the president in the field of view." A surveyor then placed his sighting equipment at the precise point of entry on the back of the president's neck, assuming that the president was struck at frame 210, and measured the angle to the end of the muzzle of the rifle positioned where it was believed to have been held by the assassin. That angle measured 2134'. From the same points of reference, the angle at frame 225 was measured at 2011', giving an average angle of 2052'30" from frame 210 to frame 225. Allowing for a downward street grade of 309', the probable angle through the president's body was calculated at 1743'30", assuming that he was sitting in a vertical position.

That angle was consistent with the trajectory of a bullet passing through the president's neck and then striking Governor Connally's back, causing the wounds which were discussed above. Shortly after that angle was ascertained, the open car and the stand-ins were taken by the agents to a nearby garage where a photograph was taken to determine through closer study whether the angle of that shot could have accounted for the wounds in the president's neck and the governor's back. A rod was placed at an angle of 1743'30" next to the stand-ins for the president and the governor, who were seated in the same relative positions. The wounds of entry and exit on the president were approximated based on information gained from the autopsy reports and photographs. The hole in the back of the jacket worn by the governor and the medical description of the wound on his back marked that entry point. That line of fire from the sixth floor of the Depository would have caused the bullet to exit under the governor's right nipple just as the bullet did. Governor Connally's doctors measured an angle of declination on his body from the entry wound on his back to the exit on the front of his chest at about 25 when he sat erect. That difference was explained by either a slight deflection of the bullet caused by striking the fifth rib or the governor's leaning slightly backward at the time he was struck. In addition, the angle could not be fixed with absolute precision, since the large wound on the front of his chest precluded an exact determination of the point of exit.

The alignment of the points of entry was only indicative and not conclusive that one bullet hit both men. The exact positions of the men could not be re-created; thus, the angle could only be approximated. Had President Kennedy been leaning forward or backward, the angle of declination of the shot to a perpendicular target would have varied. The angle of 1743'30" was approximately the angle of declination reproduced in an artist's drawing. That drawing, made from data provided by the autopsy surgeons, could not reproduce the exact line of the bullet, since the exit wound was obliterated by the tracheotomy. Similarly, if the president or the governor had been sitting in a different lateral position, the conclusion might have varied. Or if the governor had not turned in exactly the way calculated, the alignment would have been destroyed.

Additional experiments by the Army Wound Ballistics Branch further suggested that the same bullet probably passed through both President Kennedy and Governor Connally. Correlation of a test simulating the governor's chest wound with the neck and wrist experiments indicated that course. After reviewing the Parkland Hospital medical records and X-rays of the governor and discussing his chest injury with the attending surgeon, the Army ballistics experts virtually duplicated the wound using the assassination weapon and animal flesh covered by cloth. The bullet that struck the animal flesh displayed characteristics similar to the bullet found on Governor Connally's stretcher. Moreover, the imprint on the velocity screen immediately behind the animal flesh showed that the bullet was tumbling after exiting from the flesh, having lost a total average of 265 feet per second. Taking into consideration the governor's size, the reduction in velocity of a bullet passing through his body would be approximately 400 feet per second.

Based upon the medical evidence on the wounds of the governor and the president and the wound ballistics tests performed at Edgewood Arsenal, Drs Olivier and Arthur J. Dziemian, chief of the Army Wound Ballistics Branch, who had spent 17 years in that area of specialization, concluded that it was probable that the same bullet passed through the president's neck and then inflicted all the wounds on the governor. Referring to the president's neck wound and all the governor's wounds, Dr Dziemian testified: "I think the probability is very good that it is, that all the wounds were caused by one bullet." Both Drs Dziemian and Olivier believed that the wound on the governor's wrist would have been more extensive had the bullet which inflicted that injury merely passed through the governor's chest, exiting at a velocity of approximately 1,500 feet per second. Thus, the governor's wrist wound suggested that the bullet passed through the president's neck, began to yaw in the air between the president and the governor, and then lost more velocity than 400 feet per second in passing through the governor's chest. A bullet which was yawing on entering into the governor's back would lose substantially more velocity in passing through his body than a pristine bullet. In addition, the bullet that struck the animal flesh was flattened to a greater extent than the bullet which presumably struck the governor's rib, which suggests that the bullet which entered the governor's chest had already lost velocity by passing through the president's neck. Moreover, the large wound on the governor's back would be explained by a bullet which was yawing, although that type of wound might also be accounted for by a tangential striking.

Dr Frederick W. Light, Jr, the third of the wound ballistics experts, who has been engaged in that specialty at

Edgewood Arsenal since 1951, testified that the anatomical findings were insufficient for him to formulate a firm opinion as to whether the same bullet did or did not pass through the president's neck first before inflicting all the wounds on Governor Connally. Based on the other circumstances, such as the relative positions of the president and the governor in the automobile, Dr Light concluded it was probable that the same bullet traversed the president's neck and inflicted all the wounds on Governor Connally.

The subsequent bullet that hit

After a bullet penetrated President Kennedy's neck, a subsequent shot entered the back of his head and exited through the upper right portion of his skull. The Zapruder, Nix and Muchmore films show the instant in the sequence when that bullet struck. That impact was evident from the explosion of the president's brain tissues from the right side of his head. The immediately preceding frame from the Zapruder film shows the president slumped to his left, clutching at his throat, with his chin close to his chest and his head tilted forward at an angle. Based upon information provided by the doctors who conducted the autopsy, an artist's drawing depicted the path of the bullet through the president's head, with his head being in the same approximate position.

By using the Zapruder, Nix and Muchmore motion pictures, the president's location at the time the bullet penetrated his head was fixed with reasonable precision. A careful analysis of the Nix and Muchmore films led to fixing the exact location of these cameramen. The point of impact of the bullet on the president's head was apparent in all of the movies. At that point in the Nix film a straight line was plotted from the camera position to a fixed point in the background and the president's location along this line was marked on a plat map [plan of actual features]. A similar process was followed with the Muchmore film. The president's location on the plat map was identical to that determined from the Nix film. The president's location, established through the Nix and Muchmore films, was confirmed by comparing his position on the Zapruder film. This location had hitherto only been approximated, since there were no landmarks in the background of the Zapruder frame for alignment purposes other than a portion of a painted line on the curb. Through these procedures, it was determined that President Kennedy was shot in the head when he was 230.8 feet from a point on the west curbline on Houston Street where it intersected with Elm Street. The president was 265.3 feet from the rifle in the sixth-floor window and at that position the approximate angle of declination was 1521'.

NUMBER OF SHOTS

The consensus among the witnesses at the scene was that three shots were fired. However, some heard only two shots, while others testified that they heard four and perhaps as many as five or six shots. The difficulty of accurate perception of the sound of gunshots required careful scrutiny of all of this testimony regarding the number of shots. The firing of a bullet causes a number of noises: the muzzle blast, caused by the smashing of the hot gases which propel the bullet into the relatively stable air at the gun's muzzle; the noise of the bullet, caused by the shock wave built up ahead of the bullet's nose as it travels through the air; and the noise caused by the impact of the bullet on its target. Each noise can be quite sharp and may be perceived as a separate shot. The tall buildings in the area might have further distorted the sound.

The physical and other evidence examined by the Commission compels the conclusion that at least two shots were fired. As discussed previously, the nearly whole bullet

discovered at Parkland Hospital and the two larger fragments found in the presidential automobile, which were
identified as coming from the assassination rifle, came from
at least two separate bullets and possibly from three. The
most convincing evidence relating to the number of shots
was provided by the presence on the sixth floor of three
spent cartridges which were demonstrated to have been
fired by the same rifle that fired the bullets which caused
the wounds. It is possible that the assassin carried an empty
shell in the rifle and fired only two shots, with the witnesses
hearing multiple noises made by the same shot. Soon after
the three empty cartridges were found, officials at the scene
decided that three shots were fired, and that conclusion was
widely circulated by the press. The eyewitness testimony
may be subconsciously colored by the extensive publicity
given the conclusion that three shots were fired.
Nevertheless, the preponderance of the evidence, in particular the three spent cartridges, led the Commission to
conclude that there were three shots fired.

The shot that missed
From the initial findings that:

(1) one shot passed through the president's neck and then
     most probably passed through the governor's body
(2) a subsequent shot penetrated the president's head
(3) no other shot struck any part of the automobile
(4) three shots were fired

it follows that one shot probably missed the car and its
occupants. The evidence is inconclusive as to whether it
was the first, second, or third shot which missed.

The first shot
If the first shot missed, the assassin perhaps missed in an
effort to fire a hurried shot before the president passed under

the oak tree, or possibly he fired as the president passed under the tree and the tree obstructed his view. The bullet might have struck a portion of the tree and been completely deflected. On the other hand, the greatest cause for doubt that the first shot missed is the improbability that the same marksman who twice hit a moving target would be so inaccurate on the first and closest of his shots as to miss completely, not only the target, but the large automobile.

Some support for the contention that the first shot missed is found in the statement of Secret Service Agent Glen A. Bennett, stationed in the right rear seat of the president's follow-up car, who heard a sound like a firecracker as the motorcade proceeded down Elm Street. At that moment, Agent Bennett stated:

> . . . I looked at the back of the president. I heard another
> firecracker noise and saw that shot hit the president about
> four inches down from the right shoulder. A second shot
> followed immediately and hit the right rear high of the
> president's head.

Substantial weight may be given to Bennett's observations. Although his formal statement was dated November 23, 1963, his notes indicate that he recorded what he saw and heard at 5.30 pm, 22 November 1963, on the airplane en route back to Washington, prior to the autopsy, when it was not yet known that the president had been hit in the back. It is possible, of course, that Bennett did not observe the hole in the president's back, which might have been there immediately after the first noise.

Governor Connally's testimony supports the view that the first shot missed, because he stated that he heard a shot, turned slightly to his right, and, as he started to turn back toward his left, was struck by the second bullet. He never saw the president during the shooting sequence, and it is entirely possible that he heard the missed shot and that both men were struck by the second bullet. Mrs Connally testified that after the first shot she turned and saw the president's hands moving toward his throat, as seen in the films at frame 225. However, Mrs Connally further stated that she thought her husband was hit immediately thereafter by the second bullet. If the same bullet struck both the president and the governor, it is entirely possible that she saw the president's movements at the same time as she heard the second shot. Her testimony, therefore, does not preclude the possibility of the first shot having missed.

Other eyewitness testimony, however, supports the conclusion that the first of the shots fired hit the president. Special Agent Hill's testimony indicates that the president was hit by the first shot and that the head injury was caused by a second shot which followed about five seconds later. James W. Altgens, a photographer in Dallas for the Associated Press, had stationed himself on Elm Street opposite the Depository to take pictures of the passing motorcade. Altgens took a widely circulated photograph which showed President Kennedy reacting to the first of the two shots which hit him. According to Altgens, he snapped the picture "almost simultaneously" with a shot which he is confident was the first one fired. Comparison of his photograph with the Zapruder film, however, revealed that Altgens took his picture at approximately the same moment as frame 255 of the movie, 30 to 45 frames (approximately 2 seconds) later than the point at which the president was shot in the neck. Another photographer, Phillip L. Willis, snapped a picture at a time which he also asserts was simultaneous with the first shot. Analysis of his photograph revealed that it was taken at approximately frame 210 of the Zapruder film, which was the approximate time of the shot that probably hit the president and the governor. If Willis accurately recalled that there were no previous shots, this would be strong evidence that the first shot did not miss.

If the first shot did not miss, there must be an explanation for Governor Connally's recollection that he was not hit by it. There was, conceivably, a delayed reaction between the time the bullet struck him and the time he realized that he was hit, despite the fact that the bullet struck a glancing blow to a rib and penetrated his wrist bone. The governor did not even know that he had been struck in the wrist or in the thigh until he regained consciousness in the hospital the next day. Moreover, he testified that he did not hear what he thought was the second shot, although he did hear a subsequent shot which coincided with the shattering of the president's head. One possibility, therefore, would be a sequence in which the governor heard the first shot, did not immediately feel the penetration of the bullet, then felt the delayed reaction of the impact on his back, later heard the shot which shattered the president's head, and then lost consciousness without hearing a third shot which might have occurred later.

The second shot

The possibility that the second shot missed is consistent with the elapsed time between the two shots that hit their mark. From the timing evidenced by the Zapruder films, there was an interval of from 4.8 to 5.6 seconds between the shot which struck President Kennedy's neck (between frames 210 to 225) and the shot which struck his head at frame 313. Since a minimum of 2.3 seconds must elapse between shots, a bullet could have been fired from the rifle and missed during this interval. This possibility was buttressed by the testimony of witnesses who claimed that the shots were evenly spaced, since a second shot occurring within an interval of approximately five seconds would have to be almost exactly midway in this period. If Altgens' recollection is correct that he snapped his picture at the same moment as he heard a shot, then it is possible that he heard a second shot which missed, since a shot fired 2.3 seconds before he took his picture at frame 255 could have hit the president at about frame 213.

On the other hand, a substantial majority of the witnesses stated that the shots were not evenly spaced. Most witnesses recalled that the second and third shots were bunched together, although some believed that it was the first and second which were bunched. To the extent that reliance can be placed on recollection of witnesses as to the spacing of the shots, the testimony that the shots were not evenly spaced would militate against a second shot missing. Another factor arguing against the second shot missing is that the gunman would have been shooting at very near the minimum allowable time to have fired the three shots within 4.8 to 5.6 seconds, although it was entirely possible for him to have done so.

The third shot
The last possibility, of course, is that it was the third shot which missed. This conclusion conforms most easily with the probability that the assassin would most likely have missed the farthest shot, particularly since there was an acceleration of the automobile after the shot which struck the president's head. The limousine also changed direction by following the curve to the right, whereas previously it had been proceeding in almost a straight line with a rifle protruding from the sixth-floor window of the Depository Building.

One must consider, however, the testimony of the witnesses who described the head shot as the concluding event in the assassination sequence. Illustrative is the testimony of Associated Press photographer Altgens, who had an excellent vantage point near the president's car. He recalled that the shot which hit the president's head "was the last shot, that much I will say with a great degree of certainty." On the other hand, Emmett J. Hudson, the grounds-keeper of Dealey Plaza, testified that from his position on Elm Street, midway between Houston Street and the Triple Underpass, he heard a third shot after the shot which hit the president in the head. In addition, Mrs Kennedy's testimony indicated that neither the first nor the second shot missed. Immediately after the first noise she turned, because of the governor's yell, and saw her husband raise his hand to his forehead. Then the second shot struck the president's head.

Some evidence suggested that a third shot may have entirely missed and hit the turf or street by the Triple Underpass. Royce G. Skelton, who watched the motorcade from the railroad bridge, testified that after two shots "the car came on down close to the Triple Underpass" and an additional shot "hit in the left front of the president's car on the cement." Skelton thought that there had been a total of four shots, either the third or fourth of which hit in the vicinity of the underpass. Dallas Patrolman J. W. Foster, who was also on the Triple Underpass, testified that a shot hit the turf near a manhole cover in the vicinity of the underpass. Examination of this area, however, disclosed no indication that a bullet struck at the locations indicated by Skelton or Foster.

At a different location in Dealey Plaza, the evidence indicated that a bullet fragment did hit the street. James T. Tague, who got out of his car to watch the motorcade from a position between Commerce and Main streets near the Triple Underpass, was hit on the cheek by an object during the shooting. Within a few minutes Tague reported this to Deputy Sheriff Eddy R. Walthers, who was examining the area to see if any bullets had struck the turf. Walthers immediately started to search where Tague had been standing and located a place on the south curb of Main Street where it appeared a bullet had hit the cement. According to Tague, "There was a mark quite obviously that was a bullet, and it was very fresh." In Tague's opinion, it was the second shot which caused the mark, since he thinks he heard the third shot after he was hit in the face. This incident appears to have been recorded in the contemporaneous report of Dallas Patrolman L. L. Hill, who radioed in around 12.40 pm: "I have one guy that was possibly hit by a ricochet from the bullet off the concrete." Scientific examination of the mark on the south curb of Main Street by FBI experts disclosed metal smears which, "were spectrographically determined to be essentially lead with a trace of antimony." The mark on the curb could have originated from the lead core of a bullet but the absence of copper precluded "the possibility that the mark on the curbing section was made by an unmutilated military full metal-jacketed bullet such as the bullet from Governor Connally's stretcher."

It is true that the noise of a subsequent shot might have been drowned out by the siren on the Secret Service follow-up car immediately after the head shot, or the dramatic effect of the head shot might have caused so much confusion that the memory of subsequent events was blurred. Nevertheless, the preponderance of the eyewitness testimony that the head shot was the final shot must be weighed in any determination as to whether it was the third shot that missed. Even if it were caused by a bullet fragment, the mark on the south curb of Main Street cannot be identified conclusively with any of the three shots fired. Under the circumstances it might have come from the bullet which hit the president's head, or it might have been a product of the fragmentation of the missed shot upon hitting some other object in the area. Since he did not observe any of the shots striking the president, Tague's testimony that the second shot, rather than the third, caused the scratch on his cheek, does not assist in limiting the possibilities.

The wide range of possibilities and the existence of conflicting testimony, when coupled with the impossibility of scientific verification, precludes a conclusive finding by the Commission as to which shot missed.

TIME SPAN OF SHOTS

Witnesses at the assassination scene said that the shots were fired within a few seconds, with the general estimate being 5 to 6 seconds. That approximation was most probably based on the earlier publicized reports that the first shot struck the president in the neck, the second wounded the governor and the third shattered the president's head, with the time span from the neck to the head shots on the president being approximately 5 seconds. As previously indicated, the time span between the shot entering the back of the president's neck and the bullet which shattered his skull was 4.8 to 5 seconds. If the second shot missed, then 4.8 to 5.6 seconds was the total time span of the shots. If either the first or third shots missed, then a minimum of 2.3 seconds (necessary to operate the rifle) must be added to the time span of the shots which hit, giving a minimum time of 7.1 to 7.9 seconds for the three shots. If more than 2.3 seconds elapsed between a shot that missed and one that hit, then the time span would be correspondingly increased.

CONCLUSION

Based on the evidence analyzed in this chapter, the Commission has concluded that the shots which killed President Kennedy and wounded Governor Connally were fired from the sixth-floor window at the southeast corner of the Texas School Book Depository Building. Two bullets probably caused all the wounds suffered by President Kennedy and Governor Connally. Since the preponderance of the evidence indicated that three shots were fired, the Commission concluded that one shot probably missed the presidential limousine and its occupants, and that the three shots were fired in a time period ranging from approximately 4.8 to in excess of 7 seconds.

THE ASSASSIN

The preceding chapter has established that the bullets which killed President Kennedy and wounded Governor Connally were fired from the southeast corner window of the sixth floor of the Texas School Book Depository Building and that the weapon which fired these bullets was a Mannlicher-Carcano 6.5-millimeter Italian rifle bearing the serial number C2766. In this chapter the Commission evaluates the evidence upon which it has based its conclusion concerning the identity of the assassin. This evidence includes:

(1) the ownership and possession of the weapon used to commit the assassination
(2) the means by which the weapon was brought into the Depository Building

(3) the identity of the person present at the window from which the shots were fired

(4) the killing of Dallas Patrolman J. D. Tippit within 45 minutes after the assassination

(5) the resistance to arrest and the attempted shooting of another police officer by the man (Lee Harvey Oswald) subsequently accused of assassinating President Kennedy and killing Patrolman Tippit

(6) the lies told to the police by Oswald

(7) the evidence linking Oswald to the attempted killing of Major General Edwin A. Walker (Resigned, US Army) on April 10, 1963

(8) Oswald's capability with a rifle.

OWNERSHIP AND POSSESSION OF ASSASSINATION WEAPON

Purchase of rifle by Oswald

Shortly after the Mannlicher-Carcano rifle was found on the sixth floor of the Texas School Book Depository Building, agents of the FBI learned from retail outlets in Dallas that Crescent Firearms, Inc., of New York City, was a distributor of surplus Italian 6.5-millimeter military rifles. During the evening of November 22, 1963, a review of the records of Crescent Firearms revealed that the firm had shipped an Italian carbine, serial number C2766, to Klein's Sporting Goods Co., of Chicago, Illinois. After searching their records from 10 pm to 4 am the officers at Klein's discovered that a rifle bearing the serial number C2766 had been shipped to one A. Hidell, Post Office Box 2915, Dallas, Texas, on March 20, 1963. According to its microfilm records, Klein's received an order for a rifle on March 13, 1963, on a coupon clipped from the February 1963 issue of the *American Rifleman* magazine. The order coupon was signed, in hand printing, "A. Hidell, PO Box 2915, Dallas,

Texas." It was sent in an envelope bearing the same name and return address in handwriting. Document examiners for the Treasury Department and the FBI testified unequivocally that the bold printing on the face of the mail-order coupon was in the hand printing of Lee Harvey Oswald and that the writing on the envelope was also his. Oswald's writing on these and other documents was identified by comparing the writing and printing on the documents in question with that appearing on documents known to have been written by Oswald, such as his letters, passport application, and endorsements of checks. In addition to the order coupon the envelope contained a US postal money order for $21.45, purchased as No. 2, 202, 130, 462 in Dallas, Texas, on March 12, 1963. The canceled money order was obtained from the Post Office Department. Opposite the printed words "Pay To" were written the words "Kleins Sporting Goods", and opposite the printed word "From" were written the words "A. Hidell, PO Box 2915 Dallas, Texas." These words were also in the handwriting of Lee Harvey Oswald. From Klein's records it was possible to trace the processing of the order after its receipt. A bank deposit made on March 13, 1963, included an item of $21.45. Klein's shipping order form shows an imprint made by the cash register which recorded the receipt of $21.45 on March 13, 1963. This price included $19.95 for the rifle and the scope, and $1 for postage and handling. The rifle without the scope cost only $12.78.

According to the vice president of Klein's, William Waldman, the scope was mounted on the rifle by a gunsmith employed by Klein's, and the rifle was shipped fully assembled, in accordance with customary company procedures. The specific rifle shipped against the order had been received by Klein's from Crescent on February 21, 1963. It bore the manufacturer's serial number C2766. On that date, Klein's placed an internal control number VC836 on this rifle.

According to Klein's shipping order form, one Italian carbine 6.5 X-4 scope, control number VC836, serial number C2766, was shipped parcel post to "A. Hidell, PO Box 2915, Dallas, Texas," on March 20, 1963. Information received from the Italian Armed Forces Intelligence Service has established that this particular rifle was the only rifle of its type bearing serial number C2766. The post office box to which the rifle was shipped was rented to "Lee H. Oswald" from October 9, 1962, to May 14, 1963. Experts on hand-writing identification for the Treasury Department and the FBI testified that the signature and other writing on the application for that box were in the handwriting of Lee Harvey Oswald, as was a change-of-address card dated May 12, 1963, by which Oswald requested that mail addressed to that box be forwarded to him in New Orleans, where he had moved on April 24. Since the rifle was shipped from Chicago on March 20, 1963, it was received in Dallas dur-ing the period when Oswald rented and used the box. It is not known whether the application for Post Office Box 2915 listed "A. Hidell" as a person entitled to receive mail at this box. In accordance with postal regulations, the portion of the application which lists names of persons, other than the applicant, entitled to receive mail was thrown away after the box was closed on May 1963. Postal Inspector Harry D. Holmes of the Dallas Post Office testified, however, that when a package is received for a certain box, a notice is placed in that box regardless of whether the name on the package is listed on the application as a person entitled to receive mail through that box. The person having access to the box then takes the notice to the window and is given the package. Ordinarily, Inspector Holmes testified, identifica-tion is not requested because it is assumed that the person with the notice is entitled to the package.

Oswald's use of the name "Hidell" to purchase the assassination weapon was one of several instances in which he used this name as an alias. When arrested on the day of the assassination, he had in his possession a Smith & Wesson .38 caliber revolver purchased by mail-order coupon from Seaport-Traders, Inc., a mail-order division of George Rose & Co., Los Angeles. The mail-order coupon listed the purchaser as "A. J. Hidell, Age 28" with the address of Post Office Box 2915 in Dallas. Handwriting experts from the FBI and the Treasury Department testified that the writing on the mail-order form was that of Lee Harvey Oswald.

Among other identification cards in Oswald's wallet at the time of his arrest were a Selective Service notice of classification [notice of call-up for military service], a Selective Service registration certificate, and a certificate of service in the US Marine Corps, all three cards being in his own name. Also in his wallet at that time were a Selective Service notice of classification and a Marine certificate of service in the name of Alek James Hidell. On the Hidell Selective Service card there appeared a signature, "Alek J. Hidell," and the photograph of Lee Harvey Oswald. Experts on the questioned documents from the Treasury Department and the FBI testified that the Hidell cards were counterfeit photographic reproductions made by photographing the Oswald cards, retouching the resulting negatives, and producing prints from the retouched negatives.

The Hidell signature on the notice of classification was in the handwriting of Oswald. In Oswald's personal effects found in his room at 1026 North Beckley Avenue in Dallas was a purported international certificate of vaccination signed by "Dr A. J. Hidell," Post Office Box 30016, New Orleans. It certified that Lee Harvey Oswald had been vaccinated for smallpox on June 8, 1963. This, too, was a forgery. The signature of "A. J. Hidell" was in the handwriting of Lee Harvey Oswald. There is no "Dr Hidell" licensed to practice medicine in Louisiana.

There is no Post Office Box 30016 in the New Orleans Post Office but Oswald had rented Post Office Box 30061 in New Orleans on June 3, 1963, listing Marina Oswald and A. J. Hidell as additional persons entitled to receive mail in the box.

The New Orleans postal authorities had not discarded the portion of the application listing the names of those, other than the owner of the box, entitled to receive mail through the box. Expert testimony confirmed that the writing on this application was that of Lee Harvey Oswald.

Hidell's name on the post office box application was part of Oswald's use of a non-existent Hidell to serve as president of the so-called New Orleans Chapter of the Fair Play for Cuba Committee. Marina Oswald testified that she first learned of Oswald's use of the fictitious name "Hidell" in connection with his pro-Castro activities in New Orleans. According to her testimony, he compelled her to write the name "Hidell" on membership cards in the space designated for the signature of the "Chapter President." The name "Hidell" was stamped on some of the Chapter's printed literature and on the membership application blanks. Marina Oswald testified, "I knew there was no such organization. And I know Hidell is merely an altered Fidel, and I laughed at such foolishness." Hidell was a fictitious president of an organization of which Oswald was the only member.

When seeking employment in New Orleans, Oswald listed a "Sergeant Robert Hidell" as a reference on one job application and "George Hidell" as a reference on another. Both names were found to be fictitious. Moreover, the use of "Alek" as a first name for Hidell is a further link to Oswald because "Alek" was Oswald's nickname in Russia. Letters received by Marina Oswald from her husband signed "Alek" were given to the Commission.

Oswald's palmprint on rifle barrel

Based on the above evidence, the Commission concluded that Oswald purchased the rifle found on the sixth floor of the Depository Building. Additional evidence of ownership was provided in the form of palmprint identification which indicated that Oswald had possession of the rifle he had purchased. A few minutes after the rifle was discovered on the sixth floor of the Depository Building it was examined by Lieutenant J. C. Day of the identification bureau of the Dallas police. He lifted the rifle by the wooden stock after his examination convinced him that the wood was too rough to take fingerprints. Captain J. W. Fritz then ejected a cartridge by operating the bolt, but only after Day viewed the knob on the bolt through a magnifying glass and found no prints. Day continued to examine the rifle with the magnifying glass, looking for possible fingerprints. He applied fingerprint powder to the side of the metal housing near the trigger, and noticed traces of two prints. At 11.45 pm on November 22, the rifle was released to the FBI and forwarded to Washington where it was examined on the morning of November 23 by Sebastian Fritz Latona, supervisor of the Latent Fingerprint Section of the FBI's Identification Division.

In his testimony before the Commission, Latona stated that when he received the rifle, the area where prints were visible was protected by cellophane. He examined these prints, as well as photographs of them which the Dallas police had made, and concluded that:

> ... the formations, the ridge formations and characteristics were insufficient for purposes of either effecting identification or a determination that the print was not identical with the prints of people. Accordingly, my opinion simply was that the latent prints which were there were of no value.

Latona then processed the complete weapon but developed no identifiable prints. He stated that the poor quality of the wood and the metal would cause the rifle to absorb moisture from the skin, thereby making a clear print unlikely.

On November 22, however, before surrendering possession of the rifle to the FBI Laboratory, Lieutenant Day of the Dallas Police Department had "lifted" a palmprint from the underside of the gun barrel "near the firing end of the barrel about 3 inches under the woodstock when I took the woodstock loose." "Lifting" a print involves the use of adhesive material to remove the fingerprint powder which adheres to the original print. In this way the powdered impression is actually removed from the object. The lifting had been so complete in this case that there was no trace of the print on the rifle itself when it was examined by Latona. Nor was there any indication that the lift had been performed. Day, on the other hand, believed that sufficient traces of the print had been left on the rifle barrel, because he did not release the lifted print until November 26, when he received instructions to send "everything that we had" to the FBI. The print arrived in the FBI Laboratory in Washington on November 29, mounted on a card on which Lieutenant Day had written the words "off underside gun barrel near end of grip C2766." The print's positive identity as having been lifted from the rifle was confirmed by FBI Laboratory tests, which established that the adhesive material bearing the print also bore impressions of the same irregularities that appeared on the barrel of the rifle.

Latona testified that this palmprint was the right palmprint of Lee Harvey Oswald. At the request of the Commission, Arthur Mandella, fingerprint expert with the New York City Police Department, conducted an independent examination and also determined that this was the

right palmprint of Oswald. Latona's findings were also confirmed by Ronald G. Wittmus, another FBI fingerprint
expert. In the opinion of these experts, it was not possible
to estimate the time which elapsed between the placing of
the print on the rifle and the date of the lift.

Experts testifying before the Commission agreed that
palmprints are as unique as fingerprints for purposes of
establishing identification. Oswald's palmprint on the
underside of the barrel demonstrates that he handled the
rifle when it was disassembled. A palmprint could not be
placed on this portion of the rifle, when assembled, because
the wooden foregrip covers the barrel at this point.
The print is additional proof that the rifle was in Oswald's
possession.

Fibers on rifle

In a crevice between the butt plate of the rifle and the
wooden stock was a tuft of several cotton fibers of dark
blue, gray-black, and orange-yellow shades. On November
23, 1963, these fibers were examined by Paul M.
Stombaugh, a special agent assigned to the Hair and Fiber
Unit of the FBI Laboratory. He compared them with the
fibers found in the shirt which Oswald was wearing when
arrested in the Texas Theater. This shirt was also composed
of dark blue, gray-black and orange-yellow cotton fibers.
Stombaugh testified that the colors, shades, and twist of the
fibers found in the tuft on the rifle matched those in
Oswald's shirt.

Stombaugh explained in his testimony that in fiber
analysis, as distinct from fingerprint or firearms identification, it is not possible to state with scientific certainty that
a particular small group of fibers come from a certain piece
of clothing to the exclusion of all others because there are
not enough microscopic characteristics present in fibers.
Judgments as to probability will depend on the number and

types of matches. He concluded, "There is no doubt in my mind that these fibers could have come from this shirt. There is no way, however, to eliminate the possibility of the fibers having come from another identical shirt." Having considered the probabilities as explained in Stombaugh's testimony, the Commission has concluded that the fibers in the tuft on the rifle most probably came from the shirt worn by Oswald when he was arrested, and that this was the same shirt which Oswald wore on the morning of the assassination. Marina Oswald testified that she thought her husband wore this shirt to work on that day. The testimony of those who saw him after the assassination was inconclusive about the color of Oswald's shirt, but Mary Bledsoe, a former landlady of Oswald, saw him on a bus approximately 10 minutes after the assassination and identified the shirt as being the one worn by Oswald primarily because of a distinctive hole in the shirt's right elbow. Moreover, the bus transfer which he obtained as he left the bus was still in the pocket when he was arrested. Although Oswald returned to his rooming house after the assassination and when questioned by the police, claimed to have changed his shirt, the evidence indicates that he continued wearing the same shirt which he was wearing all morning and which he was still wearing when arrested.

In light of these findings the Commission evaluated the additional testimony of Stombaugh that the fibers were caught in the crevice of the rifle's butt plate "in the recent past." Although Stombaugh was unable to estimate the period of time the fibers were on the rifle he said that the fibers "were clean, they had good color to them, there was no grease on them and they were not fragmented. They looked as if they had just been picked up." The relative freshness of the fibers is strong evidence that they were caught on the rifle on the morning of the assassination or during the preceding evening. For 10 days prior to the eve of the assassination Oswald had not been present at Ruth Paine's house in Irving, Texas, where the rifle was kept. Moreover, the Commission found no reliable evidence that Oswald used the rifle at any time between September 23, when it was transported from New Orleans, and November 22, the day of the assassination. The fact that on the morning of the assassination Oswald was wearing the shirt from which these relatively fresh fibers most probably originated, provides some evidence that they were placed on the rifle that day since there was limited, if any, opportunity for Oswald to handle the weapon during the two months prior to November 22. On the other hand Stombaugh pointed out that fibers might retain their freshness if the rifle had been "put aside" after catching the fibers. The rifle used in the assassination probably had been wrapped in a blanket for about eight weeks prior to November 22. Because the relative freshness of these fibers might be explained by the continuous storage of the rifle in the blanket, the Commission was unable to reach any firm conclusion as to when the fibers were caught in the rifle. The Commission was able to conclude, however, that the fibers most probably came from Oswald's shirt. This adds to the conviction of the Commission that Oswald owned and handled the weapon used in the assassination.

Photograph of Oswald with rifle

During the period from March 2, 1963, to April 24, 1963, the Oswalds lived on Neely Street in Dallas in a rented house which had a small back yard. One Sunday, while his wife was hanging diapers, Oswald asked her to take a picture of him holding a rifle, a pistol and issues of two newspapers later identified as the *Worker* and the *Militant*. Two pictures were taken. The Commission has concluded that the rifle shown in these pictures is the same rifle which was found on the sixth floor of the Depository Building on

November 22, 1963. One of these pictures shows most of the rifle's configuration. Special Agent Lyndal L. Shaneyfelt, a photography expert with the FBI, photographed the rifle used in the assassination, attempting to duplicate the position of the rifle and the lighting. After comparing the rifle in the simulated photograph with the rifle in the first picture, Shaneyfelt testified, "I found it to be the same general configuration. All appearances were the same." He found "one notch in the stock at this point that appears very faintly in the photograph." He stated, however, that while he "found no differences" between the rifles in the two photographs, he could not make a "positive identification to the exclusion of all other rifles of the same general configuration."

The authenticity of these pictures has been established by expert testimony which links the second picture to Oswald's Imperial Reflex camera, with which Marina Oswald testified she took the pictures. The negative of that picture was found among Oswald's possessions. Using a recognized technique of determining whether a picture was taken with a particular camera, Shaneyfelt compared this negative with a negative which he made by taking a new picture with Oswald's camera. He concluded that the negative of the second picture was exposed in Oswald's Imperial Reflex camera to the exclusion of all other cameras. He could not test the first picture in the same way because the negative was never recovered. Both pictures, however, have identical backgrounds and lighting and, judging from the shadows, were taken at the same angle. They are photographs of the same scene. Since the second picture was taken with Oswald's camera, it is reasonably certain that the first picture was taken by the same camera at the same time, as Marina Oswald testified. Moreover, Shaneyfelt testified that in his opinion the photographs were not composites of two different photographs and that Oswald's face had not been superimposed on another body.

One of the photographs taken by Marina Oswald was widely published in newspapers and magazines, and in many instances the details of these pictures differed from the original, and even from each other, particularly as to the configuration of the rifle. The Commission sought to determine whether these photographs were touched prior to publication. Shaneyfelt testified that the published photographs appeared to be based on a copy of the original which the publications had each retouched differently. Several of the publications furnished the Commission with the prints they had used, or described by correspondence the retouching they had done. This information enabled the Commission to conclude that the published pictures were the same as the original except for retouching done by these publications, apparently for the purpose of clarifying the lines of the rifle and other details in the picture.

The dates surrounding the taking of this picture and the purchase of the rifle reinforce the belief that the rifle in the photograph is the rifle which Oswald bought from Klein's. The rifle was shipped from Klein's in Chicago on March 20, 1963, at a time when the Oswalds were living on Neely Street. From an examination of one of the photographs, the Commission determined the dates of the issues of the *Militant* and the *Worker* which Oswald was holding in his hand. By checking the actual mailing dates of these issues and the time usually taken to effect delivery to Dallas, it was established that the photographs must have been taken sometime after March 27. Marina Oswald testified that the photographs were taken on a Sunday about two weeks before the attempted shooting of Major General Edwin A. Walker on April 10, 1963. By Sunday, March 31, 1963, 10 days prior to the Walker attempt, Oswald had undoubtedly received the rifle shipped from Chicago on March 20, the revolver shipped from Los Angeles on the same date, and the two newspapers which he was holding in the picture.

Rifle among Oswald's possessions

Marina Oswald testified that the rifle found on the sixth floor of the Depository Building was the "fateful rifle of Lee Oswald." Moreover, it was the only rifle owned by her husband following his return from the Soviet Union in June 1962. It had been purchased in March 1963, and taken to New Orleans where Marina Oswald saw it in their rented apartment during the summer of 1963. It appears from his wife's testimony that Oswald may have sat on the screened-in porch at night practicing with the rifle by looking through the telescopic sight and operating the bolt. In September 1963, Oswald loaded their possessions into a station wagon owned by Ruth Paine, who had invited Marina Oswald and the baby to live at her home in Irving, Texas. Marina Oswald has stated that the rifle was among these possessions, although Ruth Paine testified that she was not aware of it.

From September 24, 1963, when Marina Oswald arrived in Irving from New Orleans, until the morning of the assassination, the rifle was, according to the evidence, stored in a green and brown blanket in the Paines' garage among the Oswalds' other possessions. About one week after the return from New Orleans, Marina Oswald was looking in the garage for parts to the baby's crib and thought that the parts might be in the blanket. When she started to open the blanket, she saw the stock of the rifle. Ruth and Michael Paine both noticed the rolled-up blanket in the garage during the time that Marina Oswald was living in their home. On several occasions, Michael Paine moved the blanket in the garage. He thought it contained tent poles, or possibly other camping equipment such as a folding shovel. When he appeared before the Commission, Michael Paine lifted the blanket with the rifle wrapped inside and testified that it appeared to be the same approximate weight and shape as the package in his garage.

About three hours after the assassination, a detective and deputy sheriff saw the blanket-roll, tied with a string, lying on the floor of the Paines' garage. Each man testified that he thought he could detect the outline of a rifle in the blanket, even though the blanket was empty. Paul M. Stombaugh, of the FBI Laboratory, examined the blanket and discovered a bulge approximately 10 inches long midway in the blanket. This bulge was apparently caused by a hard protruding object which had stretched the blanket's fibers. It could have been caused by the telescopic sight of the rifle which was approximately 11 inches long.

Conclusion

Having reviewed the evidence that:

(1) Lee Harvey Oswald purchased the rifle used in the assassination

(2) Oswald's palmprint was on the rifle in a position which shows that he had handled it while it was disassembled

(3) fibers found on the rifle most probably came from the shirt Oswald was wearing on the day of the assassination

(4) a photograph taken in the yard of Oswald's apartment showed him holding this rifle

(5) the rifle was kept among Oswald's possessions from the time of its purchase until the day of the assassination

the Commission concluded that the rifle used to assassinate President Kennedy and wound Governor Connally was owned and possessed by Lee Harvey Oswald.

THE RIFLE IN THE BUILDING

The Commission has evaluated the evidence tending to show how Lee Harvey Oswald's Mannlicher-Carcano rifle, serial number C2766, was brought into the Depository Building, where it was found on the sixth floor shortly after the assassination. In this connection the Commission considered:

(1) the circumstances surrounding Oswald's return to Irving, Texas, on Thursday, November 21, 1963

(2) the disappearance of the rifle from its normal place of storage

(3) Oswald's arrival at the Depository Building on November 22 carrying a long and bulky brown paper package

(4) the presence of a long handmade brown paper bag near the point from which the shots were fired

(5) the palmprint, fiber, and paper analyses linking Oswald and the assassination weapon to this bag.

The curtain rod story

During October and November of 1963, Lee Harvey Oswald lived in a rooming house in Dallas while his wife and children lived in Irving, at the home of Ruth Paine, approximately 15 miles from Oswald's place of work at the Texas School Book Depository. Oswald traveled between Dallas and Irving on weekends in a car driven by a neighbor of the Paines, Buell Wesley Frazier, who also worked at the Depository. Oswald generally would go to Irving on Friday afternoon and return to Dallas Monday morning. According to the testimony of Frazier, Marina Oswald, and Ruth Paine, it appears that Oswald never returned to Irving in midweek prior to November 21, 1963, except on Monday, October 21, when he visited his wife in the hospital after the birth of their second child.

During the morning of November 21, Oswald asked Frazier whether he could ride home with him that afternoon. Frazier, surprised, asked him why he was going to

Irving on Thursday night rather than Friday. Oswald replied, "I'm going home to get some curtain rods ... [to] put in an apartment." The two men left work at 4.40 pm and drove to Irving. There was little conversation between them on the way home. Mrs Linnie Mac Randle, Frazier's sister, commented to her brother about Oswald's unusual midweek return to Irving. Frazier told her that Oswald had come home to get curtain rods. It would appear, however, that obtaining curtain rods was not the purpose of Oswald's trip to Irving on November 21.

Mrs A. C. Johnson, his landlady, testified that Oswald's room at 1026 North Beckley Avenue had curtains and curtain rods, and that Oswald had never discussed the subject with her. In the Paines' garage, along with many other objects of a household character, there were two flat lightweight curtain rods belonging to Ruth Paine but they were still there on Friday afternoon after Oswald's arrest. Oswald never asked Mrs Paine about the use of curtain rods, and Marina Oswald testified that Oswald did not say anything about curtain rods on the day before the assassination.

No curtain rods were known to have been discovered in the Depository Building after the assassination. In deciding whether Oswald carried a rifle to work in a long paper bag on November 22, the Commission gave weight to the fact that Oswald gave a false reason for returning home on November 21, and one which provided an excuse for the carrying of a bulky package the following morning.

The missing rifle

Before dinner on November 21, Oswald played on the lawn of the Paines' home with his daughter June. After dinner Ruth Paine and Marina Oswald were busy cleaning the house and preparing their children for bed. Between the hours of 8 and 9 pm they were occupied with the children in the bedrooms located at the extreme east end of the house. On the west end of the house is the attached garage, which can be reached from the kitchen or from the outside. In the garage were the personal belongings of the Oswald family including, as the evidence has shown, the rifle wrapped in the old brown and green blanket.

At approximately 9 pm, after the children had been put to bed, Mrs Paine, according to her testimony before the Commission, "went out to the garage to paint some children's blocks, and worked in the garage for half an hour or so. I noticed when I went out that the light was on." Mrs Paine was certain that she had not left the light on in the garage after dinner. According to Mrs Paine, Oswald had gone to bed by 9 pm; Marina Oswald testified that it was between 9 and 10 pm. Neither Marina Oswald nor Ruth Paine saw Oswald in the garage. The period between 8 and 9 pm, however, provided ample opportunity for Oswald to prepare the rifle for his departure the next morning. Only if disassembled could the rifle fit into the paper bag found near the window from which the shots were fired. A firearms expert with the FBI assembled the rifle in six minutes using a 10-cent coin as a tool, and he could disassemble it more rapidly. While the rifle may have already been disassembled when Oswald arrived home on Thursday, he had ample time that evening to disassemble the rifle and insert it into the paper bag.

On the day of the assassination, Marina Oswald was watching television when she learned of the shooting. A short time later Mrs Paine told her that someone had shot the president "from the building in which Lee is working." Marina Oswald testified that at that time, "My heart dropped. I then went to the garage to see whether the rifle was there and I saw that the blanket was still there and I said 'Thank God.'" She did not unroll the blanket. She saw that it was in its usual position and it appeared to her to have something inside.

Soon afterward, at about 3 pm, police officers arrived and searched the house. Mrs Paine pointed out that most of the Oswalds' possessions were in the garage. With Ruth Paine acting as an interpreter, Detective Rose asked Marina whether her husband had a rifle. Mrs Paine, who had no knowledge of the rifle, first said "No," but when the question was translated, Marina Oswald replied "Yes." She pointed to the blanket which was on the floor very close to where Ruth Paine was standing. Mrs Paine testified:

> As she [Marina] told me about it I stepped onto the blanket roll... And she indicated to me that she had peered into this roll and saw a portion of what she took to be a gun she knew her husband to have, a rifle. And I then translated this to the officers that she knew that her husband had a gun that he had stored in here... I then stepped off of it and the officer picked it up in the middle and it bent so...

Mrs Paine had the actual blanket before her as she testified and she indicated that the blanket hung limp in the officer's hand. Marina Oswald testified that this was her first knowledge that the rifle was not in its accustomed place.

The long and bulky package

On the morning of November 22, 1963, Lee Harvey Oswald left the Paine house in Irving at approximately 7.15 am while Marina Oswald was still in bed. Neither she nor Mrs Paine saw him leave the house. About half-a-block away from the Paine house was the residence of Mrs Linnie Mac Randle, the sister of the man with whom Oswald drove to work, Buell Wesley Frazier. Mrs Randle stated that on the morning of November 22, while her brother was eating breakfast, she looked out the breakfast-room window and saw Oswald cross the street and walk toward the driveway where her brother parked his car near the carport.

He carried a "heavy brown bag." Oswald gripped the bag in his right hand near the top. "It tapered like this as he hugged it in his hand. It was ... more bulky toward the bottom" than toward the top. She then opened the kitchen door and saw Oswald open the right rear door of her brother's car and place the package in the back of the car. Mrs Randle estimated that the package was approximately 28 inches long and about 8 inches wide. She thought that its color was similar to that of the bag found on the sixth floor of the School Book Depository after the assassination.

Frazier met Oswald at the kitchen door and together they walked to the car. After entering the car, Frazier glanced over his shoulder and noticed a brown paper package on the back seat. He asked, "What's the package, Lee?" Oswald replied, "curtain rods." Frazier told the Commission "... the main reason he was going over there that Thursday afternoon was to bring back some curtain rods, so I didn't think any more about it when he told me that." Frazier estimated that the bag was 2 feet long "give and take a few inches", and about 5 or 6 inches wide. As they sat in the car, Frazier asked Oswald where his lunch was, and Oswald replied that he was going to buy his lunch that day.

Frazier testified that Oswald carried no lunch bag that day. "When he rode with me, I say he always brought lunch except that one day on November 22, he didn't bring his lunch that day." Frazier parked the car in the company parking lot about two blocks north of the Depository Building. Oswald left the car first, picked up the brown paper bag, and proceeded toward the building ahead of Frazier. Frazier walked behind and as they crossed the railroad tracks he watched the switching of the cars [i.e. rail cars]. Frazier recalled that one end of the package was under Oswald's armpit and the lower part was held with his right hand so that it was carried straight and parallel to his body. When Oswald entered the rear door of the Depository Building, he was about 50 feet ahead of Frazier. It was the first time that Oswald had not walked with Frazier from the parking lot to the building entrance. When Frazier entered the building, he did not see Oswald. One employee, Jack Dougherty, believed that he saw Oswald coming to work, but he does not remember that Oswald had anything in his hands as he entered the door. No other employee has been found who saw Oswald enter that morning.

In deciding whether Oswald carried the assassination weapon in the bag which Frazier and Mrs Randle saw, the Commission has carefully considered the testimony of these two witnesses with regard to the length of the bag. Frazier and Mrs Randle testified that the bag which Oswald was carrying was approximately 27 or 28 inches long, whereas the wooden stock of the rifle, which is its largest component, measured 34.8 inches. The bag found on the sixth floor was 33 inches long. When Frazier appeared before the Commission and was asked to demonstrate how Oswald carried the package, he said, "Like I said, I remember that I didn't look at the package very much ... but when I did look at it he did have his hands on the package like that," and at this point Frazier placed the upper part of the package under his armpit and attempted to cup his right hand beneath the bottom of the bag. The disassembled rifle was too long to be carried in this manner. Similarly, when the butt of the rifle was placed in Frazier's hand, it extended above his shoulder to ear level. Moreover, in an interview on December 1, 1963, with FBI agents, Frazier had marked the point on the back seat of his car which he believed was where the bag reached when it was laid on the seat with one edge against the door. The distance between the point on the seat and the door was 27 inches.

Mrs Randle said, when shown the paper bag, that the bag she saw Oswald carrying "wasn't that long, I mean it was folded down at the top as I told you. It definitely wasn't that long." And she folded the bag to length of about 28 inches. Frazier doubted whether the bag that Oswald carried was as wide as the bag found on the sixth floor, although Mrs Randle testified that the width was approximately the same.

The Commission has weighed the visual recollection of Frazier and Mrs Randle against the evidence here presented that the bag Oswald carried contained the assassination weapon and has concluded that Frazier and Randle are mistaken as to the length of the bag. Mrs Randle saw the bag fleetingly and her first remembrance is that it was held in Oswald's right hand "and it almost touched the ground as he carried it." Frazier's view of the bag was from the rear. He continually advised that he was not paying close attention. For example, he said,

> ... I didn't pay too much attention the way he was walking because I was walking along there looking at the railroad cars and watching the men on the diesel switch them cars and I didn't pay too much attention on how he carried the package at all.

Frazier could easily have been mistaken when he stated that Oswald held the bottom of the bag cupped in his hand with the upper end tucked into his armpit.

Location of bag

A handmade bag of wrapping paper and tape was found in the southeast corner of the sixth floor alongside the window from which the shots were fired. It was not a standard type bag which could be obtained in a store and it was presumably made for a particular purpose. It was the appropriate size to contain, in disassembled form, Oswald's Mannlicher-Carcano rifle, serial no. C2766, which was also found on the sixth floor. Three cartons had been placed at the window apparently to act as a gun rest and a fourth carton was placed behind those at the window. A person seated on the fourth carton could assemble the rifle without being seen from the rest of the sixth floor because the cartons stacked around the southeast corner would shield him. The presence of the bag in this corner is cogent evidence that it was used as the container for the rifle. At the time the bag was found, Lieutenant Day of the Dallas police wrote on it, "Found next to the sixth floor window gun fired from. May have been used to carry gun. Lt J. C. Day."

Scientific evidence linking rifle and Oswald to paper bag

Oswald's fingerprint and palmprint found on bag
Using a standard chemical method involving silver nitrates, the FBI Laboratory developed a latent palmprint and latent fingerprint on the bag. Sebastian F. Latona, supervisor of the FBI's Latent Fingerprint Section, identified these prints as the left index fingerprint and right palmprint of Lee Harvey Oswald. The portion of the palm which was identified was the heel of the right palm, ie, the area near the wrist, on the little finger side. These prints were examined independently by Ronald G. Wittmus of the FBI, and by Arthur Mandella, a fingerprint expert with the New York City Police Department. Both included that the prints were the right palm and left index finger of Lee Oswald. No other identifiable prints were found on the bag.

Oswald's palmprint on the bottom of the paper bag indicated, of course, that he had handled the bag. Furthermore, it was consistent with the bag having contained a heavy or bulky object when he handled it since a light object is usually held by the fingers. The palmprint was found on the closed end of the bag. It was from Oswald's right hand, in which he carried the long package as he walked from Frazier's car to the building.

Materials used to make bag

On the day of the assassination, the Dallas police obtained a sample of wrapping paper and tape from the shipping room of the Depository and forwarded it to the FBI Laboratory in Washington. James C. Cadigan, a questioned-documents [evidence] expert with the Bureau, compared the samples with the paper and tape in the actual bag. He testified, "In all of the observations and physical tests that I made I found ... the bag ... and the paper sample ... were the same." Among other tests, the paper and tape were submitted to fiber analysis and spectrographic examination. In addition the tape was compared to determine whether the sample tape and the tape on the bag had been taken from the tape dispensing machine at the Depository. When asked to explain the similarity of characteristics, Cadigan stated:

> Well, briefly, it would be the thickness of both the paper and the tape, the color under various lighting conditions of both the paper and the tape, the width of the tape, the knurled [ridged] markings on the surface of the fiber, the texture of the fiber, the letting pattern... I found that the paper sack found on the sixth floor ... and the sample ... had the same observable characteristics both under the microscope and all the visual tests that I could conduct. The papers I also found were similar in fiber composition, therefore, in addition to the visual characteristics, microscopic and UV [ultra violet] characteristics.

Mr Cadigan concluded that the paper and tape from the bag were identical in all respects to the sample paper and tape taken from the Texas School Book Depository shipping room on November 22, 1963. On December 1, 1963, a replica bag was made from materials found on that date in the shipping room. This was done as an investigation aid since the original bag had been discolored during various laboratory examinations and could not be used for valid identification by witnesses. Cadigan found that the paper used to make this replica sack had different characteristics from the paper in the original bag. The science of paper analysis enabled him to distinguish between different rolls of paper even though they were produced by the same manufacturer.

Since the Depository normally used approximately one roll of paper every three working days, it was not surprising that the replica sack made on December 1, 1963, had different characteristics from both the actual bag and the sample taken on November 22. On the other hand, since two rolls could be made from the same batch of paper, one cannot estimate when, prior to November 22, Oswald made the paper bag. However, the complete identity of characteristics between the paper and tape in the bag found on the sixth floor and the paper and tape found in the shipping room of the Depository on November 22 enabled the Commission to conclude that the bag was made from these materials. The Depository shipping department was on the first floor to which Oswald had access in the normal performance of his duties filling orders.

Fibers in the paper bag matched fibers in blanket

When Paul M. Stombaugh of the FBI Laboratory examined the paper bag, he found, on the inside, a single brown delustered viscose fiber and several light green cotton fibers. The blanket in which the rifle was stored was composed of brown and green cotton, viscose and woolen fibers.

The single brown viscose fiber found in the bag matched some of the brown viscose fibers from the blanket in all observable characteristics. The green cotton fibers found in the paper bag matched some of the green cotton fibers in the blanket "in all observable microscopic characteristics."

Despite these matches, however, Stombaugh was unable to render an opinion that the fibers which he found in the bag had probably come from the blanket, because other types of fibers present in the blanket were not found in the bag. He concluded:

> All I would say here is that it is possible that these fibers could have come from this blanket, because this blanket is composed of brown and green woolen fibers, brown and green delustered viscose fibers, and brown and green cotton fibers ... We found no brown cotton fibers, no green viscose fibers, and no woolen fibers. So if I found all of these then I would have been able to say these fibers probably had come from this blanket. But since I found so few, then I would say the possibility exists, these fibers could have come from this blanket.

Stombaugh confirmed that the rifle could have picked up fibers from the blanket and transferred them to the paper bag. In light of the other evidence linking Lee Harvey Oswald, the blanket, and the rifle to the paper bag found on the sixth floor, the Commission considered Stombaugh's testimony of probative value in deciding whether Oswald carried the rifle into the building in the paper bag.

Conclusion

The preponderance of the evidence supports the conclusion that Lee Harvey Oswald:

(1) told the curtain rod story to Frazier to explain both the return to Irving on a Thursday and the obvious bulk of the package which he intended to bring to work the next day

(2) took paper and tape from the wrapping bench of the Depository and fashioned a bag large enough to carry the disassembled rifle

(3) removed the rifle from the blanket in the Paines' garage on Thursday evening

(4) carried the rifle into the Depository Building, concealed in the bag

(5) left the bag alongside the window from which the shots were fired.

OSWALD AT WINDOW

Lee Harvey Oswald was hired on October 15, 1963, by the Texas School Book Depository as an "order filler". He worked principally on the first and sixth floors of the building, gathering books listed on orders and delivering them to the shipping room on the first floor. He had ready access to the sixth floor, from the southeast corner window of which the shots were fired. The Commission evaluated the physical evidence found near the window after the assassination and the testimony of eyewitnesses in deciding whether Lee Harvey Oswald was present at this window at the time of the assassination.

Palmprints and fingerprints on cartons and paper bag

Below the southeast corner window on the sixth floor was a large carton of books measuring approximately 18 by 12 by 14 inches which had been moved from a stack along the south wall. Atop this carton was a small carton marked "Rolling Readers", measuring approximately 13 by 9 by 8 inches. In front of this small carton and resting partially on the windowsill was another small "Rolling Readers" carton. These two small cartons had been moved from a stack about three aisles away. The boxes in the window appeared to have been arranged as a convenient gun rest. Behind these boxes was another carton placed on the floor on which a man sitting could look southwesterly down Elm

Street over the top of the "Rolling Readers" cartons. Next to these cartons was the handmade paper bag, previously discussed, on which appeared the print of the left index finger and right palm of Lee Harvey Oswald. The cartons were forwarded to the FBI in Washington. Sebastian F. Latona, supervisor of the Latent Fingerprint Section, testified that 20 identifiable fingerprints and eight palmprints were developed on these cartons. The carton on the windowsill and the large carton below the window contained no prints which could be identified as being those of Lee Harvey Oswald. The other "Rolling Readers" carton, however, contained a palmprint and a fingerprint which were identified by Latona as being the left palmprint and right index fingerprint of Lee Harvey Oswald.

The Commission has considered the possibility that the cartons might have been moved in connection with the work that was being performed on the sixth floor on November 22. Depository employees were laying a new floor at the west end and transferring books from the west to the east end of the building. The "Rolling Readers" cartons, however, had not been moved by the floor layers and had apparently been taken to the window from their regular position for some particular purpose. The "Rolling Readers" boxes contained, instead of books, light blocks used as reading aids.

They could be easily adjusted and were still solid enough to serve as a gun rest. The box on the floor, behind the three near the window, had been one of these moved by the floor layers from the west wall to near the east side of the building in preparation for the laying of the floor. During the afternoon of November 22, Lieutenant Day of the Dallas police dusted this carton with powder and developed a palmprint on the top edge of the carton on the side nearest the window. The position of this palmprint on the carton was parallel with the long axis of the box, and at right angles with the short axis; the bottom of the palm rested on the box. Someone sitting on the box facing the window would have his palm in this position if he placed his hand alongside his right hip. This print which had been cut out of the box was also forwarded to the FBI and Latona identified it as Oswald's right palmprint. In Latona's opinion "not too long" a time had elapsed between the time that the print was placed on the carton and the time that it had been developed by the Dallas police. Although Bureau experiments had shown that 24 hours was a likely maximum time, Latona stated that he could only testify with certainty that the print was less than three days old.

The print, therefore, could have been placed on the carton at any time within this period. The freshness of this print could be estimated only because the Dallas police developed it through the use of powder. Since cartons absorb perspiration, powder can successfully develop a print on such material only within a limited time. When the FBI in Washington received the cartons, the remaining prints, including Oswald's on the Rolling Readers carton, were developed by chemical processes. The freshness of prints developed in this manner cannot be estimated, so no conclusions can be drawn as to whether these remaining prints preceded or followed the print developed in Dallas by powder. Most of the prints were found to have been placed on the cartons by an FBI clerk and a Dallas police officer after the cartons had been processed with powder by the Dallas Police. In his independent investigation, Arthur Mandella of the New York City Police Department reached the same conclusion as Latona that the prints found on the cartons were those of Lee Harvey Oswald. In addition, Mandella was of the opinion that the print taken from the carton on the floor was probably made within a day or a day and a half of the examination on November 22. Moreover, another expert with the FBI, Ronald G.

Wittmus, conducted a separate examination and also agreed with Latona that the prints were Oswald's.

In evaluating the significance of these fingerprint and palmprint identifications, the Commission considered the possibility that Oswald handled these cartons as part of his normal duties. Since other identifiable prints were developed on the cartons, the Commission requested that they be compared with the prints of the 12 warehouse employees who, like Oswald, might have handled the cartons. They were also compared with the prints of those law enforcement officials who might have handled the cartons (see p. 189). Although a person could handle a carton and not leave identifiable prints, none of these employees except Oswald left identifiable prints on the cartons. This finding, in addition to the freshness of one of the prints and the presence of Oswald's prints on two of the four cartons and the paper bag, led the Commission to attach some probative value to the fingerprint and palmprint identifications in reaching the conclusion that Oswald was at the window from which the shots were fired, although the prints do not establish the exact time he was there.

Oswald's presence on sixth floor approximately 35 minutes before the assassination

Additional testimony linking Oswald with the point from which the shots were fired was provided by the testimony of Charles Givens, who was the last known employee to see Oswald inside the building prior to the assassination. During the morning of November 22, Givens was working with the floor-laying crew in the southwest section of the sixth floor.

At about 11.45 am the floor-laying crew used both elevators to come down from the sixth floor. The employees raced the elevators to the first floor. Givens saw Oswald standing at the gate on the fifth floor as the elevator went by.

Givens testified that after reaching the first floor, "I discovered I left my cigarettes in my jacket pocket upstairs, and I took the elevator back upstairs to get my jacket with my cigarettes in it." He saw Oswald, a clipboard in hand, walking from the southeast corner of the sixth floor toward the elevator. Givens said to Oswald, "Boy are you going downstairs? ... It's near lunch time." Oswald said, "No, sir. When you get downstairs, close the gate to the elevator." Oswald was referring to the west elevator which operates by push-button and only with the gate closed. Givens said, "Okay," and rode down in the east elevator. When he reached the first floor, the west elevator, the one with the gate, was not there. Givens thought this was about 11.55 am. None of the Depository employees is known to have seen Oswald again until after the shooting.

The significance of Givens' observation that Oswald was carrying his clipboard became apparent on December 2, 1963, when an employee, Frankie Kaiser, found a clipboard hidden by book cartons in the northwest corner of the sixth floor, at the west wall a few feet from where the rifle had been found. This clipboard had been made by Kaiser and had his name on it. Kaiser identified it as the clipboard which Oswald had appropriated from him when Oswald came to work at the Depository. Three invoices on this clipboard, each dated November 22, were for Scott Foresman books, located on the first and sixth floors. Oswald had not filled any of the three orders.

Eyewitness identification of assassin
Howard L. Brennan was an eyewitness to the shooting. As indicated previously, the Commission considered his testimony as probative in reaching the conclusion that the shots came from the sixth floor, southeast corner window of the Depository Building. Brennan also testified that Lee Harvey Oswald, whom he viewed in a police lineup on the

night of the assassination, was the man he saw fire the shots from the sixth-floor window of the Depository Building. When the shots were fired, Brennan was in an excellent position to observe anyone in the window. He was sitting on a concrete wall on the southwest corner of Elm and Houston streets, looking north at the Depository Building which was directly in front of him. The window was approximately 120 feet away. In the 6–8 minute period before the motorcade arrived, Brennan saw a man leave and return to the window "a couple of times." After hearing the first shot, which he thought was a motorcycle backfire, Brennan glanced up at the window. He testified that "this man I saw previously was aiming for his last shot ... as it appeared to me he was standing up and resting against the left window sill." Brennan saw the man fire the last shot and disappear from the window. Within minutes of the assassination, Brennan described the man to the police. This description most probably led to the radio alert sent to police cars at approximately 12.45 pm, which described the suspect as white, slender, weighing about 165 pounds, about 5'10" tall, and in his early thirties. In his sworn statement to the police later that day, Brennan described the man in similar terms, except that he gave the weight as between 165 and 175 pounds and the height was omitted. In his testimony before the Commission, Brennan described the person he saw as "... a man in his early thirties, fair complexion, slender, but neat, neat slender, possible 5 foot 10 ... 160 to 170 pounds." Oswald was 5'9", slender and 24 years old. When arrested, he gave his weight as 140 pounds. On other occasions he gave weights of both 140 and 150 pounds. The New Orleans police records of his arrest in August of 1963 show a weight of 136 pounds. The autopsy report indicated an estimated weight of 150 pounds.

Brennan's description should also be compared with the eyewitness description broadcast over the Dallas police radio at 1.22 pm of the man who shot Patrolman J. D. Tippit. The suspect was described as "a white male about 30, 5'8", black hair, slender. . ." At 1.29 pm the police radio reported that the description of the suspect in the Tippit shooting was similar to the description which had been given by Brennan in connection with the assassination. Approximately 7 or 8 minutes later the police radio reported that "an eyeball witness" described the suspect in the Tippit shooting as "a white male, 27, 5'11", 165 pounds, black wavy hair." The Commission has concluded that this suspect was Lee Harvey Oswald. Although Brennan testified that the man in the window was standing when he fired the shots, most probably he was either sitting or kneeling. The half-open window, the arrangement of the boxes, and the angle of the shots virtually preclude a standing position. It is understandable, however, for Brennan to have believed that the man with the rifle was standing. A photograph of the building taken seconds after the assassination shows three employees looking out of the fifth-floor window directly below the window from which the shots were fired. Brennan testified that they were standing, which is their apparent position in the photograph. But the testimony of these employees, together with photographs subsequently taken of them at the scene of the assassination, establishes that they were either squatting or kneeling. Since the window ledges in the Depository Building are lower than in most buildings, a person squatting or kneeling exposes more of his body than would normally be the case. From the street, this creates the impression that the person is standing.

Brennan could have seen enough of the body of a kneeling or squatting person to estimate his height. Shortly after the assassination Brennan noticed two of these employees leaving the building and immediately identified them as having been in the fifth-floor windows. When the three employees appeared before the Commission, Brennan identified the two whom he saw leave the building. The two men, Harold Norman and James Jarman, Jr, each confirmed that when they came out of the building, they saw and heard Brennan describing what he had seen.

Norman stated, "... I remember him talking and I believe I remember seeing him saying that he saw us when we first went up to the fifth-floor window, he saw us then." Jarman heard Brennan "talking to this officer about that he had heard these shots and he had seen the barrel of the gun sticking out the window, and he said that the shots came from inside the building." During the evening of November 22, Brennan identified Oswald as the person in the lineup who bore the closest resemblance to the man in the window but he said he was unable to make a positive identification. Prior to the lineup, Brennan had seen Oswald's picture on television and he told the Commission that whether this affected his identification "is something I do not know." In an interview with FBI agents on December 17, 1963, Brennan stated that he was sure that the person firing the rifle was Oswald. In another interview with FBI agents on January 7, 1964, Brennan appeared to revert to his earlier inability to make a positive identification, but, in his testimony before the Commission, Brennan stated that his remarks of January 7 were intended by him merely as an accurate report of what he said on November 22.

Brennan told the Commission that he could have made a positive identification in the lineup on November 22 but did not do so because he felt that the assassination was "a Communist activity, and I felt like there hadn't been more than one eyewitness, and if it got to be a known fact that I was an eyewitness, my family or I, either one, might not be safe." When specifically asked before the Commission whether or not he could positively identify the man he saw in the sixth-floor window as the same man he saw in the police station, Brennan stated, "I could at that time, I could, with all sincerity, identify him as being the same man." Although the record indicates that Brennan was an accurate observer, he declined to make a positive identification of Oswald when he first saw him in the police lineup. The Commission, therefore, does not base its conclusion concerning the identity of the assassin on Brennan's subsequent certain identification of Lee Harvey Oswald as the man he saw fire the rifle. Immediately after the assassination, however, Brennan described to the police the man he saw in the window and then identified Oswald as the person who most nearly resembled the man he saw. The Commission is satisfied that, at the least, Brennan saw a man in the window who closely resembled Lee Harvey Oswald, and that Brennan believes the man he saw was in fact Lee Harvey Oswald.

Two other witnesses were able to offer partial descriptions of a man they saw in the southeast corner window of the sixth floor approximately 1 minute before the assassination, although neither witness saw the shots being fired. Ronald Fischer and Robert Edwards were standing on the curb at the southwest corner of Elm and Houston streets, the same corner where Brennan was sitting on a concrete wall. Fischer testified that about 10 or 15 seconds before the motorcade turned onto Houston Street from Main Street, Edwards said, "Look at that guy there in that window." Fischer looked up and watched the man in the window for 10 or 15 seconds and then started watching the motorcade, which came into view on Houston Street. He said that the man held his attention until the motorcade came, because the man:

> . . . appeared uncomfortable for one, and secondly, he wasn't watching . . . he didn't look like he was watching for the parade. He looked like he was looking down toward the

> Trinity River and the Triple Underpass down at the end
> toward the end of Elm Street. And ... all the time I
> watched him, he never moved his head, he never, he
> never moved anything. Just was there transfixed.

Fischer placed the man in the easternmost window on the
south side of the Depository Building on either the fifth or
the sixth floor. He said that he could see the man from the
middle of his chest to the top of his head, and that as he was
facing the window, the man was in the lower right-hand
portion of the window and "seemed to be sitting a little
forward." The man was dressed in a light-colored, open-
neck shirt which could have been either a sports shirt or a
T-shirt, and he had brown hair, a slender face and neck with
light complexion, and looked to be 22 or 24 years old. The
person in the window was a white man and "looked to me
like he was looking straight at the Triple Underpass" down
Elm Street. Boxes and cases were stacked behind him.

Approximately one week after the assassination,
according to Fisher, policemen showed him a picture of
Oswald. In his testimony he said, "I told them that that
could have been the man ... That that could have been the
man that I saw in the window in the School Book
Depository Building, but that I was not sure." Fischer
described the man's hair as some shade of brown; "it wasn't
dark and it wasn't light." On November 22, Fischer had
apparently described the man as "light-headed". Fischer
explained that he did not mean by the earlier statement that
the man was blond, but rather that his hair was not black.

Robert Edwards said that, while looking at the south
side of the Depository Building shortly before the motorcade, he saw nothing of importance "except maybe one
individual who was up there in the corner room of the
sixth floor which was crowded in among boxes." He said
that this was a white man about average in size, "possibly

thin", and that he thought the man had light-brown hair. Fischer and Edwards did not see the man clearly enough or long enough to identify him.

Their testimony is of probative value, however, because their limited description is consistent with that of the man who has been found by the Commission, based on other evidence, to have fired the shots from the window. Another person who saw the assassin as the shots were fired was Amos L. Euins, age 15, who was one of the first witnesses to alert the police to the Depository as the source of the shots (see p. 105). Euins, who was on the southwest corner of Elm and Houston streets, testified that he could not describe the man he saw in the window. According to Euins, however, as the man lowered his head in order to aim the rifle down Elm Street, he appeared to have a white bald spot on his head. Shortly after the assassination, Euins signed an affidavit describing the man as "white", but a radio reporter testified that Euins described the man to him as "colored". In his Commission testimony, Euins stated that he could not ascertain the man's race and that the statement in the affidavit was intended to refer only to the white spot on the man's head and not to his race. A Secret Service agent who spoke to Euins approximately 20 to 30 minutes after the assassination confirmed that Euins could neither describe the man in the window nor indicate his race. Accordingly, Euins' testimony is considered probative as to the source of the shots but is inconclusive as to the identity of the man in the window. In evaluating the evidence that Oswald was at the southeast corner window of the sixth floor at the time of the shooting, the Commission has considered the allegation that Oswald was photographed standing in front of the building when the shots were fired. The picture which gave rise to these allegations was taken by Associated Press Photographer James W. Altgens, who was standing on the south side of Elm Street between the Triple Underpass and the Depository Building. As the motorcade started its descent down Elm Street, Altgens snapped a picture of the presidential limousine with the entrance to the Depository Building in the background. Just before snapping the picture Altgens heard a noise which sounded like the popping of a firecracker. Investigation has established that Altgens' picture was taken approximately 2 seconds after the firing of the shot which entered the back of the president's neck.

In the background of this picture were several employees watching the parade from the steps of the Depository Building. One of these employees was alleged to resemble Lee Harvey Oswald. The Commission has determined that the employee was in fact Billy Lovelady, who identified himself in the picture. Standing alongside him were Buell Wesley Frazier and William Shelley, who also identified Lovelady. The Commission is satisfied that Oswald does not appear in this photograph.

Oswald's actions in building after assassination
In considering whether Oswald was at the southeast corner window at the time the shots were fired, the Commission has reviewed the testimony of witnesses who saw Oswald in the building within minutes after the assassination. The Commission has found that Oswald's movements, as described by these witnesses, are consistent with his having been at the window at 12.30 pm.

The encounter in the lunchroom
The first person to see Oswald after the assassination was Patrolman M. L. Baker of the Dallas Police Department. Baker was riding a two-wheeled motorcycle behind the last press car of the motorcade. As he turned the corner from Main onto Houston at a speed of about 5 to 10 miles per hour, a strong wind blowing from the north

almost unseated him. At about this time he heard the first shot. Having recently heard the sounds of rifles while on a hunting trip, Baker recognized the shots as that of a high-powered rifle: "It sounded high and I immediately kind of looked up, and I had a feeling that it came from the building, either right in front of me [the Depository Building] or the one across to the right of it." He saw pigeons flutter upward. He was not certain, "but I am pretty sure they came from the building right on the northwest corner." He heard two more shots spaced "pretty well even to me." After the third shot, he "revved that motorcycle up", drove to the northwest corner of Elm and Houston, and parked approximately 10 feet from the traffic signal. As he was parking he noted that people were "falling, and they were rolling around down there ... grabbing their children" and rushing about. A woman screamed, "Oh, they have shot that man, they have shot that man."

Baker "had it in mind that the shots came from the top of this building here", so he ran straight to the entrance of the Depository Building. Baker testified that he entered the lobby of the building and "spoke out and asked where the stairs or elevator was ... and this man, Mr Truly, spoke up and says, it seems to me like he says, 'I am a building manager. Follow me, officer, and I will show you.'" Baker and building superintendent Roy Truly went through a second set of doors and stopped at a swinging door where Baker bumped into Truly's back. They went through the swinging door and continued at "a good trot" to the northwest corner of the floor where Truly hoped to find one of the two freight elevators. Neither elevator was there. Truly pushed the button for the west elevator which operates automatically if the gate is closed. He shouted twice, "Turn loose the elevator." When the elevator failed to come, Baker said, "Let's take the stairs," and he followed Truly up the stairway, which is to the west of the elevator.

The stairway is located in the northwest corner of the Depository Building. The stairs from one floor to the next are L-shaped, with both legs of the "L" approximately the same length. Because the stairway itself is enclosed, neither Baker nor Truly could see anything on the second-floor hallway until they reached the landing at the top of the stairs.

On the second-floor landing there is a small open area with a door at the east end. This door leads into a small vestibule, and another door leads from the vestibule into the second-floor lunchroom. The lunchroom door is usually open, but the first door is kept shut by a closing mechanism on the door. This vestibule door is solid except for a small glass window in the upper part of the door. As Baker reached the second floor, he was about 20 feet from the vestibule door. He intended to continue around to his left toward the stairway going up, but through the window in the door he caught a fleeting glimpse of a man walking in the vestibule toward the lunchroom.

Since the vestibule door is only a few feet from the lunchroom door, the man must have entered the vestibule only a second or two before Baker arrived at the top of the stairwell. Yet he must have entered the vestibule door before Truly reached the top of the stairwell, since Truly did not see him. If the man had passed from the vestibule into the lunchroom, Baker could not have seen him. Baker said:

> He [Truly] had already started around the bend to come to the next elevator going up, I was coming out this one on the second floor, and I don't know, I was kind of sweeping this area as I come up, I was looking from right to left and as I got to this door here I caught a glimpse of this man, just, you know, a sudden glimpse . . . and it looked to me like he was going away from me . . . I can't say whether he had gone on

through that door [the lunchroom door] or not. All I did was catch a glance at him, and evidently he was, this door might have been, you know, closing and almost shut at that time.

With his revolver drawn, Baker opened the vestibule door and ran into the vestibule. He saw a man walking away from him in the lunchroom. Baker stopped at the door of the lunchroom and commanded, "Come here." The man turned and walked back toward Baker. He had been proceeding toward the rear of the lunchroom. Along a side wall of the lunchroom was a soft drink vending machine, but at that time the man had nothing in his hands.

Meanwhile, Truly had run up several steps toward the third floor. Missing Baker, he came back to find the officer in the doorway to the lunchroom "facing Lee Harvey Oswald". Baker turned to Truly and said, "Do you know this man, does he work here?" Truly replied, "Yes." Baker stated later that the man did not seem to be out of breath; he seemed calm. "He never did say a word or nothing. In fact, he didn't change his expression one bit." Truly said of Oswald: "He didn't seem to be excited or overly afraid or anything. He might have been a bit startled, like I might have been if somebody confronted me. But I cannot recall any change in expression of any kind on his face." Truly thought that the officer's gun at that time appeared to be almost touching the middle portion of Oswald's body. Truly also noted at this time that Oswald's hands were empty.

In an effort to determine whether Oswald could have descended to the lunchroom from the sixth floor by the time Baker and Truly arrived, Commission counsel asked Baker and Truly to repeat their movements from the time of the shot until Baker came upon Oswald in the lunchroom. Baker placed himself on a motorcycle about 200 feet from the corner of Elm and Houston streets where he said he heard the shots. Truly stood in front of the building. At a given signal, they re-enacted the event. Baker's movements were timed with a stopwatch. On the first test, the elapsed time between the simulated first shot and Baker's arrival on the second-floor stair landing was 1 minute and 30 seconds. The second test run required 1 minute and 15 seconds.

A test was also conducted to determine the time required to walk from the southeast corner of the sixth floor to the second-floor lunchroom by stairway. Special Agent John Howlett of the Secret Service carried a rifle from the southeast corner of the sixth floor along the east aisle to the northeast corner. He placed the rifle on the floor near the site where Oswald's rifle was actually found after the shooting. Then Howlett walked down the stairway to the second-floor landing and entered the lunchroom. The first test, run at normal walking pace, required 1 minute, 18 seconds; the second test, at a "fast walk" took 1 minute, 14 seconds. The second test followed immediately after the first. The only interval was the time necessary to ride in the elevator from the second to the sixth floor and walk back to the southeast corner. Howlett was not short-winded at the end of either test run.

The minimum time required by Baker to park his motorcycle and reach the second-floor lunchroom was within 3 seconds of the time needed to walk from the southeast corner of the sixth floor down the stairway to the lunchroom. The time actually required for Baker and Truly to reach the second floor on November 22 was probably longer than in the test runs. For example, Baker required 15 seconds after the simulated shot to ride his motorcycle 180 to 200 feet, park it, and run 45 feet to the building. No allowance was made for the special conditions which existed on the day of the assassination, possible delayed reaction to the shot, jostling with the crowd of people on the steps and scanning the area along Elm Street and the parkway. Baker said, "We simulated the shots and by the time we got there, we did everything that I did that day, and this would be the minimum, because I am sure that I, you know, it took me a little longer." On the basis of this time test, therefore, the Commission concluded that Oswald could have fired the shots and still have been present in the second-floor lunchroom when seen by Baker and Truly. That Oswald descended by stairway from the sixth floor to the second floor lunchroom is consistent with the movements of the two elevators, which would have provided the other possible means of descent. When Truly, accompanied by Baker, ran to the rear of the first floor, he was certain that both elevators, which occupy the same shaft, were on the fifth floor. Baker, not realizing that there were two elevators, thought that only one elevator was in the shaft and that it was two or three floors above the second floor. In the few seconds which elapsed while Baker and Truly ran from the first to the second floor, neither of these slow elevators could have descended from the fifth to the second floor. Furthermore, no elevator was at the second floor when they arrived there. Truly and Baker continued up the stairs after the encounter with Oswald in the lunchroom. There was no elevator on the third or fourth floor. The east elevator was on the fifth floor when they arrived; the west elevator was not. They took the east elevator to the seventh floor and ran up a stairway to the roof where they searched for several minutes.

Jack Dougherty, an employee working on the fifth floor, testified that he took the west elevator to the first floor after hearing a noise which sounded like a backfire. Eddie Piper, the janitor, told Dougherty that the president had been shot, but in his testimony Piper did not mention either seeing or talking with Dougherty during these moments of excitement. Both Dougherty and Piper were confused witnesses. They had no exact memory of the events of that afternoon. Truly was probably correct in stating that the west elevator was on the fifth floor when he looked up the elevator shaft from the first floor. The west elevator was not on the fifth floor when Baker and Truly reached that floor, probably because Jack Dougherty took it to the first floor while Baker and Truly were running up the stairs or in the lunchroom with Oswald. Neither elevator could have been used by Oswald as a means of descent. Oswald's use of the stairway is consistent with the testimony of other employees in the building. Three employees James Jarman, Jr, Harold Norman, and Bonnie Ray Williams were watching the parade from the fifth floor, directly below the window from which the shots were fired. They rushed to the west windows after the shots were fired and remained there until after they saw Patrolman Baker's white helmet on the fifth floor moving toward the elevator.

While they were at the west windows their view of the stairwell was completely blocked by shelves and boxes. This is the period during which Oswald would have descended the stairs. In all likelihood Dougherty took the elevator down from the fifth floor after Jarman, Norman, and Williams ran to the west windows and were deciding what to do. None of these three men saw Dougherty, probably because of the anxiety of the moment and because of the books which may have blocked the view. Neither Jarman, Norman, Williams, or Dougherty saw Oswald.

Victoria Adams, who worked on the fourth floor of the Depository Building, claimed that within about 1 minute following the shots she ran from a window on the south side of the fourth floor, down the rear stairs to the first floor, where she encountered two Depository employees, William Shelley and Billy Lovelady. If her estimate of time is correct, she reached the bottom of the stairs before Truly and Baker started up, and she must have run down the stairs ahead of Oswald and would probably have seen or heard him. Actually she noticed no one on the back stairs. If she descended from the fourth to the first floor as fast as she claimed in her testimony, she would have seen Baker or Truly on the first floor or on the stairs, unless they were already in the second-floor lunchroom talking to Oswald. When she reached the first floor, she actually saw Shelley and Lovelady slightly east of the east elevator. Shelley and Lovelady, however, have testified that they were watching the parade from the top step of the building entrance when Gloria Calverly, who works in the Depository Building, ran up and said that the president had been shot.

Lovelady and Shelley moved out into the street. About this time Shelley saw Truly and Patrolman Baker go into the building. Shelley and Lovelady, at a fast walk or trot, turned west into the railroad yards and then to the west side of the Depository Building. They re-entered the building by the rear door several minutes after Baker and Truly rushed through the front entrance. On entering, Lovelady saw a girl on the first floor who he believes was Victoria Adams. If Miss Adams accurately recalled meeting Shelley and Lovelady when she reached the bottom of the stairs, then her estimate of the time when she descended from the fourth floor is incorrect, and she actually came down the stairs several minutes after Oswald and after Truly and Baker as well.

Oswald's departure from building

Within a minute after Baker and Truly left Oswald in the lunchroom, Mrs R. A. Reid, clerical supervisor for the Texas School Book Depository, saw him walk through the clerical office on the second floor toward the door leading to the front stairway. Mrs Reid had watched the parade from the sidewalk in front of the building with Truly and Mr O. V. Campbell, vice president of the Depository. She testified that she heard three shots which she thought came from the building. She ran inside and up the front stairs into the large open office reserved for clerical employees. As she approached her desk, she saw Oswald. He was walking into the office from the back hallway, carrying a full bottle of Coca-Cola in his hand, presumably purchased after the encounter with Baker and Truly. As Oswald passed Mrs Reid she said, "Oh, the president has been shot, but maybe they didn't hit him." Oswald mumbled something and walked by. She paid no more attention to him. The only exit from the office in the direction Oswald was moving was through the door to the front stairway. Mrs Reid testified that when she saw Oswald, he was wearing a T-shirt and no jacket. When he left home that morning, Marina Oswald, who was still in bed, suggested that he wear a jacket. A blue jacket, later identified by Marina Oswald as her husband's, was subsequently found in the building, apparently left behind by Oswald.

Mrs Reid believes that she returned to her desk from the street about 2 minutes after the shooting. Reconstructing her movements, Mrs Reid ran the distance three times and was timed in 2 minutes by stopwatch. The reconstruction was the minimum time. Accordingly, she probably met Oswald at about 12.32, approximately 30-45 seconds after Oswald's lunchroom encounter with Baker and Truly. After leaving Mrs Reid in the front office, Oswald could have gone down the stairs and out the front door by 12.33 pm, 3 minutes after the shooting. At that time the building had not yet been sealed off by the police.

While it was difficult to determine exactly when the police sealed off the building, the earliest estimates would still have permitted Oswald to leave the building by 12.33. One of the police officers assigned to the corner of Elm and Houston streets for the presidential motorcade, W. E. Barnett, testified that immediately after the shots he went to the rear of the building to check the fire escape. He then returned to the corner of Elm and Houston where he met a sergeant who instructed him to find out the name of the building. Barnett ran to the building, noted its name, and then returned to the corner. There he was met by a construction worker, in all likelihood Howard Brennan, who was wearing his work helmet. This worker told Barnett that the shots had been fired from a window in the Depository Building, where upon Barnett posted himself at the front door to make certain that no one left the building. The sergeant did the same thing at the rear of the building. Barnett estimated that approximately 3 minutes elapsed between the time he heard the last of the shots and the time he started guarding the front door. According to Barnett, "there were people going in and out" during this period.

Sergeant D.V. Harkness of the Dallas police said that to his knowledge the building was not sealed off at 12.36 pm when he called in on police radio that a witness (Amos Euins) had seen shots fired from a window of the building. At that time, Inspector Herbert J. Sawyer's car was parked in front of the building. Harkness did not know whether or not two officers with Sawyer were guarding the doors. At 12.34 pm Sawyer heard a call over the police radio that the shots had come from the Depository Building. He then entered the building and took the front passenger elevator as far as it would go to the fourth floor. After inspecting this floor, Sawyer returned to the street about 3 minutes after he entered the building. After he returned to the street he directed Sergeant Harkness to station two patrolmen at the front door and not let anyone in or out; he also directed that the back door be sealed off. This was no earlier than 12.37 pm and may have been later.

Special Agent Forrest V. Sorrels of the Secret Service, who had been in the motorcade, testified that after driving to Parkland Hospital, he returned to the Depository Building about 20 minutes after the shooting, found no police officers at the rear door and was able to enter through this door without identifying himself. Although Oswald probably left the building at about 12.33 pm, his absence was not noticed until at least one-half hour later. Truly, who had returned with Patrolman Baker from the roof, saw the police questioning the warehouse employees. Approximately 15 men worked in the warehouse and Truly noticed that Oswald was not among those being questioned. Satisfying himself that Oswald was missing, Truly obtained Oswald's address, phone number, and description from his employment application card. The address listed was for the Paine home in Irving. Truly gave this information to Captain Fritz who was on the sixth floor at the time. Truly estimated that he gave this information to Fritz about 15 or 20 minutes after the shots, but it was probably no earlier than 1.22 pm, the time when the rifle was found. Fritz believed that he learned of Oswald's absence after the rifle was found. The fact that Truly found Fritz in the northwest corner of the floor, near the point where the rifle was found, supports Fritz' recollection.

Conclusion

Fingerprint and palmprint evidence establishes that Oswald handled two of the four cartons next to the window and also handled a paper bag which was found near the cartons. Oswald was seen in the vicinity of the southeast corner of the sixth floor approximately 35 minutes before the assassination and no one could be found who saw Oswald anywhere else in the building until after the shooting. An eyewitness to the shooting immediately provided a description of the man in the window which was similar to Oswald's actual appearance. This witness identified Oswald in a lineup as the man most nearly resembling the man he saw and later identified Oswald as the man he observed. Oswald's known actions in the building immediately after the assassination are consistent with his having been at the southeast corner window of the sixth floor at 12.30 pm. On the basis of these findings the Commission has concluded that Oswald, at the time of the assassination, was present at the window from which the shots were fired.

THE KILLING OF PATROLMAN J. D. TIPPIT

After leaving the Depository Building at approximately 12.38 pm, Lee Harvey Oswald proceeded to his rooming house by bus and taxi. He arrived at approximately 1 pm and left a few minutes later. At about 1.16 pm, a Dallas police officer, J. D. Tippit, was shot less than one mile from Oswald's rooming house. In deciding whether Oswald killed Patrolman Tippit the Commission considered the following:

(1) positive identification of the killer by two eyewitnesses who saw the shooting and seven eyewitnesses who heard the shots and saw the gunman flee the scene with the revolver in his hand
(2) testimony of firearms identification experts establishing the identity of the murder weapon
(3) evidence establishing the ownership of the murder weapon
(4) evidence establishing the ownership of a zipper jacket found along the path of flight taken by the gunman from the scene of the shooting to the place of arrest.

Oswald's movements after leaving Depository Building

The bus ride
According to the reconstruction of time and events which the Commission found most credible, Lee Harvey Oswald

left the building approximately 3 minutes after the assassination. He probably walked east on Elm Street for seven
blocks to the corner of Elm and Murphy where he boarded
a bus which was heading back in the direction of the
Depository Building, on its way to the Oak Cliff section of
Dallas. When Oswald was apprehended, a bus transfer
marked for the Lakewood–Marsalis route was found in his
shirt pocket.

The transfer was dated "Fri. Nov. 22, '63" and was
punched in two places by the bus driver. On the basis of
this punch mark, which was distinctive to each Dallas
driver, the transfer was conclusively identified as having
been issued by Cecil J. McWatters, a bus driver for the
Dallas Transit Company. On the basis of the date and time
on the transfer, McWatters was able to testify that the
transfer had been issued by him on a trip which passed a
check-point at St Paul and Elm streets at 12.36 pm,
November 22, 1963.

McWatters was sure that he left the checkpoint on
time and he estimated that it took him 3 to 4 minutes to
drive three blocks west from the checkpoint to Field Street,
which he reached at about 12.40 pm. McWatters' recollection is that he issued this transfer to a man who entered his
bus just beyond Field Street, where a man beat on the front
door of the bus, boarded it and paid his fare. About two
blocks later, a woman asked to get off to make a 1 o'clock
train at Union Station and requested a transfer which she
might use if she got through the traffic:

> . . . So I gave her a transfer and opened the door and as she
> was going out the gentleman I had picked up about two
> blocks [back] asked for a transfer and got off at the same
> place in the middle of the block where the lady did. . . It
> was the intersection near Lamar Street, it was near Poydras
> and Lamar Street.

The man was on the bus approximately 4 minutes.

At about 6.30 pm on the day of the assassination, McWatters viewed four men in a police lineup. He picked Oswald from the lineup as the man who had boarded the bus at the "lower end of town on Elm around Houston", and who, during the ride south on Marsalis, had an argument with a woman passenger. In his Commission testimony, McWatters said he had been in error and that a teenager named Milton Jones was the passenger he had in mind. In a later interview, Jones confirmed that he had exchanged words with a woman passenger on the bus during the ride south on Marsalis.

McWatters also remembered that a man received a transfer at Lamar and Elm streets and that a man in the lineup was about the size of this man. However, McWatters' recollection alone was too vague to be a basis for placing Oswald on the bus. Riding on the bus was an elderly woman, Mary Bledsoe, who confirmed the mute evidence of the transfer. Oswald had rented a room from Mrs Bledsoe about six weeks before, on October 7, but she had asked him to leave at the end of a week. Mrs Bledsoe told him "I am not going to rent to you any more." She testified, "I didn't like his attitude ... There was just something about him I didn't like or want him ... Just didn't want him around me." On November 22, Mrs Bledsoe came downtown to watch the presidential motorcade. She boarded the Marsalis bus at St Paul and Elm streets to return home. She testified further:

> And, after we got past Akard, at Murphy I figured it out. Let's see. I don't know for sure. Oswald got on. He looks like a maniac. His sleeve was out here ... His shirt was undone ... Was a hole in it, hole, and he was dirty, and I didn't look at him. I didn't want to know I even seen him ... he looked so bad in his face, and his face was so distorted. ... Hole in his sleeve right here.

As Mrs Bledsoe said these words, she pointed to her right elbow. When Oswald was arrested in the Texas Theater, he was wearing a brown sport shirt with a hole in the right sleeve at the elbow. Mrs Bledsoe identified the shirt as the one Oswald was wearing and she stated she was certain that it was Oswald who boarded the bus. Mrs Bledsoe recalled that Oswald sat halfway to the rear of the bus which moved slowly and intermittently as traffic became heavy. She heard a passing motorist tell the driver that the president had been shot. People on the bus began talking about it. As the bus neared Lamar Street, Oswald left the bus and disappeared into the crowd.

The Marsalis bus which Oswald boarded traveled a route west on Elm, south on Houston, and southwest across the Houston viaduct to service the Oak Cliff area along Marsalis. A Beckley bus, which also served the Oak Cliff area, followed the same route as the Marsalis bus through downtown Dallas, except that it continued west on Elm, across Houston in front of the Depository Building, past the Triple Underpass into west Dallas, and south on Beckley.

Marsalis Street is seven blocks from Beckley. Oswald lived at 1026 North Beckley. He could not reach his rooming house on the Marsalis bus, but the Beckley bus stopped across the street. According to McWatters, the Beckley bus was behind the Marsalis bus, but he did not actually see it. Both buses stopped within one block of the Depository Building. Instead of waiting there, Oswald apparently went as far away as he could and boarded the first Oak Cliff bus which came along rather than wait for one which stopped across the street from his rooming house.

In a reconstruction of this bus trip, agents of the Secret Service and the FBI walked the seven blocks from the front entrance of the Depository Building to Murphy and Elm three times, averaging 6.5 minutes for the three trips. A bus moving through heavy traffic on Elm from Murphy to

Lamar was timed at 4 minutes. If Oswald left the Depository Building at 12.33 pm, walked seven blocks directly to Murphy and Elm, and boarded a bus almost immediately, he would have boarded the bus at approximately 12.40 pm and left it at approximately 12.44 pm. Roger D. Craig, a deputy sheriff of Dallas County, claimed that about 15 minutes after the assassination he saw a man, whom he later identified as Oswald, coming from the direction of the Depository Building and running down the hill north of Elm Street toward a light-colored Rambler station wagon, which was moving slowly along Elm toward the underpass. The station wagon stopped to pick up the man and then drove off. Craig testified that later in the afternoon he saw Oswald in the police interrogation room and told Captain Fritz that Oswald was the man he saw.

Craig also claimed that when Fritz pointed out to Oswald that Craig had identified him, Oswald rose from his chair, looked directly at Fritz, and said, "Everybody will know who I am now." The Commission could not accept important elements of Craig's testimony. Captain Fritz stated that a deputy sheriff whom he could not identify did ask to see him that afternoon and told him a similar story to Craig's. Fritz did not bring him into his office to identify Oswald but turned him over to Lieutenant Baker for questioning. If Craig saw Oswald that afternoon, he saw him through the glass windows of the office. And neither Captain Fritz nor any other officer can remember that Oswald dramatically arose from his chair and said, "Everybody will know who I am now." If Oswald had made such a statement, Captain Fritz and others present would probably have remembered it. Craig may have seen a person enter a white Rambler station wagon 15 or 20 minutes after the shooting and travel west on Elm Street, but the Commission concluded that this man was not Lee Harvey Oswald, because of the overwhelming evidence that Oswald was far away from the building by that time.

The taxicab ride

William Whaley, a taxicab driver, told his employer on Saturday morning, November 23, that he recognized Oswald from a newspaper photograph as a man whom he had driven to the Oak Cliff area the day before.

Notified of Whaley's statement, the police brought him to the police station that afternoon. He was taken to the lineup room where, according to Whaley, five young teenagers, all handcuffed together, were displayed with Oswald. He testified that Oswald looked older than the other boys. The police asked him whether he could pick out his passenger from the lineup. Whaley picked Oswald. He said:

> . . . you could have picked him out without identifying him by just listening to him because he was bawling out the police-man, telling them it wasn't right to put him in line with these teenagers and all of that and they asked me which one and I told them. It was him all right, the same man. He showed no respect for the policemen, he told them what he thought about them. They knew what they were doing and they were trying to railroad him and he wanted his lawyer.

Whaley believes that Oswald's conduct did not aid him in his identification "because I knew he was the right one as soon as I saw him." Whaley's memory of the lineup is inac-curate. There were four men altogether, not six men, in the lineup with Oswald. Whaley said that Oswald was the man under no. 2. Actually Oswald was under no. 3. Only two of the men in the lineup with Oswald were teenagers: John T. Horn, aged 18, was no. 1; David Knapp, aged 18, was no. 2; Lee Oswald was no. 3; and Daniel Lujan, aged 26, was no. 4.

When he first testified before the Commission, Whaley displayed a trip manifest which showed a 12 o'clock trip from Travis Hotel to the Continental bus station, unloaded at 12.15 pm; a 12.15 pm pickup at Continental to Greyhound, unloaded at 12.30 pm; and a pickup from Greyhound (bus station) at 12.30 pm, unloaded at 500 North Beckley at 12.45 pm. Whaley testified that he did not keep an accurate time record of his trips but recorded them by the quarter hour, and that sometimes he made his entry right after a trip while at other times he waited to record three or four trips. As he unloaded his Continental bus station passenger in front of Greyhound, he started to get out to buy a package of cigarettes. He saw a man walking south on Lamar from Commerce. The man was dressed in faded blue color khaki work clothes, a brown shirt, and some kind of work jacket that almost matched his pants. The man asked, "May I have the cab?" and got into the front seat. Whaley described the ensuing events as follows:

> And about that time an old lady, I think she was an old lady, I don't remember nothing but her sticking her head down past him in the door and said, "Driver, will you call me a cab down here?" She had seen him get this cab and she wanted one, too, and he opened the door a little bit like he was going to get out and he said, "I will let you have this one," and she says, "No, the driver can call me one." . . . I asked him where he wanted to go. And he said, "500 North Beckley." Well, I started up, I started to that address, and the police cars, the sirens was going, running crisscrossing everywhere, just a big uproar in that end of town and I said, "What the hell. I wonder what the hell is the uproar?" And he never said anything. So I figured he was one of these people that don't like to talk so I never said any more to him. But when I got pretty close to 500 block at Neches and North Beckley which is the 500 block, he said, "This will do fine," and I

pulled over to the curb right there. He gave me a dollar bill, the trip was 95 cents. He gave me a dollar bill and didn't say anything, just got out and closed the door and walked around the front of the cab over to the other side of the street [east side of the street]. Of course, the traffic was moving through there and I put it in gear and moved on, that is the last I saw of him.

Whaley was somewhat imprecise as to where he unloaded his passenger. He marked what he thought was the intersection of Neches and Beckley on a map of Dallas with a large "X." He said, "Yes, sir; that is right, because that is the 500 block of North Beckley." However, Neches and Beckley do not intersect. Neches is within one-half block of the rooming house at 1026 North Beckley where Oswald was living. The 500 block of North Beckley is five blocks south of the rooming house.

After a review of these inconsistencies in his testimony before the Commission, Whaley was interviewed again in Dallas. The route of the taxicab was retraced under the direction of Whaley. He directed the driver of the car to a point 20 feet north of the northwest corner of the intersection of Beckley and Neely, the point at which he said his passenger alighted. This was the 700 block of North Beckley. The elapsed time of the reconstructed run from the Greyhound Bus Station to Neely and Beckley was 5 minutes and 30 seconds by stopwatch. The walk from Beckley and Neely to 1026 North Beckley was timed by Commission counsel at 5 minutes and 45 seconds.

Whaley testified that Oswald was wearing either the gray zippered jacket or the heavy blue jacket. He was in error, however. Oswald could not possibly have been wearing the blue jacket during the trip with Whaley, since it was found in the "domino" room of the Depository late in November. Moreover, Mrs Bledsoe saw Oswald in the bus without a jacket and wearing a shirt with a hole at the elbow. On the other hand, Whaley identified the shirt taken from Oswald upon arrest as the shirt his passenger was wearing. He also stated he saw a silver identification bracelet on his passenger's left wrist. Oswald was wearing such a bracelet when he was arrested. On November 22, Oswald told Captain Fritz that he rode a bus to a stop near his home and then walked to his rooming house. When queried the following morning concerning a bus transfer found in his possession at the time of his arrest, he admitted receiving it. And when interrogated about a cab ride, Oswald also admitted that he left the slow-moving bus and took a cab to his rooming house.

The Greyhound Bus Station at Lamar and Jackson streets, where Oswald entered Whaley's cab, is three to four short blocks south of Lamar and Elm. If Oswald left the bus at 12.44 pm and walked directly to the terminal, he would have entered the cab at 12.47 or 12.48 pm. If the cab ride was approximately 6 minutes, as was the reconstructed ride, he would have reached his destination at approximately 12.54 pm. If he was discharged at Neely and Beckley and walked directly to his rooming house, he would have arrived there about 12.59 to 1 pm. From the 500 block of North Beckley, the walk would be a few minutes longer, but in either event he would have been in the rooming house at about 1 pm. This is the approximate time he entered the rooming house, according to Earlene Roberts, the housekeeper there.

Arrival and departure from rooming house

Earlene Roberts, housekeeper for Mrs A. C. Johnson at 1026 North Beckley, knew Lee Harvey Oswald under the alias of O. H. Lee. She first saw him the day he rented a room at that address on October 14, 1963. He signed his name as O. H. Lee on the rooming house register.

Mrs Roberts testified that on Thursday, November 21, Oswald did not come home. On Friday, November 22, about 1 pm, he entered the house in unusual haste. She recalled that it was subsequent to the time the president had been shot.

After a friend had called and told her, "President Kennedy has been shot," she turned on the television. When Oswald came in she said, "Oh, you are in a hurry," but Oswald did not respond. He hurried to his room and stayed no longer than 3 or 4 minutes. Oswald had entered the house in his shirt sleeves, but when he left, he was zipping up a jacket. Mrs Roberts saw him a few seconds later standing near the bus stop in front of the house on the east side of Beckley.

Oswald was next seen about $\frac{9}{10}$ mile away at the southeast corner of 10th Street and Patton Avenue, moments before the Tippit shooting. If Oswald left his rooming house shortly after 1 pm and walked at a brisk pace, he would have reached 10th and Patton shortly after 1.15 pm. Tippit's murder was recorded on the police radio tape at about 1.16 pm.

Description of shooting

Patrolman J. D. Tippit joined the Dallas Police Department in July 1952. He was described by Chief Curry as having the reputation of being "a very dedicated officer." Tippit patrolled district No. 78 in the Oak Cliff area of Dallas during daylight hours. He drove a police car painted distinctive colors with No. 10 prominently displayed on each side. Tippit rode alone, as only one man was normally assigned to a patrol car in residential areas during daylight shifts.

At about 12.44 pm on November 22, the radio dispatcher on channel 1 ordered all downtown patrol squads to report to Elm and Houston, code 3 (emergency). At 12.45 pm the dispatcher ordered No. 78 (Tippit) to "move into central Oak Cliff area." At 12.54 pm, Tippit reported that he was in the central Oak Cliff area at Lancaster and Eighth. The dispatcher ordered Tippit to be "... at large for any emergency that comes in." According to Chief Curry, Tippit was free to patrol the central Oak Cliff area. Tippit must have heard the description of the suspect wanted for the president's shooting; it was broadcast over channel 1 at 12.45 pm, again at 12.48 pm, and again at 12.55 pm. The suspect was described as a "white male, approximately 30, slender build, height 5 foot 10 inches, weight 165 pounds." A similar description was given on channel 2 at 12.45 pm.

At approximately 1.15 pm, Tippit, who was cruising east on 10th Street, passed the intersection of 10th and Patton, about eight blocks from where he had reported at 12.54 pm. About 100 feet past the intersection Tippit stopped a man walking east along the south side of Patton. The man's general description was similar to the one broadcast over the police radio. Tippit stopped the man and called him to his car. He approached the car and apparently exchanged words with Tippit through the right front or vent window. Tippit got out and started to walk around the front of the car. As Tippit reached the left front wheel the man pulled out a revolver and fired several shots. Four bullets hit Tippit and killed him instantly. The gunman started back toward Patton Avenue, ejecting the empty cartridge cases before reloading with fresh bullets.

Eyewitnesses

At least 12 persons saw the man with the revolver in the vicinity of the Tippit crime scene at or immediately after the shooting. By the evening of November 22, five of them had identified Lee Harvey Oswald in police lineups as the man they saw. A sixth did so the next day. Three others subsequently identified Oswald from a photograph. Two witnesses testified that Oswald resembled the man they had seen. One witness felt he was too distant from the gunman to make a positive identification. A taxi driver, William Scoggins, was eating lunch in his cab which was parked on Patton facing the southeast corner of 10th Street and Patton Avenue a few feet to the north. A police car moving east on 10th at about 10 or 12 miles an hour passed in front of his cab. About 100 feet from the corner the police car pulled up alongside a man on the sidewalk.

This man, dressed in a light-colored jacket, approached the car. Scoggins lost sight of him behind some shrubbery on the southeast corner lot, but he saw the policeman leave the car, heard three or four shots, and then saw the policeman fall.

Scoggins hurriedly left his seat and hid behind the cab as the man came back toward the corner with gun in hand. The man cut across the yard through some bushes, passed within 12 feet of Scoggins, and ran south on Patton. Scoggins saw him and heard him mutter either "Poor damn cop" or "Poor dumb cop." The next day Scoggins viewed a lineup of four persons and identified Oswald as the man whom he had seen the day before at 10th and Patton. In his testimony before the Commission, Scoggins stated that he thought he had seen a picture of Oswald in the newspapers prior to the lineup identification on Saturday. He had not seen Oswald on television and had not been shown any photographs of Oswald by the police.

Another witness, Domingo Benavides, was driving a pickup truck west on 10th Street. As he crossed the intersection a block east of 10th and Patton, he saw a policeman standing by the left door of the police car parked along the south side of 10th. Benavides saw a man standing at the right side of the parked police car. He then heard three shots and saw the policeman fall to the ground. By this time the pickup truck was across the street and about 25 feet from the police car.

Benavides stopped and waited in the truck until the gunman ran to the corner. He saw him empty the gun and throw the shells into some bushes on the southeast corner lot. It was Benavides, using Tippit's car radio, who first reported the killing of Patrolman Tippit at about 1.16 pm: "We've had a shooting out here." He found two empty shells in the bushes and gave them to Patrolman J. M. Poe who arrived on the scene shortly after the shooting. Benavides never saw Oswald after the arrest. When questioned by police officers on the evening of November 22, Benavides told them that he did not think that he could identify the man who fired the shots. As a result, they did not take him to the police station. He testified that the picture of Oswald which he saw later on television bore a resemblance to the man who shot Officer Tippit.

Just prior to the shooting, Mrs Helen Markham, a waitress in downtown Dallas, was about to cross 10th Street at Patton. As she waited on the northwest corner of the intersection for traffic to pass, she noticed a young man as he was "almost ready to get up on the curb" at the southeast corner of the intersection, approximately 50 feet away. The man continued along 10th Street. Mrs Markham saw a police car slowly approach the man from the rear and stop alongside of him. She saw the man come to the right window of the police car. As he talked, he leaned on the ledge of the right window with his arms. The man appeared to step back as the policeman "calmly opened the car door" and very slowly got out and walked toward the front of the car. The man pulled a gun. Mrs Markham heard three shots and saw the policeman fall to the ground near the left front wheel. She raised her hands to her eyes as the man started to walk back toward Patton. She peered through her fingers, lowered her hands, and saw the man doing something with his gun. "He was just fooling with it. I didn't know what he was doing. I was afraid he was fixing to kill me."

The man "in kind of a little trot" headed down Patton toward Jefferson Boulevard, a block away. Mrs Markham then ran to Officer Tippit's side and saw him lying in a pool of blood. Helen Markham was screaming as she leaned over the body. A few minutes later she described the gunman to a policeman. Her description and that of other eyewitnesses led to the police broadcast at 1.22 pm describing the slayer as "about 30, 5'8", black hair, slender." At about 4.30 pm, Mrs Markham, who had been greatly upset by her experience, was able to view a lineup of four men handcuffed together at the police station. She identified Lee Harvey Oswald as the man who shot the policeman. Detective L. C. Graves, who had been with Mrs Markham before the lineup testified that she was "quite hysterical" and was "crying and upset." He said that Mrs Markham started crying when Oswald walked into the lineup room. In testimony before the Commission, Mrs Markham confirmed her positive identification of Lee Harvey Oswald as the man she saw kill Officer Tippit.

In evaluating Mrs Markham's identification of Oswald, the Commission considered certain allegations that Mrs Markham described the man who killed Patrolman Tippit as "short, a little on the heavy side," and having "somewhat bushy" hair. The Commission reviewed the transcript of a phone conversation in which Mrs Markham is alleged to have provided such a description. A review of the complete transcript has satisfied the Commission that Mrs Markham strongly reaffirmed her positive identification of Oswald and denied having described the killer as short, stocky and having bushy hair. She stated that the man weighed about 150 pounds. Although she used the words "a little bit bushy" to describe the gunman's hair, the transcript establishes that she was referring to the uncombed state of his hair, a description fully supported by a photograph of Oswald taken at the time of his arrest. Although in the phone conversation she described the man as "short," on November 22, within minutes of the shooting and before the lineup, Mrs Markham described the man to the police as 5'8" tall.

During her testimony Mrs Markham initially denied that she ever had the above phone conversation. She has subsequently admitted the existence of the conversation and offered an explanation for her denial. Addressing itself solely to the probative value of Mrs Markham's contemporaneous description of the gunman and her positive identification of Oswald at a police lineup, the Commission considers her testimony reliable. However, even in the absence of Mrs Markham's testimony, there is ample evidence to identify Oswald as the killer of Tippit. Two young women, Barbara Jeanette Davis and Virginia Davis, were in an apartment of a multiple-unit house on the southeast corner of 10th and Patton when they heard the sound of gunfire and the screams of Helen Markham. They ran to the door in time to see a man with a revolver cut across their lawn and disappear around a corner of the house onto Patton. Barbara Jeanette Davis assumed that he was emptying his gun as "he had it open and was shaking it." She immediately called the police. Later in the day each woman found an empty shell on the ground near the house. These two shells were delivered to the police.

On the evening of November 22, Barbara Jeanette and Virginia Davis viewed a group of four men in a lineup and each one picked Oswald as the man who crossed their lawn while emptying his pistol. Barbara Jeanette Davis testified that no one had shown her a picture of Oswald before the identification and that she had not seen him on television. She was not sure whether she had seen his picture in a newspaper on the afternoon or evening of November 22 prior to the lineup.

Her reaction when she saw Oswald in the lineup was that "I was pretty sure it was the same man I saw. When they made him turn sideways, I was positive that was the one I seen." Similarly, Virginia Davis had not been shown pictures of anyone prior to the lineup and had not seen either television or the newspapers during the afternoon. She identified Oswald, who was the no. 2 man in the lineup, as the man she saw running with the gun. She testified, "I would say that was him for sure." Barbara Jeanette Davis and Virginia Davis were sitting alongside each other when they made their positive identifications of Oswald. Each woman whispered Oswald's number to the detective. Each testified that she was the first to make the identification.

William Arthur Smith was about a block east of 10th and Patton when he heard shots. He looked west on 10th and saw a man running to the west and a policeman falling to the ground. Smith failed to make himself known to the police on November 22. Several days later he reported what he had seen and was questioned by FBI agents. Smith subsequently told a Commission staff member that he saw Oswald on television the night of the murder and thought that Oswald was the man he had seen running away from the shooting. On television Oswald's hair looked blond, whereas Smith remembered that the man who ran away had hair that was brown or brownish black. Later, the FBI showed Smith a picture of Oswald. In the picture the hair was brown. According to his testimony, Smith told the FBI, "It looked more like him than it did on television." He stated further that from "What I saw of him" the man looked like the man in the picture.

Two other important eyewitnesses to Oswald's flight were Ted Callaway, manager of a used-car lot on the northeast corner of Patton Avenue and Jefferson Boulevard, and Sam Guinyard, a porter at the lot. They heard the sound of shots to the north of their lot. Callaway heard five shots, and Guinyard three. Both ran to the sidewalk on the east side of Patton at a point about a half a block south of 10th. They saw a man coming south on Patton with a revolver held high in his right hand. According to Callaway, the man crossed to the west side of Patton. From across the street Callaway yelled, "Hey, man, what the hell is going on?" He slowed down, halted, said something, and then kept on going to the corner, turned right, and continued west on Jefferson. Guinyard claimed that the man ran down the east side of Patton and passed within 10 feet of him before crossing to the other side. Guinyard and Callaway ran to 10th and Patton and found Tippit lying in the street beside his car. Apparently he had reached for his gun; it lay beneath him outside of the holster. Callaway picked up the gun. He and William Scoggins [a taxi driver in the vicinity] attempted to chase down the gunman in Scoggins' taxicab, but he had disappeared. Early in the evening of November 22, Guinyard and Callaway viewed the same lineup of four men from which Mrs Markham had earlier made her identification of Lee Harvey Oswald. Both men picked Oswald as the man who had run south on Patton with a gun in his hand. Callaway told the Commission: "So they brought four men in. I stepped to the back of the room, so I could kind of see him from the same distance which I had seen him before. And when he came out I knew him." Guinyard said, "I told them that was him right there. I pointed him out right there." Both Callaway and Guinyard testified that they had not been shown any pictures by the police before the lineup.

The Dallas Police Department furnished the Commission with pictures of the men who appeared in the lineups with Oswald, and the Commission has inquired into general lineup procedures used by the Dallas police as well as the specific procedures in the lineups involving Oswald. The Commission is satisfied that the lineups were conducted fairly. As Oswald ran south on Patton Avenue toward Jefferson Boulevard he was moving in the direction of a used-car lot located on the southeast corner of this intersection. Four men, Warren Reynolds, Harold Russell Pat Patterson and L. J. Lewis, were on the lot at the time, and they saw a white male with a revolver in his hands running south on Patton. When the man reached Jefferson, he turned right and headed west. Reynolds and Patterson decided to follow him. When he reached a gasoline service station one block away he turned north and walked toward a parking area in the rear of the station. Neither Reynolds nor Patterson saw the man after he turned off Jefferson at the service station. These four witnesses were interviewed by FBI agents two months after the shooting. Russell and Patterson were shown a picture of Oswald and they stated that Oswald was the man they saw on November 22, 1963. Russell confirmed this statement in a sworn affidavit for the Commission. Patterson, when asked later to confirm his identification by affidavit said he did not recall having been shown the photograph. He was then shown two photographs of Oswald and he advised that Oswald was "unquestionably" the man he saw. Reynolds did not make a positive identification when interviewed by the FBI, but he subsequently testified before a Commission staff member and, when shown two photographs of Oswald, stated that they were photographs of the man he saw. L. J. Lewis said in an interview that because of the distance from which he observed the gunman he would hesitate to state whether the man was identical with Oswald.

Murder weapon

When Oswald was arrested, he had in his possession a Smith & Wesson .38 Special caliber revolver, serial number V510210. Two of the arresting officers placed their initials on the weapon and a third inscribed his name. All three identified the revolver taken from Oswald when he was arrested. Four cartridge cases were found in the shrubbery on the corner of 10th and Patton by three of the eyewitnesses: Domingo Benavides, Barbara Jeanette Davis, and Virginia Davis. It was the unanimous and unequivocal testimony of expert witnesses before the Commission that these used cartridge cases were fired from the revolver in Oswald's possession to the exclusion of all other weapons. Cortlandt Cunningham, of the Firearms Identification Unit of the FBI Laboratory, testified that he compared the four empty cartridge cases found near the scene of the shooting with a test cartridge fired from the weapon in Oswald's possession when he was arrested. Cunningham declared that this weapon fired the four cartridges to the exclusion of all other weapons. Identification was effected through breech face marks and firing pin marks. Robert A. Frazier and Charles Killion, other FBI firearms experts, independently examined the four cartridge cases and arrived at the same conclusion as Cunningham. At the request of the Commission, Joseph D. Nicol, superintendent of the Illinois Bureau of Criminal Identification Investigation, also examined the four cartridge cases found near the site of the homicide and compared them with the test cartridge cases fired from the Smith & Wesson revolver taken from Oswald. He concluded that all of these cartridges were fired from the same weapon.

Cunningham compared four lead bullets recovered from the body of Officer Tippit with test bullets fired from Oswald's revolver. He explained that the bullets were slightly smaller than the barrel of the pistol which had fired them.

This caused the bullets to have an erratic passage through the barrel and impressed upon the lead of the bullets inconsistent individual characteristics which made identification impossible. Consecutive bullets fired from the revolver by the FBI experts could not be identified as having been fired from that revolver. Cunningham testified that all of the bullets were mutilated, one being useless for comparison purposes. All four bullets were fired from a weapon with five lands and grooves and a right twist which were the rifling characteristics of the revolver taken from Oswald.

He concluded, however, that he could not say whether the four bullets were fired from the revolver in Oswald's possession. "The only thing I can testify is they could have on the basis of the rifling characteristics, they could have been." Nicol differed with the FBI experts on one bullet taken from Tippit's body. He declared that this bullet was fired from the same weapon that fired the test bullets to the exclusion of all other weapons. But he agreed that because the other three bullets were mutilated, he could not determine if they had been fired from the same weapon as the test bullets.

The examination and testimony of the experts enabled the Commission to conclude that five shots may have been fired, even though only four bullets were recovered. Three of the bullets recovered from Tippit's body were manufactured by Winchester-Western, and the fourth bullet by Remington-Peters, but only two of the four discarded cartridge cases found on the lawn at 10th Street and Patton Avenue were of Winchester-Western manufacture. Therefore, one cartridge case of this type was not recovered. And though only one bullet of Remington-Peters manufacture was recovered, two empty cartridge cases of that make were retrieved. Therefore, either one bullet of Remington-Peters manufacture is missing or one used Remington-Peters cartridge case, which may have been in the revolver before the shooting, was discarded along with the others as Oswald left the scene. If a bullet is missing, five were fired. This corresponds with the observation and memory of Ted Callaway, and possibly Warren Reynolds, but not with the other eyewitnesses who claim to have heard from two to four shots.

Ownership of revolver

By checking certain importers and dealers after the assassination of President Kennedy and slaying of Officer Tippit, agents of the FBI determined that George Rose & Co. of Los Angeles was a major distributor of this type of revolver.

Records of Seaport Traders, Inc., a mail-order division of George Rose & Co., disclosed that on January 3, 1963, the company received from Empire Wholesale Sporting Goods, Ltd, Montreal, a shipment of 99 guns in one case. Among these guns was a .38 Special caliber Smith & Wesson revolver, serial No. V510210, the only revolver made by Smith & Wesson with this serial number. When first manufactured, it had a 5-inch barrel. George Rose & Co. had the barrel shortened by a gunsmith to $2\frac{1}{4}$ inches.

Sometime after January 27, 1963, Seaport Traders, Inc., received through the mail a mail-order coupon for one ".38 St. W. 2" Bbl.," cost $29.95. Ten dollars in cash was enclosed. The order was signed in ink by "A. J. Hidell, aged 28." The date of the order was January 27 (no year shown), and the return address was Post Office Box 2915, Dallas, Texas. Also on the order form was an order, written in ink, for one box of ammunition and one holster, but a line was drawn through these items. The mail-order form had a line for the name of a witness to attest that the person ordering the gun was a US citizen and had not been convicted of a felony. The name written in this space was D. F. Drittal.

Heinz W. Michaelis, office manager of both George Rose & Co. Inc., and Seaport Traders, Inc., identified records of Seaport Traders, Inc., which showed that a ".38 S and W Special two-inch Commando, serial number V510210" was shipped on March 20, 1963, to A. J. Hidell, Post Office Box 2915, Dallas, Texas. The invoice was prepared on March 13, 1963; the revolver was actually shipped on March 20 by Railway Express. The balance due on the purchase was $19.95.

Michaelis furnished the shipping copy of the invoice, and the Railway Express Agency shipping documents, showing that $19.95, plus $1.27 shipping charge, had been collected from the consignee, Hidell. Handwriting experts, Alwyn Cole of the Treasury Department and James C. Cadigan of the FBI, testified before the Commission that the writing on the coupon was Oswald's. The signature of the witness, D. F. Drittal, who attested that the fictitious Hidell was an American citizen and had not been convicted of a felony, was also in Oswald's handwriting.

Marina Oswald gave as her opinion that the mail-order coupon was in Oswald's handwriting. When shown the revolver, she stated that she recognized it as the one owned by her husband. She also testified that this appeared to be the revolver seen in Oswald's belt in the picture she took in late March or early April 1963 when the family was living on Neely Street in Dallas. Police found an empty revolver holster when they searched Oswald's room on Beckley Avenue after his arrest. Marina Oswald testified that this was the holster which contained the revolver in the photographs taken on Neely Street.

Oswald's jacket

Approximately 15 minutes before the shooting of Tippit, Oswald was seen leaving his rooming house. He was wearing a zipper jacket which he had not been wearing moments before when he had arrived home. When Oswald was arrested, he did not have a jacket. Shortly after Tippit was slain, policemen found a light-colored zipper jacket along the route taken by the killer as he attempted to escape. At 1.22 pm the Dallas police radio described the man wanted for the murder of Tippit as "a white male about thirty, five foot eight inches, black hair, slender, wearing a white jacket, white shirt and dark slacks."

According to Patrolman Poe this description came from Mrs Markham and Mrs Barbara Jeanette Davis. Mrs Markham told Poe that the man was a "white male, about 25, about five feet eight, brown hair, medium" and wearing a "white jacket." Mrs Davis gave Poe the same general description: a "white male in his early twenties, around five foot seven inches or eight inches, about 145 pounds" and wearing a white jacket. As has been discussed previously, two witnesses, Warren Reynolds and B. M. Patterson, saw the gunman run toward the rear of a gasoline service station on Jefferson Boulevard. Mrs Mary Brock, the wife of a mechanic who worked at the station, was there at the time and she saw "a white male, 5 feet, 10 inches ... wearing light clothing ... a light-colored jacket" walk past her at a fast pace with his hands in his pocket. She last saw him in the parking lot directly behind the service station. When interviewed by FBI agents on January 19, 1964, she identified a picture of Oswald as being the same person she saw on November 22. She confirmed this interview by a sworn affidavit.

At 1.24 pm, the police radio reported, "The suspect last seen running west on Jefferson from 400 East Jefferson." Police Captain W. R. Westbrook and several other officers concentrated their search along Jefferson Boulevard. Westbrook walked through the parking lot behind the service station and found a light-colored jacket lying under the rear of one of the cars. This jacket belonged to Lee Harvey Oswald. Marina Oswald stated that her husband owned only two jackets, one blue and the other gray. The blue jacket was found in the Texas School Book Depository and was identified by Marina Oswald as her husband's. Marina Oswald identified the jacket found by Captain Westbrook as her husband's second jacket.

The eyewitnesses vary in their identification of the jacket. Mrs Earlene Roberts, the housekeeper at Oswald's rooming house and the last person known to have seen him before he reached 10th Street and Patton Avenue, said that she may have seen the gray zipper jacket but she was not certain. It seemed to her that the jacket Oswald wore was darker. Ted Callaway, who saw the gunman moments after the shooting, testified that "I thought it had a little more tan to it." Two other witnesses, Sam Guinyard and William Arthur Smith, testified that it was the jacket worn by the man they saw on November 22. Mrs Markham and Barbara Davis thought that the jacket worn by the slayer of Tippit was darker than the jacket found by Westbrook. Scoggins thought it was lighter.

There is no doubt, however, that Oswald was seen leaving his rooming house at about 1 pm wearing a zipper jacket, that the man who killed Tippit was wearing a light-colored jacket, that he was seen running along Jefferson Boulevard, that a jacket was found under a car in a lot adjoining Jefferson Boulevard, that the jacket belonged to Lee Harvey Oswald, and that when he was arrested at approximately 1.50 pm, he was in shirt sleeves. These facts warrant the finding that Lee Harvey Oswald disposed of his jacket as he fled from the scene of the Tippit killing.

Conclusion

The foregoing evidence establishes that:

(1) two eyewitnesses who heard the shots and saw the shooting of Dallas Police Patrolman J. D. Tippit and seven eyewitnesses who saw the flight of the gunman with revolver in hand positively identified Lee Harvey Oswald as the man they saw fire the shots or flee from the scene

(2) the cartridge cases found near the scene of the shooting were fired from the revolver in the possession of Oswald at the time of his arrest, to the exclusion of all other weapons

(3) the revolver in Oswald's possession at the time of his arrest was purchased by and belonged to Oswald

(4) Oswald's jacket was found along the path of flight taken by the gunman as he fled from the scene of the killing. On the basis of this evidence the Commission concluded that Lee Harvey Oswald killed Dallas Police Patrolman J. D. Tippit.

OSWALD'S ARREST

The Texas Theater is on the north side of Jefferson Boulevard, approximately eight blocks from the scene of the Tippit shooting and six blocks from where several witnesses last saw Oswald running west on Jefferson Boulevard. Shortly after the Tippit murder, police sirens sounded along Jefferson Boulevard.

One of the persons who heard the sirens was Johnny Calvin Brewer, manager of Hardy's shoe store, a few doors east of the Texas Theater. Brewer knew from radio broadcasts that the president had been shot and that a patrolman had also been shot in Oak Cliff. When he heard police sirens, he "looked up and saw the man enter the lobby", a recessed area extending about 15 feet between the sidewalk and the front door of his store. A police car made a U-turn, and as the sirens grew fainter, the man in the lobby "looked over his shoulder and turned around and walked up West Jefferson towards the theater." The man wore a T-shirt beneath his outer shirt and he had no jacket. Brewer said, "He just looked funny to me . . . His hair was sort of messed up and looked like he had been running, and he looked scared, and he looked funny."

Mrs Julia Postal, selling tickets at the box office of the Texas Theater, heard police sirens and then saw a man as he "ducked into" the outer lobby space of the theater near the ticket office. Attracted by the sound of the sirens, Mrs Postal stepped out of the box office and walked to the curb. Shortly thereafter, Johnny Brewer, who had come from the nearby shoe store, asked Mrs Postal whether the fellow that had ducked in had bought ticket. She said, "No; by golly, he didn't," and turned around, but the man was nowhere in sight. Brewer told Mrs Postal that he had seen the man ducking into his place of business and that he had followed him to the theater. She sent Brewer into the theater to find the man and check the exits, told him about the assassination, and said "I don't know if this is the man they want ... but he is running from them for some reason." She then called the police.

At 1.45 pm, the police radio stated, "Have information a suspect just went in the Texas Theater on West Jefferson." Patrol cars bearing at least 15 officers converged on the Texas Theater. Patrolman M. N. McDonald, with Patrolmen R. Hawkins, T. A. Hutson, and C. T. Walker, entered the theater from the rear. Other policemen entered the front door and searched the balcony. Detective Paul L. Bentley rushed to the balcony and told the projectionist to turn up the house lights. Brewer met McDonald and the other policemen at the alley exit door, stepped out onto the stage with them and pointed out the man who had come into the theater without paying. The man was Oswald. He was sitting alone in the rear of the main floor of the theater near the right center aisle. About six or seven people were seated on the main floor and an equal number in the balcony.

McDonald first searched two men in the center of the main floor, about 10 rows from the front. He walked out of the row up the right center aisle. When he reached the row where the suspect was sitting, McDonald stopped abruptly and told the man to get on his feet. Oswald rose from his seat, bringing up both hands. As McDonald started to search Oswald's waist for a gun, he heard him say, "Well, it's all over now." Oswald then struck McDonald between the eyes with his left fist; with his right hand he drew a gun from his waist. McDonald struck back with his right hand and grabbed the gun with his left hand. They both fell into the seats. Three other officers, moving toward the scuffle, grabbed Oswald from the front, rear and side. As McDonald fell into the seat with his left hand on the gun, he felt something graze across his hand and heard what sounded like the snap of the hammer. McDonald felt the pistol scratch his cheek as he wrenched it away from Oswald. Detective Bob K. Carroll, who was standing beside McDonald, seized the gun from him.

The other officers who helped subdue Oswald corroborated McDonald in his testimony except that they did not hear Oswald say, "It's all over now." Deputy Sheriff Eddy R. Walthers recalled such a remark but he did not reach the scene of the struggle until Oswald had been knocked to the floor by McDonald and the others. Some of the officers saw Oswald strike McDonald with his fist. Most of them heard a click which they assumed to be a click of the hammer of the revolver. Testimony of a firearms expert before the Commission established that the hammer of the revolver never touched the shell in the chamber. Although the witnesses did not hear the sound of a misfire, they might have heard a snapping noise resulting from the police officer grabbing the cylinder of the revolver and pulling it away from Oswald while he was attempting to pull the trigger. Two patrons of the theater and John Brewer testified regarding the arrest of Oswald, as did the various police officers who participated in the fight. George Jefferson Applin, Jr, confirmed that Oswald fought with four or five officers before he was handcuffed. He added that one officer grabbed the muzzle of a shotgun, drew back, and hit Oswald with the butt end of the gun in the back. No other theater patron or officer has testified that Oswald was hit by a gun. Nor did Oswald ever complain that he was hit with a gun, or injured in the back. Deputy Sheriff Walthers brought a shotgun into the theater but laid it on some seats before helping subdue Oswald. Officer Ray Hawkins said that there was no one near Oswald who had a shotgun and he saw no one strike Oswald in the back with a rifle butt or the butt of a gun.

John Gibson, another patron in the theater, saw an officer grab Oswald, and he claims that he heard the click of a gun misfiring. He saw no shotgun in the possession of any policeman near Oswald. Johnny Brewer testified he saw Oswald pull the revolver and the officers struggle with him to take it away but that once he was subdued, no officer struck him. He further stated that while fists were flying he heard one of the officers say "Kill the president, will you." It is unlikely that any of the police officers referred to Oswald as a suspect in the assassination. While the police radio had noted the similarity in description of the two suspects, the arresting officers were pursuing Oswald for the murder of Tippit. As Oswald, handcuffed, was led from the theater, he was, according to McDonald, "cursing a little bit and hollering police brutality." At 1.51 pm, police car 2 reported by radio that it was on the way to headquarters with the suspect.

Captain Fritz returned to police headquarters from the Texas School Book Depository at 2.15 pm after a brief stop at the sheriff's office. When he entered the homicide and robbery bureau office, he saw two detectives standing there with Sergeant Gerald L. Hill, who had driven from the theater with Oswald. Hill testified that Fritz told the detective to get a search warrant, go to an address on Fifth Street in Irving, and pick up a man named Lee Oswald. When Hill asked why Oswald was wanted, Fritz replied, "Well, he was employed down at the Book Depository and he had not been present for a roll call of the employees." Hill said, "Captain, we will save you a trip ... there he sits."

STATEMENTS OF OSWALD DURING DETENTION

Oswald was questioned intermittently for approximately 12 hours between 2.30 pm on November 22 and 11 am on November 24. Throughout this interrogation he denied that he had anything to do either with the assassination of President Kennedy or the murder of Patrolman Tippit. Captain Fritz of the homicide and robbery bureau did most of the questioning, but he kept no notes and there were no stenographic or tape recordings. Representatives of other law enforcement agencies were also present, including the FBI and the US Secret Service. They occasionally participated in the questioning. A full discussion of Oswald's detention and interrogation is presented on pp. 263–275. During the evening of November 22, the Dallas Police Department performed paraffin tests on Oswald's hands and right cheek in an apparent effort to determine, by means of a scientific test, whether Oswald had recently fired a weapon.

The results were positive for the hands and negative for the right cheek. Expert testimony before the Commission was to the effect that the paraffin test was unreliable in determining whether or not a person has fired a rifle or revolver. The Commission has, therefore, placed no reliance on the paraffin tests administered by the Dallas police.

Oswald provided little information during his questioning. Frequently, however, he was confronted with evidence which he could not explain, and he resorted to statements which are known to be lies. While Oswald's untrue statements during interrogation were not considered items of positive proof by the Commission, they had probative value in deciding the weight to be given to his denials that he assassinated President Kennedy and killed

Patrolman Tippit. Since independent evidence revealed that Oswald repeatedly and blatantly lied to the police, the Commission gave little weight to his denials of guilt.

Denial of rifle ownership

From the outset, Oswald denied owning a rifle. On November 23, Fritz confronted Oswald with the evidence that he had purchased a rifle under the fictitious name of "Hidell". Oswald said that this was not true. Oswald denied that he had a rifle wrapped up in a blanket in the Paine garage. Oswald also denied owning a rifle and said that since leaving the Marine Corps he had fired only a small bore .22 rifle. On the afternoon of November 23, Officers H. M. Moore, R. S. Stovall, and G. F. Rose obtained a search warrant and examined Oswald's effects in the Paine garage. They discovered two photographs, each showing Oswald with a rifle and a pistol. These photographs were shown to Oswald on the evening of November 23 and again on the morning of the 24th. According to Fritz, Oswald sneered, saying that they were fake photographs, that he had been photographed a number of times the day before by the police, that they had superimposed upon the photographs a rifle and a revolver. He told Fritz a number of times that the smaller photograph was either made from the larger, or the larger photograph was made from the smaller and that at the proper time he would show that the pictures were fakes. Fritz told him that the two small photographs were found in the Paine garage. At that point, Oswald refused to answer any further questions. As previously indicated, Marina Oswald testified that she took the two pictures with her husband's Imperial Reflex camera when they lived on Neely Street. Her testimony was fully supported by a photography expert who testified that in his opinion the pictures were not composites.

The revolver

At the first interrogation, Oswald claimed that his only crime was carrying a gun and resisting arrest. When Captain Fritz asked him why he carried the revolver, he answered, "Well, you know about a pistol. I just carried it." He falsely alleged that he bought the revolver in Fort Worth, when in fact he purchased it from a mail-order house in Los Angeles.

The aliases "Hidell" and "O. H. Lee"

The arresting officers found a forged Selective Service card with a picture of Oswald and the name "Alek J. Hidell" in Oswald's billfold. On November 22 and 23, Oswald refused to tell Fritz why this card was in his possession, or to answer any questions concerning the card. On Sunday morning, November 24, Oswald denied that he knew A. J. Hidell. Captain Fritz produced the Selective Service card bearing the name "Alek J. Hidell." Oswald became angry and said, "Now, I've told you all I'm going to tell you about that card in my billfolds, you have the card yourself and you know as much about it as I do." At the last interrogation on November 24 Oswald admitted to Postal Inspector Holmes that he had rented Post Office Box 2915, Dallas, but denied that he had received a package in this box addressed to Hidell. He also denied that he had received the rifle through this box. Holmes reminded Oswald that A. J. Hidell was listed on Post Office Box 30061, New Orleans, as one entitled to receive mail. Oswald replied, "I don't know anything about that." When asked why he lived at his rooming house under the name O. H. Lee, Oswald responded that the landlady simply made a mistake, because he told her that his name was Lee, meaning his first name. An examination of the rooming house register revealed that Oswald actually signed the name O. H. Lee.

The curtain rod story

In concluding that Oswald was carrying a rifle in the paper bag on the morning of November 22, 1963, the Commission found that Oswald lied when he told Frazier that he was returning to Irving to obtain curtain rods. When asked about the curtain rod story, Oswald lied again. He denied that he had ever told Frazier that he wanted a ride to Irving to get curtain rods for an apartment. He explained that a party for the Paine children had been planned for the weekend and he preferred not to be in the Paine house at that time; therefore, he made his weekly visit on Thursday night. Actually, the party for one of the Paine's children was the preceding weekend, when Marina Oswald suggested that Oswald remain in Dallas. When told that Frazier and Mrs Randle had seen him carrying a long heavy package, Oswald replied, "Well, they was mistaken. That must have been some other time he picked me up." In one interview, he told Fritz that the only sack he carried to work that day was a lunch sack which he kept on his lap during the ride from Irving to Dallas. Frazier testified before the Commission that Oswald carried no lunch sack that day.

Actions during and after shooting

During the first interrogation on November 22, Fritz asked Oswald to account for himself at the time the president was shot. Oswald told him that he ate lunch in the first-floor lunchroom and then went to the second floor for a Coke which he brought downstairs. He acknowledged the encounter with the police officer on the second floor. Oswald told Fritz that after lunch he went outside, talked with Foreman Bill Shelley for 5 or 10 minutes and then left for home. He said that he left work because Bill Shelley said that there would be no more work done that day in the building. Shelley denied seeing Oswald after 12 noon or at any time after the shooting. The next day, Oswald added to his story. He stated that at the time the president was shot he was having lunch with "Junior" but he did not give Junior's last name. The only employee at the Depository Building named "Junior" was James Jarman, Jr. Jarman testified that he ate his lunch on the first floor around 5 minutes to 12, and that he neither ate lunch with nor saw Oswald. Jarman did talk to Oswald that morning:

> . . . he asked me what were the people gathering around on the corner for and I told him that the president was sup-posed to pass that morning, and he asked me did I know which way he was coming, and I told him, yes, he probably come down Main and turn on Houston and then back again on Elm. Then he said, "Oh, I see," and that was all.

PRIOR ATTEMPT TO KILL

The attempt on the life of Major General Edwin A. Walker

At approximately 9 pm, on April 10, 1963, in Dallas, Texas, Major General Edwin A. Walker, an active and controversial figure on the American political scene since his resignation from the US Army in 1961, narrowly escaped death when a rifle bullet fired from outside his home passed near his head as he was seated at his desk. There were no eyewit-nesses, although a 14-year-old boy in a neighboring house claimed that immediately after the shooting he saw two men, in separate cars, drive out of a church parking lot adja-cent to Walker's home. A friend of Walker's testified that two nights before the shooting he saw "two men around the house peeking in windows." General Walker gave this information to the police before the shooting, but it did not help solve the crime. Although the bullet was recovered from Walker's house, in the absence of a weapon it was of little investigatory value. General Walker hired two investigators to determine whether a former employee might have been involved in the shooting. Their results were negative. Until December 3, 1963, the Walker shooting remained unsolved.

The Commission evaluated the following evidence in considering whether Lee Harvey Oswald fired the shot which almost killed General Walker:

(1) a note which Oswald left for his wife on the evening of the shooting
(2) photographs found among Oswald's possessions after the assassination of President Kennedy
(3) firearm identification of the bullet found in Walker's home
(4) admissions and other statements made to Marina Oswald by Oswald concerning the shooting.

Note left by Oswald
On December 2, 1963, Mrs Ruth Paine turned over to the police some of the Oswalds' belongings, including a Russian volume entitled *Book of Useful Advice*. In this book was an undated note written in Russian. In translation, the note read as follows:

(1) This is the key to the mailbox which is located in the main post office in the city on Ervay Street. This is the same street where the drugstore, in which you always waited is located. You will find the mailbox in the post office which is located four blocks from the drugstore on that street. I paid for the box last month so don't worry about it.
(2) Send the information as to what has happened to me to the Embassy and include newspaper clippings (should there be anything about me in the newspa-

pers). I believe that the Embassy will come quickly to your assistance on learning everything.

(3) I paid the house rent on the 2d so don't worry about it.

(4) Recently I also paid for water and gas.

(5) The money from work will possibly be coming. The money will be sent to our post office box. Go to the bank and cash the check.

(6) You can either throw out or give my clothing, etc. away. Do not keep these. However, I prefer that you hold on to my personal papers (military, civil, etc.).

(7) Certain of my documents are in the small blue valise.

(8) The address book can be found on my table in the study should need same.

(9) We have friends here. The Red Cross also will help you (Red Cross in English).

(10) I left you as much money as I could, $60 on the second of the month. You and the baby [apparently] can live for another 2 months using $10 per week.

(11) If I am alive and taken prisoner, the city jail is located at the end of the bridge through which we always passed on going to the city (right in the beginning of the city after crossing the bridge).

James C. Cadigan, FBI handwriting expert, testified that this note was written by Lee Harvey Oswald.

Prior to the Walker shooting on April 10, Oswald had been attending typing classes on Monday, Tuesday, and Thursday evenings. He had quit these classes at least a week before the shooting, which occurred on a Wednesday night. According to Marina Oswald's testimony, on the night of the Walker shooting, her husband left their apartment on Neely Street shortly after dinner. She thought he was attending a class or "was on his own business." When he failed to return by 10 or 10.30 pm,

Marina Oswald went to his room and discovered the note. She testified: "When he came back I asked him what had happened. He was very pale. I don't remember the exact time, but it was very late. And he told me not to ask him any questions. He only told me he had shot at General Walker."

Oswald told his wife that he did not know whether he had hit Walker; according to Marina Oswald when he learned on the radio and in the newspapers the next day that he had missed, he said that he "was very sorry that he had not hit him." Marina Oswald's testimony was fully supported by the note itself which appeared to be the work of a man expecting to be killed, or imprisoned, or to disappear. The last paragraph directed her to the jail and the other paragraphs instructed her on the disposal of Oswald's personal effects and the management of her affairs if he should not return. It is clear that the note was written while the Oswalds were living in Dallas before they moved to New Orleans in the spring of 1963. The references to house rent and payments for water and gas indicated that the note was written when they were living in a rented apartment; therefore it could not have been written while Marina Oswald was living with the Paines. Moreover, the reference in paragraph 3 to paying "the house rent on the 2d" would be consistent with the period when the Oswalds were living on Neely Street since the apartment was rented on March 3, 1963. Oswald had paid the first month's rent in advance on March 2, 1963, and the second month's rent was paid on either April 2 or April 3. The main post office "on Ervay Street" refers to the post office where Oswald rented Box 2915 from October 9, 1962, to May 14, 1963. Another statement which limits the time when it could have been written is the reference "you and the baby," which would indicate that it was probably written before the birth of Oswald's second child on October 20, 1963.

Oswald had apparently mistaken the county jail for the city jail. From Neely Street the Oswalds would have traveled downtown on the Beckley bus, across the Commerce Street viaduct and into downtown Dallas through the Triple Underpass. Either the viaduct or the underpass might have been the "bridge" mentioned in the last paragraph of the note. The county jail is at the corner of Houston and Main streets "right in the beginning of the city" after one travels through the underpass.

Photographs

In her testimony before the Commission in February 1964, Marina Oswald stated that when Oswald returned home on the night of the Walker shooting, he told her that he had been planning the attempt for two months. He showed her a notebook three days later containing photographs of General Walker's home and a map of the area where the house was located. Although Oswald destroyed the notebook, three photographs found among Oswald's possessions after the assassination were identified by Marina Oswald as photographs of General Walker's house. Two of these photographs were taken from the rear of Walker's house. The Commission confirmed, by comparison with other photographs, that these were, indeed, photographs of the rear of Walker's house. An examination of the window at the rear of the house, the wall through which the bullet passed, and the fence behind the house indicated that the bullet was fired from a position near the point where one of the photographs was taken.

The third photograph identified by Marina Oswald depicts the entrance to General Walker's driveway from a back alley. Also seen in the picture is the fence on which Walker's assailant apparently rested the rifle. An examination of certain construction work appearing in the background of this photograph revealed that the picture was taken between March 8 and 12, 1963, and most probably on either March 9 or March 10. Oswald purchased the money order for the rifle on March 12, the rifle was shipped on March 20, and the shooting occurred on April 10. A photography expert with the FBI was able to determine that this picture was taken with the Imperial Reflex camera owned by Lee Harvey Oswald. A fourth photograph, showing a stretch of railroad tracks, was also identified by Marina Oswald as having been taken by her husband, presumably in connection with the Walker shooting. Investigation determined that this photograph was taken approximately seven-tenths of a mile from Walker's house. Another photograph of railroad tracks found among Oswald's possessions was not identified by his wife, but investigation revealed that it was taken from a point slightly less than half a mile from General Walker's house. Marina Oswald stated that when she asked her husband what he had done with the rifle, he replied that he had buried it in the ground or hidden it in some bushes and that he also mentioned a railroad track in this connection. She testified that several days later Oswald recovered his rifle and brought it back to their apartment.

Firearms identification
In the room beyond the one in which General Walker was sitting on the night of the shooting, the Dallas police recovered a badly mutilated bullet which had come to rest on a stack of paper. The Dallas City County Investigation Laboratory tried to determine the type of weapon which fired the bullet. The oral report was negative because of the battered condition of the bullet. On November 30, 1963, the FBI requested the bullet for ballistics examination; the Dallas Police Department forwarded it on December 2, 1963.

Robert A. Frazier, an FBI ballistics identification expert, testified that he was "unable to reach a conclusion" as to whether or not the bullet recovered from Walker's house had been fired from the rifle found on the sixth floor of the Texas School Book Depository Building. He concluded that "the general rifling characteristics of the rifle ... are of the same type as those found on the bullet ... and, further, on this basis ... the bullet could have been fired from the rifle on the basis of its land and groove impressions." Frazier testified further that the FBI avoids the category of "probable" identification. Unless the missile or cartridge case can be identified as coming from a particular weapon to the exclusion of all others, the FBI refuses to draw any conclusion as to probability. Frazier testified, however, that he found no microscopic characteristics or other evidence which would indicate that the bullet was not fired from the Mannlicher-Carcano rifle owned by Lee Harvey Oswald. It was a 6.5-millimeter bullet and, according to Frazier, "relatively few" types of rifles could produce the characteristics found on the bullet.

Joseph D. Nicol, superintendent of the Illinois Bureau of Criminal Identification and Investigation, conducted an independent examination of this bullet and concluded "that there is a fair probability" that the bullet was fired from the rifle used in the assassination of President Kennedy. In explaining the difference between his policy and that of the FBI on the matter of probable identification, Nicol said:

> I am aware of their position. This is not, I am sure, arrived at without careful consideration. However, to say that because one does not find sufficient marks for identification that it is a negative, I think is going overboard in the other direction. And for purposes of probative value, for whatever it might be worth, in the absence of very definite negative

evidence, I think it is permissible to say that in an exhibit such as there is enough on it to say that it could have come, and even perhaps a little stronger, to say that it probably came from this, without going so far as to say to the exclusion of all other guns. This I could not do.

Although the Commission recognizes that neither expert was able to state that the bullet which missed General Walker was fired from Oswald's rifle to the exclusion of all others, this testimony was considered probative when combined with the other testimony linking Oswald to the shooting.

Additional corroborative evidence

The admissions made to Marina Oswald by her husband are an important element in the evidence that Lee Harvey Oswald fired the shot at General Walker. As shown above, the note and the photographs of Walker's house and of the nearby railroad tracks provide important corroboration for her account of the incident. Other details described by Marina Oswald coincide with facts developed independently of her statements. She testified that her husband had postponed his attempt to kill Walker until that Wednesday because he had heard that there was to be a gathering at the church next door to Walker's house on that evening. He indicated that he wanted more people in the vicinity at the time of the attempt so that his arrival and departure would not attract great attention. An official of this church told FBI agents that services are held every Wednesday at the church except during the month of August.

Marina Oswald also testified that her husband had used a bus to return home. A study of the bus routes indicates that Oswald could have taken any one of several different buses to Walker's house or to a point near the railroad tracks where he may have concealed the rifle. It would have been possible for him to take different routes in approaching and leaving the scene of the shooting.

Conclusion
Based on:

(1) the contents of the note which Oswald left for his wife on April 10, 1963
(2) the photographs found among Oswald's possessions
(3) the testimony of firearms identification experts
(4) the testimony of Marina Oswald,

the Commission has concluded that Lee Harvey Oswald attempted to take the life of Major General Edwin A. Walker (Resigned, US Army) on April 10, 1963. The finding that Lee Harvey Oswald attempted to murder a public figure in April 1963 was considered of probative value in this investigation, although the Commission's conclusion concerning the identity of the assassin was based on evidence independent of the finding that Oswald attempted to kill General Walker.

Richard M. Nixon incident

Another alleged threat by Oswald against a public figure involved former Vice President Richard M. Nixon. In January 1964, Marina Oswald and her business manager, James Martin, told Robert Oswald, Lee Harvey Oswald's brother, that Oswald had once threatened to shoot former Vice President Richard M. Nixon. When Marina Oswald testified before the Commission on February 3–6, 1964, she had failed to mention the incident when she was asked whether Oswald had ever expressed any hostility toward any official of the United States. The Commission first learned of this incident when Robert Oswald related it to FBI agents on February 19, 1964, and to the Commission on February 21.

Marina Oswald appeared before the Commission again on June 11, 1964, and testified that a few days before her husband's departure from Dallas to New Orleans on April 24, 1963, he finished reading a morning newspaper "... and put on a good suit. I saw that he took a pistol. I asked him where he was going, and why he was getting dressed. He answered 'Nixon is coming. I want to go and have a look.'" He also said that he would use the pistol if the opportunity arose. She reminded him that after the Walker shooting he had promised never to repeat such an act. Marina Oswald related the events which followed:

> I called him into the bathroom and I closed the door and I wanted to prevent him and then I started to cry. And I told him that he shouldn't do this, and that he had promised me. ... I remember that I held him. We actually struggled for several minutes and then he quieted down.

She stated that it was not physical force which kept him from leaving the house. "I couldn't keep him from going out if he really wanted to." After further questioning she stated that she might have been confused about shutting him in the bathroom, but that "there is no doubt that he got dressed and got a gun." Oswald's revolver was shipped from Los Angeles on March 20, 1963, and he left for New Orleans on April 24, 1963. No edition of either Dallas newspaper during the period January 1, 1963, to May 15, 1963, mentioned any proposed visit by Mr Nixon to Dallas. Mr Nixon advised the Commission that the only time he was in Dallas in 1963 was on November 20–21, 1963. An investigation failed to reveal any invitation extended to Mr Nixon during the period when Oswald's threat reportedly occurred. The Commission has concluded, therefore, that regardless of what Oswald may have said to his wife he was not actually planning to shoot Mr Nixon at that time in Dallas.

On April 23, 1963, Vice President Lyndon B. Johnson was in Dallas for a visit which had been publicized in the Dallas newspapers throughout April. The Commission asked Marina Oswald whether she might have misunderstood the object of her husband's threat. She stated, "There is no question that in this incident it was a question of Mr Nixon." When asked later whether it might have been Mr Johnson, she said, "Yes, no. I am getting a little confused with so many questions. I was absolutely convinced it was Nixon and now after all these questions I wonder if I am right in my mind." She stated further that Oswald had only mentioned Nixon's name once during the incident. Marina Oswald might have misunderstood her husband. Mr Johnson was the then vice president and his visit took place on April 23. This was one day before Oswald left for New Orleans and Marina appeared certain that the Nixon incident "wasn't the day before. Perhaps three days before." Marina Oswald speculated that the incident may have been unrelated to an actual threat. She said:

> ... It might have been that he was just trying to test me. He was the kind of person who could try and wound somebody in that way. Possibly he didn't want to go out at all but was just doing this all as a sort of joke, not really as a joke but rather to simply wound me, to make me feel bad.

In the absence of other evidence that Oswald actually intended to shoot someone at this time, the Commission concluded that the incident, as described by Marina Oswald, was of no probative value in the Commission's decision concerning the identity of the assassin of President Kennedy.

OSWALD'S RIFLE CAPABILITY

In deciding whether Lee Harvey Oswald fired the shots which killed President Kennedy and wounded Governor Connally, the Commission considered whether Oswald, using his own rifle, possessed the capability to hit his target with two out of three shots under the conditions described on pp. 142–159. The Commission evaluated:

(1) the nature of the shots
(2) Oswald's Marine training in marksmanship
(3) his experience and practice after leaving the Marine Corps
(4) the accuracy of the weapon and the quality of the ammunition.

The nature of the shots

For a rifleman situated on the sixth floor of the Texas School Book Depository Building the shots were at a slow-moving target proceeding on a downgrade in virtually a straight line with the alignment of the assassin's rifle, at a range of 177 to 266 feet. An aerial photograph of Dealey Plaza shows that Elm Street runs at an angle so that the president would have been moving in an almost straight line away from the assassin's rifle. In addition, the three downward slope of Elm Street was of assistance in eliminating at least some of the adjustment which is ordinarily required when a marksman must raise his rifle as a target moves farther away.

Four marksmanship experts testified before the Commission. Major Eugene D. Anderson, assistant head of the Marksmanship Branch of the US Marine Corps, testified that the shots which struck the president in the neck and in the head were "not ... particularly difficult". Robert A. Frazier, FBI expert in firearms identification and training, said:

> From my own experience in shooting over the years, when you shoot at 175 feet or 260 feet, which is less than 100 yards, with a telescopic sight, you should not have any difficulty in hitting your target. I mean it requires no training at all to shoot a weapon with a telescopic sight once you

know that you must put the crosshairs on the target and that is all that is necessary.

Ronald Simmons, chief of the US Army Infantry Weapons Evaluation Branch of the Ballistics Research Laboratory, said: "Well, in order to achieve three hits, it would not be required that a man be an exceptional shot. A proficient man with this weapon, yes." The effect of a four-power telescopic sight on the difficulty of these shots was considered in detail by Major Sergeant James A. Zahm, non-commissioned officer in charge of the Marksmanship Training Unit in the Weapons Training Battalion of the Marine Corps School at Quantico, Virginia. Referring to a rifle with a four-power telescope, Sergeant Zahm said:

> ... this is the ideal type of weapon for moving targets...
> Using the scope, rapidly working a bolt and using the
> scope to relocate your target quickly and at the same time
> when you locate that target you identify it and the
> crosshairs are in close relationship to the point you want to
> shoot at, it just takes a minor move in aiming to bring the
> crosshairs to bear, and then it is a quick squeeze.
>
> I consider it a real advantage, particularly at the range of
> 100 yards, in identifying your target. It allows you to see
> your target clearly, and it is still of a minimum amount of
> power that it doesn't exaggerate your own body move-
> ments. It just is an aid in seeing in the fact that you only
> have the one element, the crosshair, in relation to the target
> as opposed to iron sights with aligning the sights and then
> aligning them on the target.

Characterizing the four-power scope as "a real aid, an extreme aid" in rapid fire shooting, Sergeant Zahm expressed the opinion that the shot which struck President Kennedy in the neck at 176.9 to 190.8 feet was "very easy" and the shot which struck the president in the head at a distance of 265.3 feet was "an easy shot". After viewing photographs depicting the alignment of Elm Street in relation to the Texas School Book Depository Building, Zahm stated further:

> This is a definite advantage to the shooter, the vehicle moving directly away from him and the downgrade of the street, and he being in an elevated position made an almost stationary target while he was aiming in, very little movement if any.

Oswald's Marine training

In accordance with standard Marine procedures, Oswald received extensive training in marksmanship. During the first week of an intensive eight-week training period he received instruction in sighting, aiming, and manipulation of the trigger. He went through a series of exercises called "dry firing" where he assumed all positions which would later be used in the qualification course. After familiarization with live ammunition in the .22 rifle and .22 pistol, Oswald, like all Marine recruits, received training on the rifle range at distances up to 500 yards, firing 50 rounds each day for five days.

Following that training, Oswald was tested in December of 1956, and obtained a score of 212, which was two points above the minimum for qualifications as a "sharpshooter" in a scale of marksman/sharpshooter/expert. In May of 1959, on another range, Oswald scored 191, which was one point over the minimum for ranking as a "marksman". The Marine Corps records maintained on Oswald further show that he had fired and was familiar with the Browning Automatic rifle, .45 caliber pistol, and 12-gage riot gun.

Based on the general Marine Corps ratings, Lieutenant Colonel A. G. Folsom, Jr, head, Records Branch, Personnel

Department, Headquarters US Marine Corps, evaluated the sharpshooter qualification as a "fairly good shot" and a low marksman rating as a "rather poor shot". When asked to explain the different scores achieved by Oswald on the two occasions when he fired for record, Major Anderson said:

> ... when he fired that [212] he had just completed a very intensive preliminary training period. He had the services of an experienced highly trained coach. He had high motivation. He had presumably a good to excellent rifle and good ammunition. We have nothing here to show under what conditions the B course was fired. It might well have been a bad day for firing the rifle – windy, rainy, dark. There is little probability that he had a good, expert coach, and he probably didn't have as high a motivation because he was no longer in recruit training and under the care of the drill instructor. There is some possibility that the rifle he was firing might not have been as good a rifle as the rifle that he was firing in his A course firing, because [he] may well have carried this rifle for quite some time, and it got banged around in normal usage.

Major Anderson concluded:

> I would say that as compared to other Marines receiving the same type of training, that Oswald was a good shot, somewhat better than or equal to better than the average, let us say. As compared to a civilian who had not received this intensive training, he would be considered as a good to excellent shot.

When Sergeant Zahm was asked whether Oswald's Marine Corps training would have made it easier to operate a rifle with a four-power scope, he replied:

> Based on that training, his basic knowledge in sight manipulation and trigger squeeze and what not, I would say that

he would be capable of sighting that rifle in well, firing it, with 10 rounds.

After reviewing Oswald's marksmanship scores, Sergeant Zahm concluded:

> I would say in the Marine Corps he is a good shot, slightly above average, and as compared to the average male of his age throughout the civilian, throughout the United States, that he is an excellent shot.

Oswald's rifle practice outside the Marines

During one of his leaves from the Marines, Oswald hunted with his brother Robert, using a .22 caliber bolt-action rifle belonging either to Robert or Robert's in-laws. After he left the Marines and before departing for Russia, Oswald, his brother, and a third companion went hunting for squirrels and rabbits. On that occasion Oswald again used a bolt-action .22 caliber rifle; and according to Robert, Lee Oswald exhibited an average amount of proficiency with that weapon. While in Russia, Oswald obtained a hunting license, joined a hunting club and went hunting about six times. Soon after Oswald returned from the Soviet Union he again went hunting with his brother, Robert, and used a borrowed .22 caliber bolt-action rifle. After Oswald purchased the Mannlicher-Carcano rifle, he told his wife that he practiced with it. Marina Oswald testified that on one occasion she saw him take the rifle, concealed in a raincoat, from the house on Neely Street. Oswald told her he was going to practice with it. According to George De Mohrenschildt [an acquaintance of The Oswalds in Texas], Oswald said that he went target shooting with that rifle.

Marina Oswald testified that in New Orleans in May of 1963, she observed Oswald sitting with the rifle on their screened porch at night, sighting with the telescopic lens and operating the bolt. Examination of the cartridge cases found on the sixth floor of the Depository Building established that they had been previously loaded and ejected from the assassination rifle, which would indicate that Oswald practiced operating the bolt.

Accuracy of weapon

It will be recalled from the discussion on pp. 142–159 that the assassin in all probability hit two out of the three shots during the maximum time span of 4.8 to 5.6 seconds if the second shot missed, or, if either the first or third shots missed, the assassin fired the three shots during a minimum time span of 7.1 to 7.9 seconds. A series of tests were performed to determine whether the weapon and ammunition used in the assassination were capable of firing the shots which were fired by the assassin on November 22, 1963. The ammunition used by the assassin was manufactured by Western Cartridge Co of East Alton, IIlinois. In tests with the Mannlicher-Carcano C2766 rifle, over 100 rounds of this ammunition were fired by the FBI and the Infantry Weapons Evaluation Branch of the US Army. There were no misfires.

In an effort to test the rifle under conditions which simulated those which prevailed during the assassination, the Infantry Weapons Evaluation Branch of the Ballistics Research Laboratory had expert riflemen fire the assassination weapon from a tower at three silhouette targets at distances of 175, 240, and 265 feet. The target at 265 feet was placed to the right of the 240-foot target which was in turn placed to the right of the closest silhouette. Using the assassination rifle mounted with the telescopic sight, three marksmen, rated as master by the National Rifle Association, each fired two series of three shots. In the first series the firers required time spans of 4.6, 6.75, and 8.25 seconds respectively. On the second series they required 5.15, 6.45, and 7 seconds. None of the marksmen had any practice with the assassination weapon except for exercising the bolt for 2 or 3 minutes on a dry run. They had not even pulled the trigger because of concern about breaking the firing pin.

The marksmen took as much time as they wanted for the first target and all hit the target. For the first four attempts, the firers missed the second shot by several inches. The angle from the first to the second shot was greater than from the second to the third shot and required a movement in the basic firing position of the marksmen. This angle was used in the test because the majority of the eyewitnesses to the assassination stated that there was a shorter interval between shots two and three than between shots one and two. As has been shown earlier, if the three shots were fired within a period of from 4.8 to 5.6 seconds, the shots would have been evenly spaced and the assassin would not have incurred so sharp an angular movement.

Five of the six shots hit the third target where the angle of movement of the weapon was small. On the basis of these results, Simmons testified that in his opinion the probability of hitting the targets at the relatively short range at which they were hit was very high. Considering the various probabilities which may have prevailed during the actual assassination, the highest level of firing performance which would have been required of the assassin and the C2766 rifle would have been to fire three times and hit the target twice within a span of 4.8 to 5.6 seconds. In fact, one of the firers in the rapid fire test in firing his two series of three shots, hit the target twice within a span of 4.6 and 5.15 seconds. The others would have been able to reduce their times if they had been given the opportunity to become familiar with the movement of the bolt and the trigger pull. Simmons testified that familiarity with the bolt could be achieved in dry practice and, as has been indicated above, Oswald engaged in such practice. If the assassin missed either the first or third shot, he had a total of between 4.8 and 5.6 seconds between the two shots which hit and a total minimum time period of from 7.1 to 7.9 seconds for all three shots. All three of the firers in these tests were able to fire the rounds within the time period which would have been available to the assassin under those conditions.

Three FBI firearms experts tested the rifle in order to determine the speed with which it could be fired. The purpose of this experiment was not to test the rifle under conditions which prevailed at the time of the assassination but to determine the maximum speed at which it could be fired. The three FBI experts each fired three shots from the weapon at 15 yards in 6, 7, and 9 seconds, and one of these agents, Robert A. Frazier, fired two series of three shots at 25 yards in 4.6 and 4 seconds. At 15 yards each man's shots landed within the size of a dime. The shots fired by Frazier at the range of 25 yards landed within an area of 2 inches and 5 inches respectively. Frazier later fired four groups of three shots at a distance of 100 yards in 5.9, 6.2, 5.6, and 6.5 seconds. Each series of three shots landed within areas ranging in diameter from 3 to 5 inches. Although all of the shots were a few inches high and to the right of the target, this was because of a defect in the scope which was recognized by the FBI agents and which they could have compensated for if they were aiming to hit a bull's-eye. They were instead firing to determine how rapidly the weapon could be fired and the area within which three shots could be placed.

Frazier testified that while he could not tell when the defect occurred, a person familiar with the weapon could compensate for it. Moreover, the defect was one which would have assisted the assassin aiming at a target which was moving away. Frazier said, "The fact that the crosshairs are set high would actually compensate for any lead which had to be taken. So that if you aimed with this weapon as it actually was received at the laboratory, it would not be necessary to take any lead whatsoever in order to hit the intended object. The scope would accomplish the lead for you." Frazier added that the scope would cause a slight miss to the right. It should be noted, however, that the president's car was curving slightly to the right when the third shot was fired. Based on these tests the experts agreed that the assassination rifle was an accurate weapon. Simmons described it as "quite accurate", in fact, as accurate as current military rifles. Frazier testified that the rifle was accurate, that it had less recoil than the average military rifle and that one would not have to be an expert marksman to have accomplished the assassination with the weapon which was used.

Conclusion

The various tests showed that the Mannlicher-Carcano was an accurate rifle and that the use of a four-power scope was a substantial aid to rapid, accurate firing. Oswald's Marine training in marksmanship, his other rifle experience and his established familiarity with this particular weapon show that he possessed ample capability to commit the assassination. Based on the known facts of the assassination, the Marine marksmanship experts, Major Anderson and Sergeant Zahm, concurred in the opinion that Oswald had the capability to fire three shots, with two hits, within 4.8 and 5.6 seconds. Concerning the shots which struck the president in the back of the neck, Sergeant Zahm testified: "With the equipment he [Oswald] had and with his ability I consider it a very easy shot." Having fired this slot the assassin was then required to hit the target one more time within a space of from 4.8 to 5.6 seconds. On the basis of Oswald's training and the accuracy of the weapon as established by the tests, the Commission concluded that Oswald was capable of accomplishing this second hit even if there was an intervening shot which missed. The probability of hitting the president a second time would have been markedly increased if, in fact, he had missed either the first or third shots thereby leaving a time span of 4.8 to 5.6 seconds between the two shots which struck their mark. The Commission agrees with the testimony of Marine marksmanship expert Zahm that it was "an easy shot" to hit some part of the president's body, and that the range where the rifleman would be expected to hit would include the president's head.

CONCLUSION ON THE IDENTITY OF ASSASSIN

On the basis of the evidence reviewed in this chapter, the Commission has found that Lee Harvey Oswald:

(1) owned and possessed the rifle used to kill President Kennedy and wound Governor Connally

(2) brought this rifle into the Depository Building on the morning of the assassination

(3) was present, at the time of the assassination, at the window from which the shots were fired

(4) killed Dallas Police Officer J. D. Tippit in an apparent attempt to escape

(5) resisted arrest by drawing a fully loaded pistol and attempting to shoot another police officer

(6) lied to the police after his arrest concerning important substantive matters

(7) attempted, in April 1963, to kill Major General Edwin A. Walker

(8) possessed the capability with a rifle which would have enabled him to commit the assassination.

On the basis of these findings the Commission has concluded that Lee Harvey Oswald was the assassin of President Kennedy.

DETENTION AND DEATH OF OSWALD

Lee Harvey Oswald spent almost all of the last 48 hours of his life in the Police and Courts Building, a gray stone structure in downtown Dallas that housed the headquarters of the Dallas Police Department and the city jail.

Following his arrest early Friday afternoon, Oswald was brought immediately to this building and remained there until Sunday morning, November 24, when he was scheduled to be transferred to the county jail. At 11.21 that morning, in full view of millions of people watching on television, Oswald was fatally wounded by Jack Ruby, who emerged suddenly from the crowd of newsmen and policemen witnessing the transfer and fired a single shot at Oswald. Whether the killing of Oswald was part of a conspiracy involving the assassination of President Kennedy is considered in the next chapter. Aside from that question, the occurrences within the Police and Courts Building between November 22 and 24 raise other important issues concerning the conduct of law enforcement officials, the responsibilities of the press, the rights of accused persons, and the administration of criminal justice in the United States. The Commission has therefore deemed it necessary to determine the facts concerning Oswald's detention and death and to evaluate the actions and responsibilities of the police and press involved in these events.

TREATMENT OF OSWALD IN CUSTODY

The focal center of the Police and Courts Building during Oswald's detention was the third floor, which housed the main offices of the Dallas Police Department. The public elevators on this floor opened into a lobby midpoint of a corridor that extended along the length of the floor for about 140 feet. At one end of this 7-foot-wide corridor were the offices occupied by Chief of Police Jesse E. Curry and his immediate subordinates; at the other end was a small pressroom that could accommodate only a handful of reporters. Along this corridor were other police offices, including those of the major detective bureaus. Between the pressroom and the lobby was the complex of offices belonging to the homicide and robbery bureau, headed by Captain J. Will Fritz.

Chronology

The policemen who seized Oswald at the Texas Theater arrived with him at the police department building at about 2 pm and brought him immediately to the third floor offices of the homicide and robbery bureau to await the arrival of Captain Fritz from the Texas School Book

Depository. After about 15 or 20 minutes Oswald was ush-
ered into the office of Captain Fritz for the first of several
interrogation sessions. At 4.05 pm he was taken to the basement assembly room for his first lineup. While waiting
outside the lineup room, Oswald was searched, and five cartridges and other items were removed from his pockets.
After the lineup, at about 4.20, Oswald was returned to
Captain Fritz office for further questioning. Two hours
later, at 6.20 pm, Oswald was taken downstairs for a second
lineup and returned to Captain Fritz' office within 15 minutes for additional interrogation. Shortly after 7 pm,
Captain Fritz signed a complaint charging Oswald with the
murder of Patrolman Tippit. Oswald was formally
arraigned, i.e. advised of the charges, at 7.10 pm, before
Justice of the Peace David L. Johnston, who came to the
Captain's office for the occasion.

After a third lineup at about 7.40 pm, Oswald was
returned to Fritz' office. About an hour later, after further
questioning, Oswald's fingerprints and palmprints were
taken and a paraffin test administered in Fritz' office, after
which the questioning resumed. At 11.26 pm Fritz signed
the complaint charging Oswald with the murder of
President Kennedy. Shortly after midnight, detectives
took Oswald to the basement assembly room for an
appearance of several minutes before members of the
press. At about 12.20 am Oswald was delivered to the
jailer who placed him in a maximum security cell on the
fifth floor. His cell was the center one in a block of three
cells that were separated from the remainder of the jail
area. The cells on either side of Oswald were empty and
a guard was nearby whenever Oswald was present.
Shortly after 1.30 am Oswald was brought to the identification bureau on the fourth floor and arraigned before
Justice of the Peace Johnston, this time for the murder
President Kennedy.

Questioning resumed in Fritz' office on Saturday morning at about 10.25 am, and the session lasted nearly an hour and 10 minutes. Oswald was then returned to his cell for an hour, and at 12.35 pm he was brought back to Fritz' office for an additional half-hour of questioning. From 1.10 to 1.30 pm, Oswald's wife and mother visited him in the fourth floor visiting area; at 1.40 pm he attempted to call an attorney in New York. He appeared in another lineup at 2.15 pm. At 2.45 pm, with Oswald's consent, a member of the identification bureau obtained fingernail scrapings and specimens of hair from him. He returned to the fourth floor at 3.30 pm for a 10-minute visit with his brother, Robert.

Between 4 and 4.30 pm, Oswald made two telephone calls to Mrs Ruth Paine at her home in Irving; at about 5.30 pm he was visited by the president of the Dallas Bar Association with whom he spoke for about five minutes. From 6 to 7.15 pm Oswald was interrogated once again in Captain Fritz' office and then returned to his cell. At 8 pm he called the Paine residence again and asked to speak to his wife, but Mrs Paine told him that his wife was no longer there.

Oswald was signed out of jail at 9.30 am on Sunday, November 24, and taken to Captain Fritz' office for a final round of questioning. The transfer party left Fritz' office at about 11.15 am; at 11.21 am Oswald was shot. He was declared dead at Parkland Hospital at 1.07 pm.

Interrogation sessions

During the period between 2.30 pm on Friday afternoon and 11.15 am Sunday morning, Oswald was interrogated for a total of approximately 12 hours. Though subject to intermittent questioning for more than 7 hours on Friday, Oswald was given 8 to 9 hours to rest that night. On Saturday he was questioned for a total of only 3 hours during three interrogation sessions, and on Sunday he was questioned for less than 2 hours. (These interrogations are discussed on pp. 237–241.)

Captain Fritz' office, within which the interrogations took place, was a small room, 14 feet by $9\frac{1}{2}$ feet in size. In addition to the policemen guarding the prisoner, those present usually included Dallas detectives, investigators from the FBI and the Secret Service, and occasionally other officials, particularly a post office inspector and the US marshal. As many as seven or eight people crowded into the small office. In all, more than 25 different persons participated in or were present at some time during interrogations. Captain Fritz, who conducted most of the interrogations, was frequently called from the room. He said, "I don't believe there was any time when I went through a very long period without having to step to the door, or step outside, to get a report from some pair of officers, or to give them additional assignments." In his absence, others present would occasionally question Oswald.

The interrogators differ on whether the confusion prevailing in the main third floor corridor penetrated Fritz' office and affected the atmosphere within. Oswald's processions through the third floor corridor, described more fully below, tended, in Fritz' opinion, to keep Oswald upset, and the remarks and questions of newsmen sometimes caused him to become annoyed. Despite the confusion that frequently prevailed, Oswald remained calm most of the time during the interrogations. According to Captain Fritz:

> You know I didn't have trouble with him. If we would just talk to him quietly like we are talking right now, we talked all right until I asked him a question that meant something, every time I asked him a question that meant something, that would produce evidence, he immediately told me he wouldn't tell me about it and he seemed to anticipate what I was going to ask.

Special Agent James W. Bookhout, who represented the FBI at most of the interrogations, stated, "I think generally you might say anytime that you asked a question that would be pertinent to the investigation, that would be the type of question he would refuse to discuss." The number of people in the interrogation room and the tumultuous atmosphere throughout the third floor made it difficult for the interrogators to gain Oswald's confidence and to encourage him to be truthful. As Chief Curry has recognized in his testimony, "we were violating every principle of interrogation ... it was just against all principles of good interrogation practice."

Oswald's legal rights

All available evidence indicates that Oswald was not subjected to any physical hardship during the interrogation sessions or at any other time while he was in custody. He was fed and allowed to rest. When he protested on Friday against being handcuffed from behind, the cuffs were removed and he was handcuffed in front. Although he made remarks to newsmen about desiring a shower and demanding his "civil rights", Oswald did not complain about his treatment to any of the numerous police officers and other persons who had much to do with him during the two days of his detention. As described on pp. 234–236, Oswald received a slight cut over his right eye and a bruise under his left eye during the scuffle in the Texas Theater with the arresting officers, three of whom were injured and required medical treatment. These marks were visible to all who saw him during the two days of his detention and to millions of television viewers.

Before the first questioning session on Friday afternoon, Fritz warned Oswald that he was not compelled to make any statement and that statements he did make could be used against him. About 5 hours later, he was arraigned for the Tippit murder and within an additional $6\frac{1}{2}$ hours he was arraigned for the murder of President Kennedy. On each occasion the justice of the peace advised Oswald of his right to obtain counsel and the right to remain silent.

Throughout the period of detention, however, Oswald was not represented by counsel. At the Friday midnight press conference in the basement assembly room, he made the following remarks:

A: Well, I was questioned by Judge [Johnston]. However, I protested at that time that I was not allowed legal representation during that very short and sweet hearing. I really don't know what the situation is about. Nobody has told me anything except that I am accused of, of murdering a policeman. I know nothing more than that and I do request someone to come forward to give me legal assistance.

Q: Did you kill the president?

A: No. I have not been charged with that. In fact nobody has said that to me yet. The first thing I heard about it was when the newspaper reporters in the hall asked me that question.

Q: Mr Oswald, how did you hurt your eye?

A: A policeman hit me.

At this time Oswald had been arraigned only for the murder of Patrolman Tippit, but questioning by Captain Fritz and others had been substantially concerned with Oswald's connection with the assassination.

On Friday evening, representatives of the American Civil Liberties Union visited the police department to determine whether Oswald was being deprived of counsel. They were assured by police officials and Justice of the Peace Johnston that Oswald had been informed of his rights and was being allowed to seek a lawyer. On Saturday

Oswald attempted several times to reach John Abt, a New York lawyer, by telephone, but with no success. In the afternoon, he called Ruth Paine and asked her to try to reach Abt for him, but she too failed. Later in the afternoon, H. Louis Nichols, president of the Dallas Bar Association, visited Oswald in his cell and asked him whether he wanted the association to obtain a lawyer for him. Oswald declined the offer, stating a first preference for Abt and a second preference for a lawyer from the American Civil Liberties Union. As late as Sunday morning, according to Postal Inspector Harry D. Holmes, Oswald said that he preferred to get his own lawyer.

ACTIVITY OF NEWSMEN

Within an hour of Oswald's arrival at the police department on November 22, it became known to newsmen that he was a possible suspect in the slaying of President Kennedy as well as in the murder of Patrolman Tippit. At least as early as 3.26 pm a television report carried this information. Reporters and cameramen flooded into the building and congregated in the corridor of the third floor, joining those few who had been present when Oswald first arrived.

On the third floor

Felix McKnight, editor of the Dallas *Times-Herald*, who handled press arrangements for the president's visit, estimated that within 24 hours of the assassination more than 800 representatives of news media were in Dallas, including correspondents from foreign newspapers and press associations. District Attorney Henry M. Wade thought that the crowd in the third floor hallway itself may have numbered as many as 300. Most estimates, including those based on examination of video tapes, place upwards of 100 newsmen and cameramen in the third floor corridor of the police department by the evening of November 22. In the words of an FBI agent who was present, the conditions at the police station were "not too much unlike Grand Central Station at rush hour, maybe like the Yankee Stadium during the World Series games..." In the lobby of the third floor, television cameramen set up two large cameras and floodlights in strategic positions that gave them a sweep of the corridor in either direction. Technicians stretched their television cables into and out of offices, running some of them out of the windows of a deputy chief's office and down the side of the building. Men with newsreel cameras, still cameras, and microphones, more mobile than the television cameramen, moved back and forth seeking information and opportunities for interviews. Newsmen wandered into the offices of other bureaus located on the third floor, sat on desks, and used police telephones; indeed, one reporter admits hiding a telephone behind a desk so that he would have exclusive access to it if something developed.

By the time Chief Curry returned to the building in the middle of the afternoon from Love Field where he had escorted President Johnson from Parkland Hospital, he found that "there was just pandemonium on the third floor." The news representatives, he testified:

> ... were jammed into the north hall of the third floor,
> which are the offices of the criminal investigation division.
> The television trucks, there were several of them around
> the city hall. I went into my administrative offices, I saw
> cables coming through the administrative assistant's office
> and through the deputy chief of traffic through his office,
> and running through the hall. They had a live TV set up
> on the third floor, and it was a bedlam of confusion.

According to Special Agent Winston G. Lawson of the Secret Service:

At least by 6 or 7 o'clock ... [the reporters and cameramen] were quite in evidence up and down the corridors, cameras on the tripods, the sound equipment, people with still cameras, motion picture-type hand cameras, all kinds of people with tape recorders, and they were trying to interview people, anybody that belonged in police headquarters that might know anything about Oswald...The corridor became so jammed that policemen and newsmen had to push and shove if they wanted to get through, stepping over cables, wires, and tripods. The crowd in the hallway was so dense that District Attorney Wade found it a "strain to get the door open" to get into the homicide office. According to Lawson, "You had to literally fight your way through the people to get up and down the corridor." A witness who was escorted into the homicide offices on Saturday afternoon related that he tried to get by the reporters, stepping over television cables and "you couldn't hardly get by, they would grab you and wanted to know what you were doing down here, even with the detectives one in front and one behind you."

The television cameras continued to record the scene on the third floor as some of the newsmen kept vigil through the night.

Such police efforts as there were to control the newsmen were unavailing. Captain Glen D. King, administrative assistant to Chief Curry, witnessed efforts to clear an aisle through the hallway, but related that "this was a constant battle because of the number of newsmen who were there. They would move back into the aisle way that had been cleared. They interfered with the movement of people who had to be there." According to one detective, "they would be asked to stand back and stay back but it wouldn't do much good, and they would push forward and you had to hold them off physically." The detective recalled that on one occasion when he was escorting a witness through the corridor he "stopped ... and looked down and there was a joker who had a camera stuck between ... [his] legs taking pictures..."

Forrest V. Sorrels of the Secret Service had the impression that the "press and the television people just ... took over." Police control over the access of other than newsmen to the third floor was of limited but increasing effectiveness after Oswald's arrival at the police department. Initially no steps were taken to exclude unauthorized persons from the third floor corridor, but late Friday afternoon Assistant Chief Charles Batchelor stationed guards at the elevators and the stairway to prevent the admission of such persons. He also directed the records room in the basement to issue passes, after verification by the bureaus involved, to people who had legitimate business on the third floor.

Throughout the three days of Oswald's detention, the police were obliged to continue normal business in all five bureaus located along the third floor hallway. Thus many persons – relatives of prisoners, complainants, witnesses – had occasion to visit police offices on the third floor on business unrelated to the investigation of the assassination. Newsmen seeking admission to the third floor were required to identify themselves by their personal press cards; however, the department did not follow its usual procedure of checking the authenticity of press credentials. Captain King felt that this would have been impossible in light of "the atmosphere that existed over there, the tremendous pressures that existed, the fact that telephones were ringing constantly, that there were droves of people in there ... the fact that the method by which you positively identify someone ... it's not easy." Police officers on the third floor testified that they carefully checked all persons for credentials, and most newsmen indicated that after Batchelor imposed security they were required to identify themselves by their press cards. Special Agent Sorrels of the

Secret Service stated that he was requested to present credentials on some of his visits to the third floor. However, other newsmen apparently went unchallenged during the entire period before Oswald was killed, although some of them were wearing press badges on their lapels and some may have been known to the police officers.

According to some reporters and policemen, people who appeared to be unauthorized were present on the third floor after security procedures were instituted, and video tapes seem to confirm their observations. Jack Ruby was present on the third floor on Friday night. Assistant Chief of Police N. T. Fisher testified that even on Saturday "anybody could come up with a plausible reason for going to one of the third floor bureaus and was able to get in."

Oswald and the press

When the police car bringing Oswald from the Texas Theater drove into the basement of police headquarters at about 2 pm on Friday, some reporters and cameramen, principally from local papers and stations, were already on hand. The policemen formed a wedge around Oswald and conducted him to the elevator, but several newsmen crowded into the elevator with Oswald and the police. When the elevator stopped at the third floor, the cameramen ran ahead down the corridor, and then turned around and backed up, taking pictures of Oswald as he was escorted toward the homicide and robbery bureau office. According to one escorting officer, some six or seven reporters followed the police into the bureau office so from Friday afternoon, when Oswald arrived in the building, until Sunday, newspaper reporters and television cameras focused their attention on the homicide office. In full view and within arm's length of the assembled newsmen, Oswald traversed the 20 feet of corridor between the homicide office and the locked door leading to the jail elevator at least 15 times after his initial arrival. The jail elevator, sealed off from public use, took him to his fifth floor cell and to the assembly room in the basement for lineups and the Friday night news conference.

On most occasions, Oswald's escort of three to six detectives and policemen had to push their way through the newsmen who sought to surround them. Although the Dallas press normally did not take pictures of a prisoner without first obtaining permission of the police, who generally asked the prisoner, this practice was not followed by any of the newsmen with Oswald. Generally when Oswald appeared the newsmen turned their cameras on him, thrust microphones at his face, and shouted questions at him. Sometimes he answered. Reporters in the forefront of the throng would repeat his answers for the benefit of those behind them who could not hear. On Saturday, however, in response to police admonitions, the reporters exercised more restraint and shouted fewer questions at Oswald when he passed through the corridor.

Oswald's most prolonged exposure occurred at the midnight press conference on Friday night. In response to demands of newsmen, District Attorney Wade, after consulting with Chief Curry and Captain Fritz, had announced shortly before midnight that Oswald would appear at a press conference in the basement assembly room. An estimated 70 to 100 people, including Jack Ruby and other unauthorized persons, crowded into the small downstairs room. No identification was required. The room was so packed that Deputy Chief M. W. Stevenson and Captain Fritz who came down to the basement after the crowd had assembled could not get in and were forced to remain in the doorway.

Oswald was brought into the room shortly after midnight. Curry had instructed policemen not to permit newsmen to touch Oswald or get close to him, but no steps were taken to shield Oswald from the crowd. Captain Fritz had asked that Oswald be placed on the platform used for line-ups so that he could be more easily removed "if anything happened". Chief Curry, however, insisted that Oswald stand on the floor in front of the stage, where he was also in front of the one-way nylon-cloth screen customarily used to prevent a suspect from seeing those present in the room. This was done because cameramen had told Curry that their cameras would not photograph well through the screen.

Curry had instructed the reporters that they were not to "ask any questions and try to interview . . . [Oswald] in any way," but when he was brought into the room, immediately they began to shoot questions at him and "shove micro-phones into his face." It was difficult to hear Oswald's answers above the uproar. Cameramen stood on the tables to take pictures and others pushed forward to get close-ups. The noise and confusion mounted as reporters shouted at each other to get out of the way and cameramen made fran-tic efforts to get into position for pictures. After Oswald had been in the room only a few minutes, Chief Curry inter-vened and directed that Oswald be taken back to the jail because, he testified, the newsmen "tried to overrun him."

THE ABORTIVE TRANSFER

In Dallas, after a person is charged with a felony, the county sheriff ordinarily takes custody of the prisoner and assumes responsibility for his safekeeping. Normally, the Dallas Police Department notifies the sheriff when a prisoner has been charged with a felony and the sheriff dispatches his deputies to transport the accused to the county jail. This is usually done within a few hours after the complaint has been filed. In cases of unusual importance, however, the Dallas city police sometimes transport the prisoners to the county jail.

The decision to move Oswald to the county jail on Sunday morning was reached by Chief Curry the preceding evening. Sometime after 7.30 Saturday evening, according to Assistant Chief Batchelor, two reporters told him that they wanted to go out to dinner but that "they didn't want to miss anything if we were going to move the prisoner." Curry came upon them at that point and told the two newsmen that if they returned by 10 o'clock in the morning, they wouldn't "miss anything". A little later, after checking with Captain Fritz, Curry made a similar announcement to the assembled reporters. Curry reported the making of his decision to move Oswald as follows:

> Then, I talked to Fritz about when he thought he would transfer the prisoner, and he didn't think it was a good idea to transfer him at night because of the fact you couldn't see, and if anybody tried to cause them any trouble, they needed to see who they were and where it was coming from and so forth, and he suggested that we wait until daylight, so this was normal procedure, I mean, for Fritz to determine when he is going to transfer his prisoners, so I told him "Okay." I asked him, I said, "What time do you think you will be ready tomorrow?" And he didn't know exactly and I said, "Do you think about 10 o'clock?" and he said, "I believe so," and this is when I went out and told the newspaper people ... "I believe if you are back here by 10 o'clock you will be back in time to observe anything you care to observe."

During the night, between 2.30 and 3 am, the local office of the FBI and the sheriff's office received telephone calls from an unidentified man who warned that a committee had decided "to kill the man that killed the president." Shortly after, an FBI agent notified the Dallas police of the anonymous threat. The police department and ultimately Chief Curry were informed of both threats.

Immediately after his arrival at the building on Sunday morning between 8.30 and 8.45 am, Curry spoke by telephone with Sheriff J. E. Decker about the transfer. When Decker indicated that he would leave to Curry the decision on whether the sheriff's office or the police would move Oswald, Curry decided that the police would handle it because "we had so much involved here, we were the ones that were investigating the case and we had the officers set up downstairs to handle it." After talking with Decker, Curry began to discuss plans for the transfer. With the threats against Oswald in mind, Curry suggested to Batchelor and Deputy Chief Stevenson that Oswald be transported to the county jail in an armored truck, to which they agreed. While Batchelor made arrangements to have an armored truck brought to the building, Curry and Stevenson tentatively agreed on the route the armored truck would follow from the building to the county jail.

Curry decided that Oswald would leave the building via the basement. He stated later that he reached this decision shortly after his arrival at the police building Sunday morning, when members of the press had already begun to gather in the basement. There is no evidence that anyone opposed this decision. Two members of the Dallas police did suggest to Captain Fritz that Oswald be taken from the building by another exit, leaving the press "waiting in the basement and on Commerce Street, and we could be to the county jail before anyone knew what was taking place." However, Fritz said that he did not think Curry would agree to such a plan because he had promised that Oswald would be transferred at a time when newsmen could take pictures. Forrest Sorrels also suggested to Fritz that Oswald be moved at an unannounced time when no one was around, but Fritz again responded that Curry "wanted to go along with the press and not try to put anything over on them." Preliminary arrangements to obtain additional personnel to assist with the transfer were begun Saturday evening. On Saturday night, the police reserves were requested to provide 8 to 10 men on Sunday, and additional reservists were sought in the morning. Captain C. E. Talbert, who was in charge of the patrol division for the city of Dallas on the morning of November 24, retained a small number of policemen in the building when he took charge that morning and later ordered other patrolmen from several districts to report to the basement. At about 9 am Deputy Chief Stevenson instructed all detectives within the building to remain for the transfer. Sheriff Decker testified that his men were ready to receive Oswald at the county jail from the early hours of Sunday morning.

With the patrolmen and reserve policemen available to him, Captain Talbert, on his own initiative, undertook to secure the basement of the police department building. He placed policemen outside the building at the top of the Commerce Street ramp to keep all spectators on the opposite side of Commerce Street. Later, Talbert directed that patrolmen be assigned to all street intersections the transfer vehicle would cross along the route to the county jail. His most significant security precautions, however, were steps designed to exclude unauthorized persons from the basement area. The spacious basement of the Police and Courts Building contains, among other things, the jail office and the police garage. The jail office, into which the jail elevator opens, is situated on the west side of an auto ramp cutting across the length of the basement from Main Street, on the north side of the building, to Commerce Street, on the south side. From the foot of this ramp, on the east side, midway through the basement, a decline runs down a short distance to the L-shaped police garage. In addition to the auto ramp, five doors to the garage provide access to the basement from the Police and Courts Building on the west side of the garage and the attached Municipal Building on the east. Three of these five doors provide access to three elevators opening into the garage, two for passengers near the central part of the garage and one for service at the east end of the garage. A fourth door near the passenger elevator opens into the municipal building; the fifth door, at the Commerce Street side of the garage, opens into a sub-basement that is connected with both buildings.

Shortly after 9 o'clock Sunday morning, policemen cleared the basement of all but police personnel. Guards were stationed at the top of the Main and Commerce streets auto ramps leading down into the basement, at each of the five doorways into the garage, and at the double doors leading to the public hallway adjacent to the jail office. Then, Sergeant Patrick T. Dean, acting under instructions from Talbert, directed 14 men in a search of the garage. Maintenance workers were directed to leave the area. The searchers examined the rafters, tops of air conditioning ducts, and every closet and room opening off the garage. They searched the interior and trunk compartment of automobiles parked in the garage. The two passenger elevators in the central part of the garage were not in service and the doors were shut and locked; the service elevator was moved to the first floor, and the operator was instructed not to return it to the basement.

Despite the thoroughness with which the search was conducted, there still existed one and perhaps two weak points in controlling access to the garage. Testimony did not resolve positively whether or not the stairway door near the public elevators was locked both from the inside and outside as was necessary to secure it effectively. And although guards were stationed near the double doors, the hallway near the jail office was accessible to people from inside the Police and Courts Building without the necessity of presenting identification. Until seconds before Oswald was shot, newsmen hurrying to photograph Oswald were able to run without challenge through those doors into the basement.

After the search had been completed, the police allowed news representatives to re-enter the basement area and gather along the entrance to the garage on the east side of the ramp. Later, the police permitted the newsmen to stand in front of the railing on the east side of the ramp leading to Main Street. The policemen deployed by Talbert and Dean had instructions to allow no one but identified news media representatives into the basement. As before, the police accepted any credentials that appeared authentic, though some officers did make special efforts to check for pictures and other forms of corroborating identification. Many newsmen reported that they were checked on more than one occasion while they waited in the basement. A small number did not recall that their credentials were ever checked.

Shortly after his arrival on Sunday morning, Chief Curry issued instructions to keep reporters and cameramen out of the jail office and to keep television equipment behind the railing separating the basement auto ramp from the garage.

Curry observed that in other respects Captain Talbert appeared to have security measures in hand and allowed him to proceed on his own initiative. Batchelor and Stevenson checked progress in the basement during the course of the morning, and the officials were generally satisfied with the steps Talbert had taken.

At about 11 am, Deputy Chief Stevenson requested that Captain O. A. Jones of the forgery bureau bring all available detectives from the third-floor offices to the basement. Jones instructed the detectives who accompanied him to the basement to line the walls on either side of the passageway cleared for the transfer party. According to Detective T. D. McMillon,

... Captain Jones explained to us that, when they brought the prisoner out, that he wanted two lines formed and we were to keep these two lines formed: you know, a barrier on either side of them, kind of an aisle ... for them to walk through, and when they came down this aisle, we were to keep this line intact and move along with them until the man was placed in the car.

With Assistant Chief Batchelor's permission, Jones removed photographers who had gathered once again in the basement jail office. Jones recalled that he instructed all newsmen along the Main Street ramp to remain behind an imaginary line extending from the southeast corner of the jail office to the railing on the east side of the ramp; other officers recalled that Jones directed the newsmen to move away from the foot of the Main Street ramp and to line up against the east railing. In any event, newsmen were allowed to congregate along the foot of the ramp after Batchelor observed that there was insufficient room along the east of the ramp to permit all the news representatives to see Oswald as he was brought out. By the time Oswald reached the basement, 40 to 50 newsmen and 70 to 75 police officers were assembled there.

Three television cameras stood along the railing and most of the newsmen were congregated in that area and at the top of the adjacent decline leading into the garage. A group of newsmen and police officers, best estimated at about 20, stood strung across the bottom of the Main Street ramp. Along the south wall of the passageway outside the jail office door were about eight detectives, and three detectives lined the north wall. Two officers stood in front of the double doors leading into the passageway from the corridor next to the jail office. Beginning Saturday night, the public had been kept informed of the approximate time of the transfer. At approximately 10.20 am Curry told a press conference that Oswald would be moved in an armored truck and gave a general description of other security precautions. Apparently no newsmen were informed of the transfer route, however, and the route was not disclosed to the driver of the armored truck until the truck arrived at the Commerce Street exit at about 11.07 am. When they learned of its arrival, many of the remaining newsmen who had waited on the third floor descended to the basement. Shortly after, newsmen may have had another indication that the transfer was imminent if they caught a glimpse through the glass windows of Oswald putting on a sweater in Captain Fritz' office.

Because the driver feared that the truck might stall if it had to start from the bottom of the ramp and because the overhead clearance appeared to be inadequate, Assistant Chief Batchelor had it backed only into the entranceway at the top of the ramp. Batchelor and others then inspected the inside of the truck.

When Chief Curry learned that the truck had arrived, he informed Captain Fritz that security controls were in effect and inquired how long the questioning of Oswald would continue. At this point, Fritz learned for the first time of the plan to convey Oswald by armored truck and immediately expressed his disapproval. He urged the use of an unmarked police car driven by a police officer, pointing out that this would be better from the standpoint of both speed and maneuverability.

Curry agreed to Fritz' plan; the armored truck would be used as a decoy. They decided that the armored truck would leave the ramp first, followed by a car which would contain only security officers. A police car bearing Oswald would follow. After proceeding one block, the car with Oswald would turn off and proceed directly to the county jail; the armored truck would follow a lead car to the jail along the previously agreed upon and more circuitous route.

Captain Fritz instructed Detectives C. W. Brown and C. N. Dhority and a third detective to proceed to the garage and move the follow-up car and the transfer car into place on the auto ramp. He told Lieutenant Rio S. Pierce to obtain another automobile from the basement and take up a lead position on Commerce Street. Deputy Chief Stevenson went back to the basement to inform Batchelor and Jones of the change in plans. Oswald was given his sweater, and then his right hand was handcuffed to the left hand of Detective J. R. Leavelle. Detective T. L. Baker called the jail office to check on security precautions in the basement and notify officials that the prisoner was being brought down.

On arriving in the basement, Pierce asked Sergeant James A. Putnam and Billy Joe Maxey to accompany him in the lead car. Since the armored truck was blocking the Commerce Street ramp, it would be necessary to drive out the Main Street ramp and circle the block to Commerce Street. Maxey sat on the back seat of Pierce's car, and Putnam helped clear a path through reporters on the ramp so that Pierce could drive up toward Main Street. When the car passed by the reporters at about 11.20 am, Putnam entered the car on the right front side. Pierce drove to the top of the Main Street ramp and slowed momentarily as Patrolman Roy E. Vaughn stepped from his position at the top of the ramp toward the street to watch for traffic. After Pierce's car left the garage area, Brown drove another police car out of the garage, moved part way up the Commerce Street ramp, and began to back down into position to receive Oswald. Dhority also proceeded to drive the follow-up car into position ahead of Brown.

As Pierce's car started up the ramp at about 11.20 am, Oswald, accompanied by Captain Fritz and four detectives, arrived at the jail office. Cameramen in the hallway of the basement took pictures of Oswald through the interior glass windows of the jail office as he was led through the office to the exit. Some of these cameramen then ran through the double doors near the jail office and squeezed into the line which had formed across the Main Street ramp.

Still others remained just inside the double doors or proceeded through the double doors after Oswald and his escort emerged from the jail office. When Fritz came to the jail office door, he asked if everything was ready, and a detective standing in the passageway answered "yes". Someone shouted, "Here he comes!"; additional spotlights were turned on in the basement, and the din increased. A detective stepped from the jail office and proceeded toward the transfer car. Seconds later Fritz and then Oswald, with Detective Leavelle at his right, Detective L. C. Graves at his left, and Detective L. D. Montgomery at his rear, came through the door. Fritz walked to Brown's car, which had not yet backed fully into position; Oswald followed a few feet behind. Newsmen near the double door moved forward after him. Though movie films and video tapes indicate that the front line newsmen along the Main Street ramp remained fairly stationary, it was the impression of many who were close to the scene that with Oswald's appearance the crowd surged forward. According to Detective Montgomery, who was walking directly behind Oswald, "soon as we came out this door . . . this bunch here just moved in on us." To Detective B. H. Combest, standing on the Commerce Street side of the passageway from the jail office door, it appeared that:

> Almost the whole line of people pushed forward when Oswald started to leave the jail office, the door, the hall – all the newsmen were poking their sound mikes across to him and asking questions, and they were everywhere sticking their flashbulbs up and around and over him and in his face.

After Oswald had moved about 10 feet from the door of the jail office, Jack Ruby passed between a newsman and a detective at the edge of the straining crowd on the Main Street ramp. With his right hand extended and holding a caliber revolver, Ruby stepped quickly forward and fired a single fatal bullet into Oswald's abdomen.

POSSIBLE ASSISTANCE TO JACK RUBY

The killing of Lee Harvey Oswald in the basement of police headquarters in the midst of more than 70 police officers gave rise to immediate speculation that one or more members of the police department provided Jack Ruby assistance which had enabled him to enter the basement and approach within a few feet of the accused presidential assassin. On pp. 336–371, the Commission has considered whether there is any evidence linking Jack Ruby with a conspiracy to kill the president. At this point, however, it is appropriate to consider whether there is evidence that Jack Ruby received assistance from Dallas policemen or others in gaining access to the basement on the morning of November 24. An affirmative answer would require that the evidence be evaluated for possible connection with the assassination itself. While the Commission has found no evidence that Ruby received assistance from any person in entering the basement, his means of entry is significant in evaluating the adequacy of the precautions taken to protect Oswald. Although more than a hundred policemen and newsmen were present in the basement of police headquarters during the 10 minutes before the shooting of Oswald, none has been found who definitely observed Jack Ruby's entry into the basement. After considering all the evidence, the Commission has concluded that Ruby entered the basement unaided, probably via the Main Street ramp, and no more than 3 minutes before the shooting of Oswald.

Ruby's account of how he entered the basement by the Main Street ramp merits consideration in determining his means of entry. Three Dallas policemen testified that approximately 80 minutes after his arrest, Ruby told them that he had walked to the top of the Main Street ramp from the nearby Western Union office and that he walked down the ramp at the time the police car driven by Lieutenant Pierce emerged into Main Street. This information did not come to light immediately because the policemen did not report it to their superiors until some days later. Ruby refused to discuss his means of entry in interrogations with other investigators later on the day of his arrest. Thereafter, in a lengthy interview on December 21 and in a sworn deposition taken after his trial, Ruby gave the same explanation he had given to the three policemen.

The Commission has been able to establish with precision the time of certain events leading up to the shooting. Minutes before Oswald appeared in the basement, Ruby was in the Western Union office located on the same block of Main Street some 350 feet from the top of the Main Street ramp. The time stamp on a money order which he sent and on the receipt found in his pocket establish that the order was accepted for transmission at almost exactly 11.17 am. Ruby was then observed to depart the office walking in the direction of the police building. Video tapes taken without interruption before the shooting establish that Lieutenant Pierce's car cleared the crowd at the foot of the ramp 55 seconds before the shooting. They also show Ruby standing at the foot of the ramp on the Main Street side before the shooting.

The shooting occurred very close to 11.21 am. This time has been established by observing the time on a clock appearing in motion pictures of Oswald in the basement jail office, and by records giving the time of Oswald's departure from the city jail and the time at which an ambulance was summoned for Oswald.

The Main Street ramp provided the most direct route to the basement from the Western Union office. At normal stride, it requires approximately 1 minute to walk from that office to the top of the Main Street ramp and about 20–25 seconds to descend the ramp. It is certain, therefore, that Ruby entered the basement no more than 2–3 minutes before the shooting. This timetable indicates that a little more than 2 of the 4 minutes between Ruby's departure from the Western Union office and the time of the shooting are unaccounted for. Ruby could have consumed this time in loitering along the way, at the top of the ramp, or inside the basement. However, if Ruby is correct that he passed Pierce's car at the top of the ramp, he could have been in the basement no more than 30 seconds before the shooting.

The testimony of two witnesses partially corroborates Ruby's claim that he entered by the Main Street ramp. James Turner, an employee of WBAP-TV Fort Worth, testified that while he was standing near the railing on the east side of the Main Street ramp, perhaps 30 seconds before the shooting, he observed a man he is confident was Jack Ruby moving slowly down the Main Street ramp about 10 feet from the bottom. Two other witnesses testified that they thought they had seen Ruby on the Main Street side of the ramp before the shooting.

One other witness has testified regarding the purported movements of a man on the Main Street ramp, but his testimony merits little credence. A former police officer, N. J. Daniels, who was standing at the top of the ramp with the single patrolman guarding this entrance, R. E. Vaughn, testified that "3 or 4 minutes, I guess" before the shooting, a man walked down the Main Street ramp in full view of Vaughn but was not stopped or questioned by the officer. Daniels did not identify the man as Ruby. Moreover, he gave a description which differed in important respects

from Ruby's appearance on November 24, and he has testified that he doesn't think the man was Ruby. On
November 24, Vaughn telephoned Daniels to ask him if he
had seen anybody walk past him on the morning of the
24th and was told that he had not; it was not until
November 29 that Daniels came forward with the statement that he had seen a man enter.

Although the sum of this evidence tends to support
Ruby's claim that he entered by the Main Street ramp,
there is other evidence not fully consistent with Ruby's
story. Patrolman Vaughn stated that he checked the credentials of all unknown persons seeking to enter the basement,
and his testimony was supported by several persons. Vaughn
denied that the emergence of Lieutenant Pierce's car from
the building distracted him long enough to allow Ruby to
enter the ramp unnoticed, and neither he nor any of the
three officers in Lieutenant Pierce's car saw Ruby enter.

Despite Vaughn's denial the Commission has found no
credible evidence to support any other entry route. Two
Dallas detectives believed they observed three men pushing
a WBAP-TV camera into the basement minutes before the
shooting, while only two were with the camera after
Oswald had been shot. However, films taken in the basement show the WBAP-TV camera being pushed past the
detectives by only two men. The suspicion of the detectives
is probably explained by testimony that a third WBAP-TV
employee ran to help steady the incoming camera as it
entered the basement, probably just before the camera
became visible on the films. Moreover, since the camera
entered the basement close to 4 minutes before the shooting, it is virtually impossible that Ruby could have been in
the basement at that time. The possibility that Ruby
entered the basement by some other route has been investigated, but the Commission has found no evidence to
support it. Ruby could have walked from the Western

Union office to the Commerce Street ramp on the other side of the building in about $2\frac{1}{2}$ minutes. However, during the minutes preceding the shooting, video tapes show the armored truck in the entranceway to this ramp with only narrow clearance on either side. Several policemen were standing near the truck and a large crowd of spectators was gathered across the street.

It is improbable that Ruby could have squeezed past the truck without having been observed. If Ruby entered by any other means, he would have had to pass first through the Police and Courts Building or the attached Municipal Building, and then secondly through one of the five doors into the basement, all of which, according to the testimony of police officers, were secured. The testimony was not completely positive about one of the doors.

There is no evidence to support the speculations that Ruby used a press badge to gain entry to the basement or that he concealed himself in a police car. Police found no form of press card on Ruby's person after his apprehension, nor any discarded badges within the basement. There is no evidence that any police officer admitted Ruby on the pretense that he was a member of the press or any other pretense.

Police vehicles in the basement were inspected during the course of the search supervised by Sergeant Dean. According to Patrolman Vaughn, the only vehicles that entered the basement while he was at the top of the Main Street ramp were two patrol cars, one of which entered twice, and a patrol wagon which was searched by another policeman after it entered the basement. All entered on official police business and considerably more than 4 minutes before Oswald was shot. None of the witnesses at the top of the Main Street ramp recalled any police car entering the basement in the 4-minute period after Ruby left the Western Union office and preceding the shooting. The possibility that Ruby could have entered the basement in a car may therefore be completely discounted. The Dallas Police Department, concerned at the failure of its security measures, conducted an extensive investigation that revealed no information indicating complicity between any police officer and Jack Ruby. Ruby denied to the Commission that he received any form of assistance. The FBI interviewed every member of the police department who was on duty in the basement on November 24, and Commission staff members took sworn depositions from many. With few exceptions, newsmen who were present in the basement at the time also gave statements and/or depositions. As the record before the Commission indicated, Ruby had had rather free access to the Dallas police quarters during the period subsequent to the assassination, but there was no evidence that implicated the police or newsmen in Ruby's actions on that day.

Ruby was known to have a wide acquaintanceship with Dallas policemen and to seek their favor. According to testimony from many sources, he gave free coffee at his clubs to many policemen while they were on duty and free admittance and discounts on beverages when they were off duty. Although Chief Curry's estimate that approximately 25 to 50 of the 1,175 men in the Dallas Police Department knew Ruby may be too conservative, the Commission found no evidence of any suspicious relationships between Ruby and any police officer. The Commission found no substantial evidence that any member of the Dallas Police Department recognized Jack Ruby as an unauthorized person in the basement prior to the time Sergeant P. T. Dean, according to his testimony, saw Ruby dart forward toward Oswald. But Dean was then part way up the Commerce Street ramp, too far removed to act.

Patrolman W. J. Harrison, Captain Glen King, and reserve officers Captain C. O. Arnett and Patrolman W. M.

Croy were among those in front of Ruby at the time Dean saw him. They all faced away from Ruby, toward the jail office. Video tapes show that Harrison turned in the direction of the ramp at the time Lieutenant Pierce's car passed, and once again 25 seconds later, but there is no indication that he observed or recognized Ruby. The policemen standing on the south side of the passageway from the jail office, who might have been looking in Ruby's direction, had the glare of television and photographer's lights in their eyes.

The Commission also considered the possibility that a member of the police department called Ruby at his apartment and informed him, either intentionally or unintentionally, of the time of the planned transfer. From at least 10.19 am until close to 11 am on Sunday, Ruby was at his apartment, where he could have received a call that the transfer was imminent. He apparently left his apartment between 10.45 and 11 am. However, the drive from Ruby's apartment to the Western Union office takes approximately 15 minutes. Since the time of the contemplated transfer could not have been known to anyone until a few minutes before 11.15 am, a precise time could not have been conveyed to Ruby while he was at his apartment. Moreover, the television and radio publicized the transfer plans throughout the morning, obviating the need for Ruby to obtain information surreptitiously.

ADEQUACY OF SECURITY PRECAUTIONS

The shooting of Lee Harvey Oswald obviously resulted from the failure of the security precautions which the Dallas Police Department had taken to protect their prisoner. In assessing the causes of the security failure, the Commission has not overlooked the extraordinary circumstances which prevailed during the days that the attention of the world was turned on Dallas. Confronted with a unique situation, the Dallas police took special security measures to insure Oswald's safety.

Unfortunately these did not include adequate control of the great crowd of newsmen that inundated the police department building. The Dallas police had in custody a man whose alleged act had brought upon him immediate and universal opprobrium.

There were many possible reasons why people might have attempted to kill him if given the opportunity. Concerned that there might be an attempt on Oswald's life, FBI Director J. Edgar Hoover sent a message to Chief Curry on November 22 through Special Agent Manning C. Clements of the FBI's Dallas office, urging that Oswald be afforded the utmost security. Curry does not recall receiving the message.

Although the presence of a great mass of press representatives created an extraordinary security problem in the building, the police department pursued its normal policy of admitting the press. That policy, set forth in General Order No. 81 of the Dallas Police Department, provided:

> . . . that members of this department render every assistance,
> except such as obviously may seriously hinder or delay the
> proper functioning of the department, to the accredited
> members of the official newsgathering agencies and this
> includes newspaper, television cameramen and newsreel
> photographers.

In a letter to all members of the police department, dated February 7, 1963, Chief Curry explained the general order, in part, as follows:

> The General Order covering this subject is not merely
> permissive. It does not state that the officer may, if he so
> chooses, assist the press. It rather places on him a respon-
> sibility to lend active assistance.

... as a Department we deal with public affairs. It is the right of the public to know about these affairs, and one of the most accurate and useful avenues we have of supplying this information is through the newspapers and radio and television stations. Implied in the General Order is a prohibition for the officer to improperly attempt to interfere with the news media representative, who is functioning in his capacity as such. Such activity on the part of any police officer is regarded by the press as an infringement of rights, and the department shares this view.

Under this policy, news representatives ordinarily had access to the Police and Courts Building. The first newsmen to arrive on Friday afternoon were admitted in accordance with the policy; others who came later simply followed behind them. Shortly after Oswald arrived, Captain King granted permission to bring television cameras to the third floor. By the time the unwieldy proportions of the crowd of newsmen became apparent, it had already become well entrenched on the third floor. No one suggested reversing the department's policy expressed in General Order No. 81. Chief Curry testified that at no time did he consider clearing the crowd from the building; he "saw no particular harm in allowing the media to observe the prisoner." Captain King later stated candidly that he simply became "accustomed to the idea of them being out there." The general policy of the Dallas police recognized that the rule of full cooperation did not apply when it might jeopardize an investigation. In retrospect, most members of the department believed that the general rule allowing admittance of the press to the police quarters should not have been followed after the assassination. Few, if any, thought this at the time. By failing to exclude the press from the building on Friday and Saturday, the Dallas police made it possible for the uncontrolled crowd to nearly surround Oswald on the frequent occasions that he moved through the third-floor corridor. The decision to allow newsmen to observe the transfer on Sunday followed naturally the policy established during these first two days of Oswald's detention. The reporters and cameramen descended upon the third floor of the Police and Courts Building in such numbers that the pressroom on the third floor proved wholly inadequate. Rather than the "two or three or maybe a half dozen reporters" who normally appeared to cover local police stories, the police were faced with upward of 100. Bringing with them cameras, microphones, cables, and spotlights, the newsmen inevitably spilled over into areas where they interfered with the transaction of police business and the maintenance of security.

Aside from numbers, the gathering of reporters presented a problem because most of them were representatives of the national and foreign press, rather than the local press. These newsmen carried individual press cards rather than identification cards issued by the Dallas police. Therefore, it was impossible for the police to verify quickly the identity of this great number of unfamiliar people who appeared almost simultaneously. Because of the close physical proximity of the milling mass of insistent newsmen to the prisoner, the failure to authenticate press credentials subjected the prisoner to a serious security risk. Although steps were taken on Friday afternoon to insure that persons seeking entry to the third floor were there for a legitimate purpose, reasons could be fabricated. Moreover, because of the large crowd, it was easier for unauthorized persons to slip by those guarding the entrances. Jack Ruby, for one, was able to gain entry to the third-floor corridor on Friday night. The third-floor corridor provided the only passageway between the homicide and robbery bureau and the jail elevator.

No thought seems to have been given, however, to the possibility of questioning Oswald on some other floor. Moreover, Oswald's most extended exposure to the press, at the Friday evening press conference, was unrelated to any phase of the investigation and was motivated primarily by the desire to satisfy the demands of the news media to see the prisoner. The risks attendant upon this appearance were emphasized by the presence of unauthorized persons, including Jack Ruby, at the press conference in the basement assembly room.

Although Oswald was repeatedly exposed to possible assaults on Friday and Saturday, he met his death on Sunday, when police took the most extensive security precautions. The assembly of more than 70 police officers, some of them armed with tear gas, and the contemplated use of an armored truck, appear to have been designed primarily to repel an attempt of a mob to seize the prisoner. Chief Curry's own testimony indicated that such a focus resulted not from any appraisal of the varied risks to Oswald's life but came about in response to the telephone threat Sunday morning that a hundred men were going to attack Oswald.

A more balanced appraisal would have given thought to protection against any attack. For example, the acceptance of inadequate press credentials posed a clear avenue for a one-man assault. The likelihood of an unauthorized person obtaining entry by such means is confirmed not alone by the fact that Jack Ruby managed to get by a guard at one entrance. Several newsmen related that their credentials were not checked as they entered the basement Sunday morning. Seconds before Oswald was shot, the double doors from the hallway next to the jail office afforded a means of entry to the basement without presentation of credentials earlier demanded of newsmen.

The swarm of news people in the basement also substantially limited the ability of the police to detect an unauthorized person once he had entered the basement. While Jack Ruby might have been easily spotted if only police officers had been in the basement, he remained apparently unnoticed in the crowd of newsmen until he lunged forward toward Oswald.

The near-blinding television and motion picture lights which were allowed to shine upon the escort party further increased the difficulty of observing unusual movements in the basement. Moreover, by making public the plans for the transfer, the police attracted to the city jail many persons who otherwise might not have learned of the move until it had been completed. This group included the onlookers gathered on Commerce Street and a few people on Main Street. Also, continuous television and radio coverage of the activities in the basement might have resulted in compromise of the transfer operation. These risks to Oswald's safety, growing in part out of adherence to the general policy of the police department, were also accepted for other reasons. Many members of the police department believed that the extraordinary public attention aroused by the tragic death of President Kennedy obliged them to make special efforts to accommodate the press. Captain King carefully articulated one reason why the newsmen were permitted

> . . . to remain in the hallways . . . to view the investigation and to keep in constant touch with progress of the investigation.
>
> We realized that if we arrested a suspect, that if we brought him into the police station and then conducted all of our investigations behind closed doors, that if we gave no reports on the progress of our investigation and did not permit the newsmen to see the suspect – if we excluded them from it – we would leave ourselves open not only to criticisms that we were fabricating a suspect and were attempting to pin something on someone, but even more

importantly, we would cause people to lose faith in our fairness and, through losing faith in our fairness, to lose faith to a certain extent in the processes of law. We felt it was mandatory that as many people knew about it as possible. We knew, too, that if we did exclude the newsmen, we would be leaving ourselves open to a charge that we were using improper action, duress, physical abuse, all of these things.

While Oswald was in custody, the Dallas police kept the press informed about the treatment Oswald was receiving.

The public could have been assured that the prisoner was not mistreated and that his rights were fully respected by the police, without each one of hundreds of cameramen and reporters being permitted to satisfy himself that the police had not abused the prisoner. This result could have been accomplished by obtaining reports from members of the family who visited him, or by a committee of the bar or other substantial citizens of the community. When it became known on Saturday that Oswald did not have an attorney, the president of the Dallas Bar Association visited him to inquire whether he wished assistance in obtaining counsel.

Moreover, the right of the public to know does not give the press license to interfere with the efficient operation of law-enforcement agencies. Permitting the press to remain on the third floor of the building served no valid purpose that could not have been met if the press had been excluded from the third floor, as it was from the fourth and fifth floors, and informed of developments either through press releases or at press conferences elsewhere in the building. Having failed to exclude the mass of the press from the basement during the transfer of Oswald, the police department's security measures could not be completely effective. Despite the pressures that prevailed, planning and coordination of security arrangements could have been more thorough and precise. No single member of the Dallas

Police Department ever assumed full responsibility for the details of Oswald's transfer. Chief Curry participated in some of the planning, but he felt that primary authority for the transfer should be Fritz', since Fritz had charge of the investigation.

According to Chief Curry:

> Fritz and I, I think, discussed this briefly, the possibility of getting that prisoner out of the city hall during the night hours and by another route and slipping him to the jail, but actually Fritz was not too much in favor of this and I more or less left this up to Fritz as to when and how this transfer would be made, because he has in the past transferred many of his prisoners to the county jail and I felt that since it was his responsibility, the prisoner was, to let him decide when and how he wanted to transfer this prisoner.

Fritz, on the other hand, felt that Curry was directing the transfer arrangements: "I was transferring him like the chief told me to transfer him." When Captain W. B. Frazier notified Fritz by telephone early Sunday morning about the threats to Oswald's life, Fritz replied that Curry should be notified, since he was handling the transfer. When urged to modify the transfer plans to avoid the press, as he later testified he would have preferred to do, Fritz declined on the ground that Curry had already decided to the contrary. Hence, if the recollection of both officials is accurate, the basic decision to move Oswald at an announced time and in the presence of the news media was never carefully thought through by either man. Curry and Fritz had agreed Saturday evening that Oswald should not be moved at night, but their discussion apparently went little further.

Perhaps the members of the Dallas Police Department were, as many testified, accustomed to working together so that formal instructions were sometimes unnecessary. On the other hand, it is clear, at least in retrospect, that this particular occasion demanded more than the usual informal unspoken understandings. The evidence indicates that no member of the department at any time considered fully the implications of moving Oswald through the basement. Nor did any single official or group of officials coordinate and direct where the transfer vehicle would be stationed to accept Oswald, where the press would stand, and the number and positioning of police officers in the basement. Captain Jones indicated that there were to be two solid lines of policemen from the jail office door to the transfer vehicle, but lines were formed only along the walls of the areaway between the jail office door and the ramp. The newsmen were not kept east of the auto ramp where a railing would have separated them from Oswald. No strong ranks of policemen were ever placed in front of the newsmen once they were allowed to gather in the area of the Main Street ramp. Many policemen in the basement did not know the function they were supposed to perform. No instructions were given that certain policemen should watch the crowd rather than Oswald. Apparently no one gave any thought to the blinding effect of television and other camera lights upon the escort party. Largely on his own initiative, Captain Talbert undertook to secure the basement, with only minimal coordination with those responsible for and familiar with the route Oswald would take through the basement.

Several officials recalled that Lieutenant Woodrow Wiggins was directed to clear the basement jail office, but Wiggins testified that he received no such assignment. In any event, less than 20 minutes before the transfer, Captain Jones observed newsmen in the jail office and had them removed. But no official removed news personnel from the corridor beside the jail office; indeed, cameramen took pictures through the glass windows of the jail office as Oswald walked through it toward the basement, and then approached to within 20 feet of Oswald from the rear at the same time that Jack Ruby moved toward Oswald from the front.

A clear example of the inadequacy of coordination was the last-minute change in plans to transfer Oswald in an unmarked police car rather than by armored truck. The plan to use an armored vehicle was adopted without informing Fritz. When Fritz was told of the arrangement shortly after 11 o'clock, he objected, and hurried steps were taken to modify the arrangements. Fritz was then prematurely informed that the basement arrangements were complete. When Oswald and the escorting detectives entered the basement, the transfer car had not yet been backed into position, nor had the policemen been arranged to block the newsmen's access to Oswald's path. If the transfer car had been carefully positioned between the press and Oswald, Ruby might have been kept several yards from his victim and possibly without a clear view of him.

Detective Leavelle, who accompanied Oswald into the basement, testified:

> . . . I was surprised when I walked to the door and the car was not in the spot it should have been, but I could see it was in back, and backing into position, but had it been in position where we were told it would be, that would have eliminated a lot of the area in which anyone would have access to him, because it would have been blocked by the car. In fact, if the car had been sitting where we were told it was going to be, see it would have been sitting directly upon the spot where Ruby was standing when he fired the shot.

Captain Jones described the confusion with which Oswald's entry into the basement was in fact received:

Then the change – going to put two cars up there. There is
no reason why that back car can't get all the way back to
the jail office. The original plan would be that the line of
officers would be from the jail door to the vehicle. Then
they say, "Here he comes." . . . It is too late to get the people
out of the way of the car and form the line. I am aware that
Oswald is already coming because of the furor, so, I was
trying to keep everybody out of the way and keep the way
clear and I heard a shot.

Therefore, regardless of whether the press should have been
allowed to witness the transfer, security measures in the
basement for Oswald's protection could and should have
been better organized and more thorough. These additional
deficiencies were directly related to the decision to admit
newsmen to the basement. The Commission concludes that
the failure of the police to remove Oswald secretly or to
control the crowd in the basement at the time of the transfer were the major causes of the security breakdown which
led to Oswald's death.

NEWS COVERAGE AND POLICE POLICY

Consistent with its policy of allowing news representatives to remain within the working quarters of the Police
and Courts Building, the police department made every
effort to keep the press fully informed about the progress
of the investigation. As a result, from Friday afternoon
until after the killing of Oswald on Sunday, the press was
able to publicize virtually all of the information about
the case which had been gathered until that time. In the
process, a great deal of misinformation was disseminated
to a worldwide audience. As administrative assistant to
Chief Curry, Captain King also handled departmental
press relations and issued press releases. According to

King, it was "the responsibility of each member of the department to furnish to the press information on incidents in which they, themselves, were involved, except on matters which involved ... personnel policies of the department, or ... unless it would obviously interfere with an investigation underway." In Oswald's case, Chief Curry released most of the information to the press. He and Assistant Chief Batchelor agreed on Friday that Curry would make all announcements to the press. However, there is no evidence that this decision was ever communicated to the rest of the police force. The chief consequence appears to have been that Batchelor refrained from making statements to the news media during this period. Most of the information was disclosed through informal oral statements or answers to questions at impromptu and clamorous press conferences in the third floor corridor. Written press releases were not employed. The ambulatory press conference became a familiar sight during these days. Whenever Curry or other officials appeared in the hallway, newsmen surrounded them, asking questions and requesting statements. Usually the officials complied. Curry appeared in interviews on television and radio at least a dozen times during November 22–24. He did not attend any of the interrogations of Oswald in Captain Fritz' office except at the beginning and toward the end of Sunday morning's session; he received his information through Captain Fritz and other sources. Nevertheless, in sessions with the newsmen on Friday and Saturday, he gave detailed information on the progress of the case against Oswald. Recorded statements of television and radio interviews with Curry and other officials in Dallas during November 22–24 have been transcribed. An example of these interviews is the following transcript of remarks made by Curry to newsmen on Saturday:

Q: Chief Curry, I understand you have some new information in this case. Could you relate what that is?

A: Yes, we've just been informed by the Federal Bureau of Investigation, that they, the FBI, have the order letter from a mail order house, and the order was sent to their laboratory in Washington and the writing on this order was compared with known samples of our suspect, Oswald's handwriting and found to be the same.

Q: This order was for the rifle?

A: This order was for the rifle to a mail order house in Chicago. It was [inaudible]. The return address was to Dallas, Texas, to the post office box under the name of A. Hidell, H-I-D-E-double L. This is the post office box of our suspect. This gun was mailed parcel post March 20, 1963. I understand he left Dallas shortly after this and didn't come back until I think about two months ago.

Q: Do you know again on what date this rifle was ordered and are you able to link it definitely as the rifle which you confiscated at the School Book Depository?

A: That we have not done so far. If the FBI has been able to do it I have not been informed of it yet. We do know that this man ordered a rifle of the type that was used in the assassination of the president from this mail order house in Chicago and the FBI has definitely identified the writing as that of our suspect.

Q: On another subject – I understand you have photographs of the suspect, Oswald, with a rifle like that used. Could you describe that picture?

A: This is the picture of Oswald standing facing a camera with a rifle in his hand which is very similar to the rifle that we have in our possession. He also had a pistol strapped on his hip. He was holding two papers in his hand, with one of them seemed to be *The Worker* and the other says *Be Militant* – I don't know whether that was headlines or the name of the paper.

Q: How much did the gun cost from the mail order house?

A: I understand the gun was advertised for $12.78, I believe.

Q: Have you received any results on the ballistics test conducted on the gun and on Oswald?

A: They're going to be favorable. I don't have a formal report yet.

Q: But you are sure at this time they will be favorable?

A: Yes.

Q: Do you feel now that you have the case completely wrapped up, or are you continuing?

A: We will continue as long as there is a shred of evidence to be gathered. We have a strong case at this time.

Q: I believe you said earlier this afternoon that you have a new development which does wrap up the case – the first time you said the case definitely is secure. Is that correct?

A: That was this morning. This additional evidence just makes a stronger case.

Q: But this is not the same evidence you were referring to then?

A: No, that's true.

Q: Would you be willing to say what that evidence was?

A: No, sir. I don't wish to reveal it. It might jeopardize our case.

Commentator: Thank you very much Chief Jesse Curry of the Dallas Police Department.

Although Captain Fritz permitted himself to be interviewed by the news media less frequently than did Chief Curry, he nevertheless answered questions and ventured opinions about the progress of the investigation. On

Saturday he told reporters that he was convinced beyond a doubt that Oswald had killed the president. He discussed some of the evidence in the case, especially the rifle, but his contribution to the knowledge of the reporters was small compared with that of Chief Curry.

Many other members of the police department, including high officials, detectives, and patrolmen, were also interviewed by news representatives during these days. Some of these men had participated in specific aspects of the case, such as the capture of Oswald at the Texas Theater and the search for evidence at the Texas School Book Depository Building. Few, if any, seemed reluctant to submit to questions and to being televised. It seemed to District Attorney Wade that the newsmen "just followed everybody everywhere they went ... they interviewed some of your patrolmen ... on the corner ... they were interviewing anybody." Wade himself also made several statements to the press. He visited police headquarters twice on Friday, twice on Saturday, and twice on Sunday. On most of these occasions he was interviewed by the press and appeared on television. After Oswald had appeared before the press on Friday night, Wade held an impromptu conference with reporters in the overflowing assembly room. Wade told the press on Saturday that he would not reveal any evidence because it might prejudice the selection of a jury. On other occasions, however, he mentioned some items of evidence and expressed his opinions regarding Oswald's guilt. He told the press on Friday night that Oswald's wife had told the police that her husband had a rifle in the garage at the house in Irving and that it was missing the morning of the assassination. On one occasion he repeated the error that the murder rifle had been a Mauser. Another time, he stated his belief that Oswald had prepared for the assassination months in advance, including what he would tell the police. He also said that Oswald had practiced with the rifle to improve his marksmanship.

The running commentary on the investigation by the police inevitably carried with it the disclosure of many details that proved to be erroneous. In their efforts to keep the public abreast of the investigation, the police reported hearsay items and unverified leads; further investigation proved many of these to be incorrect or inaccurate. For example, the rifle found on the sixth floor of the Texas School Book Depository Building was initially identified as a Mauser 7.65 rather than a Mannlicher–Carcano 6.5 because a deputy constable who was one of the first to see it thought it looked like a Mauser [see p. 120]. He neither handled the weapon nor saw it at close range.

Police sources were also responsible for the mistaken notion that the chicken bones found on the sixth floor were the remains of Oswald's lunch. They had in fact been left by another employee who ate his lunch there at least 15 minutes before the assassination. Curry repeated the erroneous report that a Negro had picked up Oswald near the scene of the assassination and driven him across town. It was also reported that the map found in Oswald's room contained a marked route of the presidential motorcade when it actually contained markings of places where Oswald may have applied for jobs, including, of course, the Texas School Book Depository.

Concern about the effects of the unlimited disclosures was being voiced by Saturday morning. According to District Attorney Wade, he received calls from lawyers in Dallas and elsewhere expressing concern about providing an attorney for Oswald and about the amount of information being given to the press by the police and the district attorney. Curry continued to answer questions on television and radio during the remainder of the day and Sunday morning.

FBI Director J. Edgar Hoover became concerned because "almost as soon as ... [FBI Laboratory reports] would reach the Dallas Police Department, the chief of police or one of the representatives of the department would go on TV or radio and relate findings of the FBI, giving information such as the identification of the gun and other items of physical evidence." On Sunday, after Oswald was shot, Hoover dispatched a personal message to Curry requesting him "not to go on the air any more until this case ... [is] resolved." Hoover testified later that Curry agreed not to make any more statements.

The shooting of Oswald shocked the Dallas police, and after the interviews that immediately followed the shooting they were disposed to remain silent. Chief Curry made only one more television appearance after the shooting. At 1.30 pm, he descended to the assembly room where, tersely and grimly, he announced Oswald's death. He refused to answer any of the questions shouted at him by the persistent reporters, concluding the conference in less than a minute.

District Attorney Wade also held one more press conference. Before doing so on Sunday evening, he returned once more to the police station and held a meeting with "all the brass" except Curry. Wade told them that "people are saying ... you had the wrong man and you all were the ones who killed him or let him out here to have him killed intentionally." Wade told the police that "somebody ought to go out on television and lay out the evidence that you had on Oswald, and tell them everything." He sat down and listed from memory items of evidence in the case against Oswald. According to Wade, Chief Curry refused to make any statements because he had told an FBI inspector that he would say no more. The police refused to furnish Wade with additional details of the case.

Wade nonetheless proceeded to hold a lengthy formal press conference that evening, in which he attempted to list all of the evidence that had been accumulated at that point tending to establish Oswald as the assassin of President Kennedy.

Unfortunately, at that time, as he subsequently testified, he lacked a thorough grasp of the evidence and made a number of errors. He stated that Oswald had told a woman on a bus that the president had been killed, an error apparently caused by the bus driver having confused Oswald with another passenger who was on the bus after Oswald had left. Wade also repeated the error about Oswald's having a map marked with the route of the motorcade. He told reporters that Oswald's description and name "went out by the police to look for him." The police never mentioned Oswald's name in their broadcast descriptions before his arrest.

Wade was innocent of one error imputed to him since November 24. The published transcript of part of the press conference furnished to newspapers by the Associated Press represented Wade as having identified the cabdriver who took Oswald to North Beckley Avenue after the shooting, as one named "Darryl Click". The transcript as it appeared in the *New York Times* and the *Washington Post* of November 26 reads:

> A: [Wade] A lady. He then [caught] the bus, he asked the
> bus driver to stop, got off at a stop, caught a taxicab
> driver, Darryl Click, don't have his exact place – and
> went to his home in Oak Cliff, changed his clothes
> hurriedly, and left.

The correct transcript, taken from an audio tape supplied by station WBAP, Fort Worth, is as follows:

> A: [Wade] A lady. He then [caught] the bus, he asked the bus
> driver to stop, got off at a stop, caught a taxicab driver.

Q: Where?

A: In Oak Cliff. I don't have the exact place and went to his home in Oak Cliff, changed his clothes hurriedly and left.

In this manner, a section of Dallas, "Oak Cliff", became a non-existent taxicab driver, "Darryl Click." Wade did not mention the cabdriver by name at any time. In transcribing the conference from the sound tape, a stenographer apparently made an error that might have become permanently imbedded in the literature of the event but for the preservation and use of an original sound tape. Though many of the inaccuracies were subsequently corrected by the police and are negated by findings of the Commission included elsewhere in this report, the publicizing of unchecked information provided much of the basis for the myths and rumors that came into being soon after the president's death. The erroneous disclosures became the basis for distorted reconstructions and interpretations of the assassination. The necessity for the Dallas authorities to correct themselves or to be corrected by other sources gave rise not only to criticism of the police department's competence but also to doubts regarding the veracity of the police. Skeptics sought to cast doubt on much of the correct evidence later developed and to find support for their own theories in these early police statements.

The immediate disclosure of information by the police created a further risk of injuring innocent citizens by unfavorable publicity. This was the unfortunate experience of Joe R. Molina, a Dallas-born Navy veteran who had been employed by the Texas School Book Depository since 1947 and on November 22, 1963, held the position of credit manager. Apparently because of Molina's employment at the Depository and his membership in a veterans' organization, the American GI Forum, that the Dallas police considered possibly subversive, Dallas policemen searched Molina's home, with his permission, at about 1.30 am, Saturday, November 23. During the day Molina was intermittently interrogated at police headquarters for 6 or 7 hours, chiefly about his membership in the American GI Forum, and also about Oswald. He was never arrested, charged, or held in custody.

While Molina was being questioned, officials of the police department made statements or answered questions that provided the basis for television reports about Molina during the day. These reports spoke of a "second suspect being picked up", insinuated that the Dallas police had reason to suspect another person who worked in the Texas School Book Depository, stated that the suspect had been arrested and his home searched, and mentioned that Molina may have been identified by the US Department of Justice as a possible subversive.

No evidence was ever presented to link Molina with Oswald except as a fellow employee of the Texas School Book Depository. According to Molina, he had never spoken to Oswald. The FBI notified the Commission that Molina had never been the subject of an investigation by it and that it had never given any information about Molina to the Dallas police concerning any alleged subversive activities by him. The Dallas police explained in a statement to the FBI that they had never had a file on Molina, but that they did have one on the American GI Forum.

Molina lost his job in December. He felt that he was being discharged because of the unfavorable publicity he had received, but officials of the Depository claimed that automation was the reason. Molina testified that he had difficulty in finding another position, until finally, with the help of a fellow church member, he secured a position at a lower salary than his previous one.

If Oswald had been tried for his murders of November 22, the effects of the news policy pursued by the Dallas authorities would have proven harmful both to the prosecution and the defense. The misinformation reported after the shootings might have been used by the defense to cast doubt on the reliability of the State's entire case. Though each inaccuracy can be explained without great difficulty, the number and variety of misstatements issued by the police shortly after the assassination would have greatly assisted a skillful defense attorney attempting to influence the attitudes of jurors. A fundamental objection to the news policy pursued by the Dallas police, however, is the extent to which it endangered Oswald's constitutional right to a trial by an impartial jury. Because of the nature of the crime, the widespread attention which it necessarily received, and the intense public feelings which it aroused, it would have been a most difficult task to select an unprejudiced jury, either in Dallas or elsewhere. But the difficulty was markedly increased by the divulgence of the specific items of evidence with which the police linked Oswald to the two killings. The disclosure of evidence encouraged the public, from which a jury would ultimately be impaneled, to prejudge the very questions that would be raised at trial. Moreover, rules of law might have prevented the prosecution from presenting portions of this evidence to the jury.

For example, though expressly recognizing that Oswald's wife could not be compelled to testify against him, District Attorney Wade revealed to the Nation that Marina Oswald had affirmed her husband's ownership of a rifle like that found on the sixth floor of the Texas School Book Depository. Curry stated that Oswald had refused to take a lie detector test, although such a statement would have been inadmissible in a trial. The exclusion of such evidence, however, would have been meaningless if jurors were already familiar with the same facts from previous television or newspaper reports. Wade might have influenced prospective jurors by his mistaken statement that the paraffin test showed that Oswald had fired a gun. The tests merely showed that he had nitrate traces on his hands, which did not necessarily mean that he had fired either a rifle or a pistol.

The disclosure of evidence was seriously aggravated by the statements of numerous responsible officials that they were certain of Oswald's guilt. Captain Fritz said that the case against Oswald was "cinched." Curry reported on Saturday that "we are sure of our case." Curry announced that he considered Oswald sane, and Wade told the public that he would ask for the death penalty.

The American Bar Association declared in December 1963 that "widespread publicizing of Oswald's alleged guilt, involving statements by officials and public disclosures of the details of 'evidence', would have made it extremely difficult to impanel an unprejudiced jury and afford the accused a fair trial." Local bar associations expressed similar feelings. The Commission agrees that Lee Harvey Oswald's opportunity for a trial by 12 jurors free of preconception as to his guilt or innocence would have been seriously jeopardized by the premature disclosure and weighing of the evidence against him. The problem of disclosure of information and its effect on trials is, of course, further complicated by the independent activities of the press in developing information on its own from sources other than law enforcement agencies. Had the police not released the specific items of evidence against Oswald, it is still possible that the other information presented on television and in the newspapers, chiefly of a biographical nature, would itself have had a prejudicial effect on the public. In explanation of the news policy adopted by the Dallas authorities, Chief Curry observed that "it seemed like there was a great demand by the general public to know what was going on." In a prepared statement, Captain King wrote:

> At that time we felt a necessity for permitting the newsmen as much latitude as possible. We realized the magnitude of the incident the newsmen were there to cover. We realized that not only the nation but the world would be greatly interested in what occurred in Dallas. We believed that we had an obligation to make as widely known as possible everything we could regarding the investigation of the assassination and the manner in which we undertook that investigation.

The Commission recognizes that the people of the United States, and indeed the world, had a deep-felt interest in learning of the events surrounding the death of President Kennedy, including the development of the investigation in Dallas. An informed public provided the ultimate guarantee that adequate steps would be taken to apprehend those responsible for the assassination and that all necessary precautions would be taken to protect the national security. It was therefore proper and desirable that the public know which agencies were participating in the investigation and the rate at which their work was progressing. The public was also entitled to know that Lee Harvey Oswald had been apprehended and that the State had gathered sufficient evidence to arraign him for the murders of the president and Patrolman Tippit, that he was being held pending action of the grand jury, that the investigation was continuing, and that the law enforcement agencies had discovered no evidence which tended to show that any other person was involved in either slaying. However, neither the press nor the public had a right to be contemporaneously informed by the police or prosecuting authorities of the details of the evidence being accumulated against Oswald. Undoubtedly the public was interested in these disclosures, but its curiosity should not have been satisfied at the expense of the accused's right to a trial by an impartial jury. The courtroom, not the newspaper or television screen, is the appropriate forum in our system for the trial of a man accused of a crime. If the evidence in the possession of the authorities had not been disclosed, it is true that the public would not have been in a position to assess the adequacy of the investigation or to apply pressures for further official undertakings. But a major consequence of the hasty and at times inaccurate divulgence of evidence after the assassination was simply to give rise to groundless rumors and public confusion. Moreover, without learning the details of the case, the public could have been informed by the responsible authority of the general scope of the investigation and the extent to which State and Federal agencies were assisting in the police work.

RESPONSIBILITY OF NEWS MEDIA

While appreciating the heavy and unique pressures with which the Dallas Police Department was confronted by reason of the assassination of President Kennedy, primary responsibility for having failed to control the press and to check the flow of undigested evidence to the public must be borne by the police department. It was the only agency that could have established orderly and sound operating procedures to control the multitude of newsmen gathered in the police building after the assassination. The Commission believes, however, that a part of the responsibility for the unfortunate circumstances following the president's death must be borne by the news media. The crowd of newsmen generally failed to respond properly to the demands of the police. Frequently without permission, news representatives used police offices on the third floor, tying up facilities and interfering with normal police operations. Police efforts to preserve order and to clear passageways in the corridor were usually unsuccessful. On Friday night the reporters completely ignored Curry's injunction against asking Oswald questions in the assembly room and crowding in on him. On Sunday morning, the newsmen were instructed to direct no questions at Oswald; nevertheless, several reporters shouted questions at him when he appeared in the basement.

Moreover, by constantly pursuing public officials, the news representatives placed an insistent pressure upon them to disclose information. And this pressure was not without effect, since the police attitude toward the press was affected by the desire to maintain satisfactory relations with the news representatives and to create a favorable image of themselves.

Chief Curry frankly told the Commission that:

> I didn't order them out of the building, which if I had it to do over I would. In the past like I say, we had always maintained very good relations with our press, and they had always respected us...

Curry refused Fritz' request to put Oswald behind the screen in the assembly room at the Friday night press conference because this might have hindered the taking of pictures. Curry's subordinates had the impression that an unannounced transfer of Oswald to the county jail was unacceptable because Curry did not want to disappoint the newsmen; he had promised that they could witness the transfer. It seemed clear enough that any attempt to exclude the press from the building or to place limits on the information disclosed to them would have been resented and disputed by the newsmen, who were constantly and aggressively demanding all possible information about anything related to the assassination. Although the

Commission has found no corroboration in the video and audio tapes, police officials recall that one or two representatives of the press reinforced their demands to see Oswald by suggesting that the police had been guilty of brutalizing him. They intimated that unless they were given the opportunity to see him, these suggestions would be passed on to the public. Captain King testified that he had been told that:

> A short time after Oswald's arrest one newsman held up a photograph and said, "This is what the man charged with the assassination of the president looks like. Or at least this is what he did look like. We don't know what he looks like after an hour in the custody of the Dallas Police Department."

City Manager Elgin Crull stated that when he visited Chief Curry in his office on the morning of November 23, Curry told him that he "felt it was necessary to cooperate with the news media representatives, in order to avoid being accused of using Gestapo tactics in connection with the handling of Oswald." Crull agreed with Curry. The Commission deems any such veiled threats to be absolutely without justification.

The general disorder in the Police and Courts Building during November 22–24 reveals a regrettable lack of self-discipline by the newsmen. The Commission believes that the news media, as well as the police authorities, who failed to impose conditions more in keeping with the orderly process of justice, must share responsibility for the failure of law enforcement which occurred in connection with the death of Oswald. On previous occasions, public bodies have voiced the need for the exercise of self-restraint by the news media in periods when the demand for information must be tempered by other fundamental requirements of our society. At its annual meeting in Washington in April 1964, the American Society of Newspaper Editors discussed the role of the press in Dallas immediately after President Kennedy's assassination. The discussion revealed the strong misgivings among the editors themselves about the role that the press had played and their desire that the press display more self-discipline and adhere to higher standards of conduct in the future. To prevent a recurrence of the unfortunate events which followed the assassination, however, more than general concern will be needed. The promulgation of a code of professional conduct governing representatives of all news media would be welcome evidence that the press had profited by the lesson of Dallas. The burden of insuring that appropriate action is taken to establish ethical standards of conduct for the news media must also be borne, however, by state and local governments, by the bar, and ultimately by the public. The experience in Dallas during November 22–24 is a dramatic affirmation of the need for steps to bring about a proper balance between the right of the public to be kept informed and the right of the individual to a fair and impartial trial.

INVESTIGATION OF POSSIBLE CONSPIRACY

This chapter sets forth the findings of the Commission as to whether Lee Harvey Oswald had any accomplices in the planning or execution of the assassination. Particularly after the slaying of Oswald by Jack Ruby under the circumstances described in the preceding chapter, rumors and suspicions developed regarding the existence of a conspiracy to assassinate President Kennedy. Many of these rumors were based on a lack of information as to the nature and extent of evidence that Oswald alone fired the shots which killed President Kennedy and wounded Governor Connally. Others of the more widely publicized rumors maintained that Oswald must have received aid from one or more persons or political groups, ranging from the far left to the far right of the political spectrum, or from a foreign government, usually either the Castro regime in Cuba or the Soviet Union.

The Commission faced substantial difficulties in determining whether anyone conspired with or assisted the person who committed the assassination. Prior to his own death Oswald had neither admitted his own involvement nor implicated any other persons in the assassination of the president. The problem of determining the existence or non-existence of a conspiracy was compounded because of the possibility of subversive activity by a foreign power. Witnesses and evidence located in other countries were not subject to subpoena, as they would have been if they had been located in the United States. When evidence was obtained from a foreign nation, it could not be appraised as effectively as if it had been derived from a domestic source. The Commission has given the closest scrutiny to all available evidence which related or might have related to a foreign country. All such evidence was tested, whenever possible, against the contingency that it had been fabricated or slanted to mislead or confuse.

In order to meet its obligations fully, the Commission has investigated each rumor and allegation linking Oswald to a conspiracy which has come to its attention, regardless of source. In addition, the Commission has explored the details of Lee Harvey Oswald's activities and life, especially in the months immediately preceding the assassination, in order to develop any investigative lead relevant to the issue of conspiracy. All of Oswald's known writings or other possessions which might have been used for code or other espionage purposes have been examined by either the Federal Bureau of Investigation or the National Security Agency, or both agencies, to determine whether they were so used.

In setting forth the results of this investigation, the first section of this chapter reviews the facts related to the assas-

sination itself, previously considered in more detail on pp.
63–101. If any conspiracy did exist, it might have mani-
fested itself at some point during Oswald's preparation for
the shooting, his execution of the plan, or his escape from
the scene of the assassination. The Commission has therefore studied the precise means by which the assassination
occurred for traces of evidence that Oswald received any
form of assistance in effecting the killing.

The second section of the chapter deals more
broadly with Oswald's life since 1959. During the
period following his discharge from the Marines in
1959, Oswald engaged in several activities which
demand close scrutiny to determine whether, through
these pursuits, he developed any associations which were
connected with the planning or execution of the assassination. Oswald professed commitment to Marxist
ideology; he defected to the Soviet Union in 1959; he
attempted to expatriate himself and acquire Soviet citizenship; and he resided in the Soviet Union until June
of 1962. After his return to the United States he sought
to maintain contacts with the Communist Party, Socialist
Workers Party, and the Fair Play for Cuba Committee;
he associated with various Russian-speaking citizens in
the Dallas-Fort Worth area – some of whom had resided
in Russia; he traveled to Mexico City where he visited
both the Cuban and Soviet Embassies seven weeks
before the assassination; and he corresponded with the
Soviet Embassy in Washington, DC. In view of these
activities, the Commission has instituted a thorough
investigation to determine whether the assassination was
in some manner directed or encouraged through contacts made abroad or through Oswald's politically
oriented activities in this country. The Commission has
also considered whether any connections existed
between Oswald and certain right-wing activity in

Dallas which, shortly before the assassination, led to the publication of hostile criticism of President Kennedy.

The final section of this chapter considers the possibility that Jack Ruby was part of a conspiracy to assassinate President Kennedy. The Commission explored Ruby's background and his activities in the months prior to the assassination, and especially his activities in the two days after the assassination, in an effort to determine whether there was any indication that Ruby was implicated in that event. The Commission also sought to ascertain the truth or falsity of assertions that Oswald and Ruby were known to one another prior to the assassination. In considering the question of foreign involvement, the Commission has received valuable assistance from the Department of State, the Central Intelligence Agency, the Federal Bureau of Investigation, and other Federal agencies with special competence in the field of foreign investigation. Some of the information furnished by these agencies is of a highly confidential nature. Nevertheless, because the disclosure of all facts relating to the assassination of President Kennedy is of great public importance, the Commission has included in this report all information furnished by these agencies which the Commission relied upon in coming to its conclusions, or which tended to contradict those conclusions. Confidential sources of information, as contrasted with the information itself, have, in a relatively few instances, been withheld.

CIRCUMSTANCES SURROUNDING THE ASSASSINATION

Earlier chapters have set forth the evidence upon which the Commission concluded that President Kennedy was fired upon from a single window in the southeast corner of the sixth floor of the Texas School Book Depository, and that

Lee Harvey Oswald was the person who fired the shots from this point. As reflected in those chapters, a certain sequence of events necessarily took place in order for the assassination to have occurred as it did. The motorcade traveled past the Texas School Book Depository; Oswald had access to the sixth floor of the building; Oswald brought the rifle into the building; the cartons were arranged at the sixth-floor window; and Oswald escaped from the building before the police had sealed off the exits. Accordingly, the Commission has investigated these circumstances to determine whether Oswald received help from any other person in planning or performing the shooting.

Selection of motorcade route

The factors involved in the choice of the motorcade route by the Secret Service have been discussed on pp. 68–72. It was there indicated that after passing through a portion of suburban Dallas, the motorcade was to travel west on Main Street, and then to the Trade Mart by way of the Stemmons Freeway, the most direct route from that point. This route would take the motorcade along the traditional parade route through downtown Dallas; it allowed the maximum number of persons to observe the president; and it enabled the motorcade to cover the distance from Love Field to the Trade Mart in the 45 minutes allocated by members of the White House staff planning the president's schedule in Dallas. No member of the Secret Service, the Dallas Police Department, or the local host committee who was consulted felt that any other route would be preferable.

To reach Stemmons Freeway from Main Street, it was determined that the motorcade would turn right from Main Street onto Houston Street for one block and then left onto Elm Street, proceeding through the Triple Underpass to the Stemmons Freeway access road. This route took the motorcade past the Texas School Book

Depository Building on the northwest corner of Elm and Houston streets. Because of the sharp turn at this corner, the motorcade also reduced its speed. The motorcade would have passed approximately 90 yards further from the Depository Building and made no turn near the building if it had attempted to reach the Stemmons Freeway directly from Main Street. The road plan in Dealey Plaza, however, is designed to prevent such a turn. In order to keep motorists from reaching the freeway from Main Street, a concrete barrier has been erected between Main and Elm streets extending beyond the freeway entrance. Hence, it would have been necessary for the motorcade either to have driven over this barrier or to have made a sharp S-turn in order to have entered the freeway from Main Street. Selection of the motorcade route was thus entirely appropriate and based on such legitimate considerations as the origin and destination of the motorcade, the desired opportunity for the president to greet large numbers of people, and normal patterns of traffic.

Oswald's presence in the Depository Building

Oswald's presence as an employee in the Texas School Book Depository Building was the result of a series of happenings unrelated to the president's trip to Dallas. He obtained the Depository job after almost two weeks of job hunting which began immediately upon his arrival in Dallas from Mexico on October 8, 1963. At that time he was in poor financial circumstances, having arrived from Mexico City with approximately $133 or less, and with his unemployment compensation benefits due to expire on October 8. Oswald and his wife were expecting the birth of their second child, who was in fact born on October 20. In attempting to procure work, Oswald utilized normal channels, including the Texas Employment Commission.

On October 4, 1963, Oswald applied for a position with Padgett Printing Corp., which was located at 1313 Industrial Boulevard, several blocks from President Kennedy's parade route. Oswald favorably impressed the plant superintendent who checked his prior job references, one of which was Jaggars-Chiles-Stovall, the firm where Oswald had done photography work from October 1962 to April 1963. The following report was written by Padgett's plant superintendent on the reverse side of Oswald's job application: "Bob Stovall does not recommend this man. He was released because of his record as a troublemaker. Has Communistic tendencies." Oswald received word that Padgett Printing had hired someone else.

Oswald's employment with the Texas School Book Depository came about through a chance conversation on Monday, October 14, between Ruth Paine, with whom his family was staying while Oswald was living in a rooming house in Dallas, and two of Mrs Paine's neighbors. During a morning conversation over coffee, at which Marina Oswald was present, Oswald's search for employment was mentioned. The neighbors suggested several places where Oswald might apply for work. One of the neighbors present, Linnie Mac Randle, said that her brother had recently been hired as a schoolbook order filler at the Texas School Book Depository and she thought the Depository might need additional help. She testified, "and of course you know just being neighborly and everything, we felt sorry for Marina because her baby was due right away as we understood it, and he didn't have any work..."

When Marina Oswald and Mrs Paine returned home, Mrs Paine promptly telephoned the Texas School Book Depository and spoke to Superintendent Roy Truly, whom she did not know. Truly agreed to interview Oswald, who at the time was in Dallas seeking employment. When Oswald called that evening, Mrs Paine told him of her conversation with Truly. The next morning Oswald went to the Texas School Book Depository where he was interviewed and hired for the position of order filler.

On the same date, the Texas Employment Commission attempted to refer Oswald to an airline company which was looking for baggage and cargo handlers at a salary which was $100 per month higher than that offered by the Depository Co. The Employment Commission tried to advise Oswald of this job at 10.30 am on October 16, 1963. Since the records of the Commission indicate that Oswald was then working, it seems clear that Oswald was hired by the Depository Co. before the higher paying job was available. It is unlikely that he ever learned of this second opportunity.

Although publicity concerning the president's trip to Dallas appeared in Dallas newspapers as early as September 13, 1963, the planning of the motorcade route was not started until after November 4, when the Secret Service was first notified of the trip. A final decision as to the route could not have been reached until November 14, when the Trade Mart was selected as the luncheon site. Although news reports on November 15 and November 16 might have led a person to believe that the motorcade would pass the Depository Building, the route was not finally selected until November 18; it was announced in the press on November 19, only three days before the president's arrival. Based on the circumstances of Oswald's employment and the planning of the motorcade route, the Commission has concluded that Oswald's employment in the Depository was wholly unrelated to the president's trip to Dallas.

Bringing rifle into building

On the basis of the evidence developed on pp. 175–187, the Commission concluded that Lee Harvey Oswald carried the rifle used in the assassination into the Depository

Building on Friday, November 22, 1963, in the handmade brown paper bag found near the window from which the shots were fired. The arrangement by which Buell Wesley Frazier drove Oswald between Irving and Dallas was an innocent one, having commenced when Oswald first started working at the Depository. As noted above, it was Frazier's sister, Linnie Mac Randle, who had suggested to Ruth Paine that Oswald might be able to find employment at the Depository. When Oswald started working there, Frazier, who lived only a half block away from the Paines, offered to drive Oswald to and from Irving whenever he was going to stay at the Paines' home. Although Oswald's request for a ride to Irving on Thursday, November 21, was a departure from the normal weekend pattern, Oswald gave the explanation that he needed to obtain curtain rods for an "apartment" in Dallas.

This served also to explain the long package which he took with him from Irving to the Depository Building the next morning. Further, there is no evidence that Ruth Paine or Marina Oswald had reason to believe that Oswald's return was in any way related to an attempt to shoot the president the next day. Although his visit was a surprise, since he arrived on Thursday instead of Friday for his usual weekend visit, both women testified that they thought he had come to patch up a quarrel which he had with his wife a few days earlier when she learned that he was living in Dallas under an assumed name.

It has also been shown that Oswald had the opportunity to work in the Paines' garage on Thursday evening and prepare the rifle by disassembling it, if it were not already disassembled, and packing it in the brown bag. It has been demonstrated that the paper and tape from which the bag was made came from the shipping room of the Texas School Book Depository and that Oswald had access to this material. Neither Ruth Paine nor Marina Oswald saw the paper bag or the paper and tape out of which the bag was constructed. Oswald actually prepared the bag in the Depository out of materials available to him there, he could have concealed it in the jacket or shirt which he was wearing. The Commission has found no evidence which suggests that Oswald required or in fact received any assistance in bringing the rifle into the building other than the innocent assistance provided by Frazier in the form of the ride to work.

Accomplices at the scene of the assassination

The arrangement of boxes at the window from which the shots were fired was studied to determine whether Oswald required any assistance in moving the cartons to the window. Cartons had been stacked on the floor, a few feet behind the window, thus shielding Oswald from the view of anyone on the sixth floor who did not attempt to go behind them. Most of those cartons had been moved there by other employees to clear an area for laying a new flooring on the west end of the sixth floor. Superintendent Roy Truly testified that the floor-laying crew moved a long row of books parallel to the windows on the south side and had "quite a lot of cartons" in the southeast corner of the building. He said that there was not any particular pattern that the men used in putting them there. "They were just piled up there more or less at that time." According to Truly, "several cartons" which had been in the extreme southeast corner had been placed on top of the ones that had been piled in front of the southeast corner window.

The arrangement of the three boxes in the window and the one on which the assassin may have sat has been described previously. Two of these four boxes, weighing approximately 55 pounds each, had been moved by the floor-laying crew from the west side of the floor to thearea near the southwest corner. The carton on which the assassin may have sat might not even have been moved by the assassin at all. A photograph of the scene depicts this carton on the floor alongside other similar cartons. Oswald's right palmprint on this carton may have been placed there as he was sitting on the carton rather than while carrying it. In any event both of these 55-pound cartons could have been carried by one man. The remaining two cartons contained light block-like reading aids called "Rolling Readers" weighing only about 8 pounds each. Although they had been moved approximately 40 feet from their normal locations at the southeast corner window, it would appear that one man could have done this in a matter of seconds.

In considering the possibility of accomplices at the window, the Commission evaluated the significance of the presence of fingerprints other than Oswald's on the four cartons found in and near the window. Three of Oswald's prints were developed on two of the cartons. In addition a total of 25 identifiable prints were found on the four cartons. Moreover, prints were developed which were considered as not identifiable, i.e. the quality of the print was too fragmentary to be of value for identification purposes.

As has been explained on pp. 188–190, the Commission determined that none of the warehouse employees who might have customarily handled these cartons left prints which could be identified. This was considered of some probative value in determining whether Oswald moved the cartons to the window. All but one of the 25 definitely identifiable prints were the prints of two persons – an FBI employee and a member of the Dallas Police Department who had handled the cartons during the course of the investigation. One identifiable palmprint was not identified.

The presence on these cartons of unidentified prints, whether or not identifiable, does not appear to be unusual since these cartons contained commercial products which had been handled by many people throughout the normal course of manufacturing, warehousing, and shipping. Unlike other items of evidence such as, for example, a ransom note in a kidnapping, these cartons could contain the prints of many people having nothing to do with the assassination. Moreover, the FBI does not maintain a filing system for palmprints because, according to the supervisor of the Bureau's latent fingerprint section, Sebastian F. Latona, the problems of classification make such a system impracticable. Finally, in considering the significance of the unidentified prints, the Commission gave weight to the opinion of Latona to the effect that people could handle these cartons without leaving prints which were capable of being developed.

Though the fingerprints other than Oswald's on the boxes thus provide no indication of the presence of an accomplice at the window, two Depository employees are known to have been present briefly on the sixth floor during the period between 11.45 am, when the floor-laying crew stopped for lunch, and the moment of the assassination. One of these was Charles Givens, a member of the floor-laying crew, who went down on the elevator with the others and then returned to the sixth floor to get his jacket and cigarettes. He saw Oswald walking away from the southeast corner, but saw no one else on the sixth floor at that time. He then took one of the elevators back to the first floor at approximately 11.55 am.

Bonnie Ray Williams, who was also working with the floor-laying crew, returned to the sixth floor at about noon to eat his lunch and watch the motorcade. He looked out on Elm Street from a position in the area of the third or fourth set of windows from the east wall. At this point he was approximately 20–30 feet away from the southeast corner window. He remained for about "5, 10, maybe 12 minutes" eating his lunch which consisted of chicken and a bottle of soda pop. Williams saw no one on the sixth floor during this period, although the stacks of books prevented his seeing the east side of the building. After finishing his lunch Williams took the elevator down because no one had joined him on the sixth floor to watch the motorcade. He stopped at the fifth floor where he joined Harold Norman and James Jarman, Jr, who watched the motorcade with him from a position on the fifth floor directly below the point from which the shots were fired. Williams left the remains of his lunch, including chicken bones and a bottle of soda, near the window where he was eating.

Several witnesses outside the building claim to have seen a person in the southeast corner window of the sixth floor. As has already been indicated, some were able to offer better descriptions than others and one, Howard L. Brennan, made a positive identification of Oswald as being the person at the window. Although there are differences among these witnesses with regard to their ability to describe the person they saw, none of these witnesses testified to seeing more than one person in the window.

One witness, however, offered testimony which, if accurate, would create the possibility of an accomplice at the window at the time of the assassination. The witness was 18-year-old Arnold Rowland, who testified in great detail concerning his activities and observations on November 22, 1963. He and his wife were awaiting the motorcade, standing on the east side of Houston Street between Maine and Elm, when he looked toward the Depository Building and noticed a man holding a rifle standing back from the southwest corner window on the sixth floor. The man was rather slender in proportion to his size and of light complexion with dark hair. Rowland said that his wife was looking elsewhere at the time and when they looked back to the window the man "was gone from our vision". They thought the man was most likely someone protecting the president. After the assassination Rowland signed an affidavit in which he told of seeing this man, although Rowland was unable to identify him.

When Rowland testified before the Commission on March 10, 1964, he claimed for the first time to have seen another person on the sixth floor. Rowland said that before he had noticed the man with the rifle on the southwest corner of the sixth floor he had seen an elderly Negro man "hanging out that window" on the southeast corner of the sixth floor. Rowland described the Negro man as "very thin, an elderly gentleman, bald or practically bald, very thin hair if he wasn't bald," between 50 and 60 years of age, 5 feet 8 inches to 5 feet 10 inches tall, with fairly dark complexion. Rowland claimed that he looked back two or three times and noticed that the man remained until 5 or 6 minutes prior to the time the motorcade came. Rowland did not see him thereafter. He made no mention of the Negro man in his affidavit. And, while he said he told FBI agents about the man in the southeast corner window when interviewed on the Saturday and Sunday following the assassination, no such statement appears in any FBI report.

Mrs Rowland testified that her husband never told her about seeing any other man on the sixth floor except the man with the rifle in the southwest corner that he first saw. She also was present during Rowland's interview with representatives of the FBI and said she did not hear him make such a statement, although she also said that she did not hear everything that was discussed. Mrs Rowland testified that after her husband first talked about seeing a man with the rifle, she looked back more than once at the Depository Building and saw no person looking out of any window on the sixth floor. She also said that "At times my husband is prone to exaggerate." Because of inconsistencies in Rowland's testimony and the importance of his testimony to the question of a possible accomplice, the Commission requested the FBI to conduct an inquiry into the truth of a broad range of statements made by Rowland to the Commission.

The investigation showed that numerous statements by Rowland concerning matters about which he would not normally be expected to be mistaken – such as subjects he studied in school, grades he received, whether or not he had graduated from high school, and whether or not he had been admitted to college – were false.

The only possible corroboration for Rowland's story is found in the testimony of Roger D. Craig, a deputy sheriff of Dallas County, whose testimony on other aspects of the case has been discussed on p. 213. Craig claimed that about 10 minutes after the assassination he talked to a young couple, Mr and Mrs Rowland:

> ... and the boy said he saw two men on the sixth floor of the Book Depository Building over there; one of them had a rifle with a telescopic sight on it – but he thought they were Secret Service agents or guards and didn't report it. This was about – oh, he said, 15 minutes before the motor-cade ever arrived.

According to Craig, Rowland said that he looked back a few minutes later and "the other man was gone, and there was just one man – the man with the rifle." Craig further testified that Rowland told him that when he first saw the two men, they were walking back and forth in front of the window for several minutes. They were both white men and one of them had a rifle with a scope on it. This report by Craig is contradicted by the testimony of both the Rowlands, and by every recorded interview with them conducted by law enforcement agencies after the assassination.

As part of its investigation of Rowland's allegation and of the general question of accomplices at the scene of the assassination, the Commission undertook an investigation of every person employed in the Texas School Book Depository Building. Two employees might possibly fit the general description of an elderly Negro man, bald or balding. These two men were on the first floor of the building during the period before and during the assassination. Moreover, all of the employees were asked whether they saw any strangers in the building on the morning of November 22. Only one employee saw a stranger whom he described as a feeble individual who had to be helped up the front steps of the building. He went to a public restroom and left the building 5 minutes later, about 40 minutes before the assassination.

Rowland's failure to report his story despite several interviews until his appearance before the Commission, the lack of probative corroboration, and the serious doubts about his credibility, have led the Commission to reject the testimony that Rowland saw an elderly balding Negro man in the southeast corner window of the sixth floor of the Depository Building several minutes before the assassination.

Oswald's escape

The Commission has analyzed Oswald's movements between the time of the assassination and the shooting of Patrolman Tippit to determine whether there is any evidence that Oswald had assistance in his flight from the building. Oswald's activities during this period have been traced through the testimony of seven witnesses and discussed in detail on pp. 191–218. Patrolman M. L. Baker and Depository superintendent Roy Truly saw him within 2 minutes of the assassination on the second floor of the building. Mrs R. A. Reid saw him less than 1 minute later walking through the second-floor offices toward the front of the building. A bus driver, Cecil J. McWatters, and Oswald's former landlady, Mrs Mary Bledsoe, saw him board a bus at approximately 12.40 pm, and get off about 4 minutes later. A cabdriver, William W. Whaley, drove Oswald from a cab stand located a few blocks from where Oswald left the bus to a point in Oak Cliff about four blocks from his rooming house; and Earlene Roberts, the housekeeper at Oswald's rooming house, saw him enter the rooming house at about 1 pm and leave a few minutes later. When seen by these seven witnesses Oswald was always alone.

Particular attention has been directed to Oswald's departure from the Depository Building in order to determine whether he could have left the building within approximately 3 minutes of the assassination without assistance. As discussed more fully on pp. 206–207, the building was probably first sealed off no earlier than 12.37 by Inspector Herbert Sawyer. The shortest estimate of the time taken to seal off the building comes from Police Officer W. E. Barnett, one of the officers assigned to the corner of Elm and Houston streets for the presidential motorcade, who estimated that approximately 3 minutes elapsed between the time he heard the last of the shots and the time he started guarding the front door. According to Barnett, "there were people going in and out" during this period. The evidence discussed on pp. 201–204 shows that 3 minutes would have been sufficient time for Oswald to have descended from the sixth floor and left the building without assistance.

One witness, James R. Worrell, Jr, claims to have seen a man running from the rear of the building shortly after the assassination, but in testimony before the Commission he stated that he could not see his face. Two other witnesses who watched the rear of the building during the first 5 minutes after the shooting saw no one leave. The claim of

Deputy Sheriff Roger Craig that he saw Oswald leave the Depository Building approximately 15 minutes after the assassination has been discussed on p. 213. Although Craig may have seen someone enter a station wagon 15 minutes after the assassination, the person he saw was not Lee Harvey Oswald, who was far removed from the building at that time.

The possibility that accomplices aided Oswald in connection with his escape was suggested by the testimony of Earlene Roberts, the housekeeper at the 1026 North Beckley rooming house. She testified that at about 1 pm on November 22, after Oswald had returned to the rooming house, a Dallas police car drove slowly by the front of the 1026 North Beckley premises and stopped momentarily; she said she heard its horn several times. Mrs Roberts stated that the occupants of the car were not known to her even though she had worked for some policemen who would occasionally come by. She said the policeman she knew drove car No. 170 and that this was not the number on the police car that honked on November 22. She testified that she first thought the car she saw was No. 106 and then said that it was No. 107. In an FBI interview she had stated that she looked out the front window and saw police car No. 207. Investigation has not produced any evidence that there was a police vehicle in the area of 1026 North Beckley at about 1 pm on November 22. Squad car 207 was at the Texas School Book Depository Building, as was car 106. Squad cars 170 and 107 were sold in April 1963 and their numbers were not reassigned until February 1964.

Whatever may be the accuracy of Mrs Roberts' recollection concerning the police car, it is apparent from Mrs Roberts' further testimony that she did not see Oswald enter a car when he hurriedly left the house. She has stated that when she last saw Oswald, shortly after 1 pm, he was standing at a bus stop in front of the house. Oswald was next seen less than one mile away, at the point where he shot Patrolman Tippit. Oswald could have easily reached this point on foot by about 1.16 pm, when Tippit was shot. Finally, investigation has produced no evidence that Oswald had prearranged plans for a means to leave Dallas after the assassination or that any other person was to have provided him assistance in hiding or in departing the city.

POSSIBLE CONSPIRACY INVOLVING JACK RUBY

Jack Ruby shot Lee Harvey Oswald at 11.21 am, on Sunday, November 24, 1963, shortly after Ruby entered the basement of the Dallas Police Department. Almost immediately, speculation arose that Ruby had acted on behalf of members of a conspiracy who had planned the killing of President Kennedy and wanted to silence Oswald. This section sets forth the Commission's investigation into the possibility that Ruby, together with Oswald or with others, conspired to kill the president, or that Ruby, though not part of any such conspiracy, had accomplices in the slaying of Oswald. Presented first are the results of the Commission's detailed inquiry into Ruby's actions from November 21 to November 24. In addition, this section analyzes the numerous rumors and suspicions that Ruby and Oswald were acquainted and examines Ruby's background and associations for evidence of any conspiratorial relationship or motive.

Ruby's activities from November 21 to November 24, 1963
The Commission has attempted to reconstruct as precisely as possible the movements of Jack Ruby during the period November 21–November 24, 1963. It has done so on the premise that, if Jack Ruby were involved in a conspiracy, his

activities and associations during this period would, in some way, have reflected the conspiratorial relationship. The Commission has not attempted to determine the time at which Ruby first decided to make his attack on Lee Harvey Oswald, nor does it purport to evaluate the psychiatric and related legal questions which have arisen from the assault upon Oswald. Ruby's activities during this three-day period have been scrutinized, however, for the insight they provide into whether the shooting of Oswald was grounded in any form of conspiracy.

The eve of the president's visit
On Thursday, November 21, Jack Ruby was attending to his usual duties as the proprietor of two Dallas night spots – the Carousel Club, a downtown nightclub featuring striptease dancers, and the Vegas Club, a rock-and-roll establishment in the Oaklawn section of Dallas. Both clubs opened for business each day in the early evening and continued seven days a week until after midnight. Ruby arrived at the Carousel Club at about 3 pm Thursday afternoon, as was his custom, and remained long enough to chat with a friend and receive messages from Larry Crafard, a handyman and helper who lived at the Carousel. Earlier in the day Ruby had visited with a young lady who was job hunting in Dallas, paid his rent for the Carousel premises, conferred about a peace bond he had been obliged to post as a result of a fight with one of his striptease dancers, consulted with an attorney about problems he was having with Federal tax authorities, distributed membership cards for the Carousel Club, talked with Dallas County Assistant District Attorney William F. Alexander about insufficient fund checks which a friend had passed, and submitted advertising copy for his nightclubs to the Dallas *Morning News*.

Ruby's evening activities on Thursday, November 21, were a combination of business and pleasure. At approximately 7.30 pm, he drove Larry Crafard to the Vegas Club which Crafard was overseeing because Ruby's sister, Eva Grant, who normally managed the club, was convalescing from a recent illness. Thereafter, Ruby returned to the Carousel Club and conversed for about an hour with Lawrence Meyers, a Chicago businessman. Between 9.45 and 10.45 pm, Ruby had dinner with Ralph Paul, his close friend and financial backer. While dining Ruby spoke briefly with a Dallas *Morning News* employee, Don Campbell, who suggested that they go to the Castaway Club, but Ruby declined. Thereafter, Ruby returned to the Carousel Club where he acted as master of ceremonies for his show and peacefully ejected an unruly patron. At about midnight Ruby rejoined Meyers at the Bon Vivant Room of the Dallas Cabana where they met Meyers' brother and sister-in-law. Neither Ralph Paul nor Lawrence Meyers recalled that Ruby mentioned the president's trip to Dallas. Leaving Meyers at the Cabana after a brief visit, Ruby returned to close the Carousel Club and obtain the night's receipts. He then went to the Vegas Club which he helped Larry Crafard close for the night; and, as late as 2.30 am, Ruby was seen eating at a restaurant near the Vegas Club.

Friday morning at the Dallas Morning News
Jack Ruby learned of the shooting of President Kennedy while in the second-floor advertising offices of the Dallas *Morning News*, five blocks from the Texas School Book Depository, where he had come Friday morning to place regular weekend advertisements for his two nightclubs. On arriving at the newspaper building at about 11 or 11.30 am, he talked briefly with two newspaper employees concerning some diet pills he had recommended to them. Ruby then went to the office of *Morning News* columnist, Tony Zoppi, where he states he obtained a brochure on his new master of ceremonies that he wanted to use in preparing

copy for his advertisements. Proceeding to the advertising department, he spoke with advertising employee Don Campbell from about noon until 12.25 pm when Campbell left the office. In addition to the business at hand, much of the conversation concerned Ruby's unhappiness over the financial condition of his clubs and his professed ability to handle the physical fights which arose in connection with the clubs. According to Campbell, Ruby did not mention the presidential motorcade nor did he display any unusual behavior.

About 10 minutes after the president had been shot but before word had spread to the second floor, John Newnam, an advertising department employee, observed Ruby sitting at the same spot where Campbell had left him. At that time Ruby had completed the advertisement, which he had apparently begun to compose when Campbell departed, and was reading a newspaper. To Newnam, Ruby voiced criticism of the black-bordered advertisement entitled "Welcome, Mr Kennedy" appearing in the morning paper and bearing the name of Bernard Weissman as the chairman of the committee sponsoring the advertisement. According to Eva Grant, Ruby's sister, he had telephoned her earlier in the morning to call her attention to the ad. At about 12.45 pm, an employee entered the office and announced that shots had been fired at the president. Newham remembered that Ruby responded with a look of "stunned disbelief".

Shortly afterward, according to Newnam, "confusion reigned" in the office as advertisers telephoned to cancel advertising they had placed for the weekend. Ruby appears to have believed that some of those cancellations were motivated by the Weissman advertisement. After Newnam accepted a few telephone calls, he and Ruby walked toward a room where other persons were watching television. One of the newspaper employees recalled that Ruby then appeared "obviously shaken, and an ashen color – just very pale. . .", showed little disposition to converse, and sat for a while with a dazed expression in his eyes.

After a few minutes, Ruby placed telephone calls to Andrew Armstrong, his assistant at the Carousel Club, and to his sister, Mrs Grant. He told Armstrong, "If anything happens we are going to close the club" and said he would see him in about 30 minutes. During the call to his sister, Ruby again referred to the Weissman advertisement; at one point he put the telephone to Newnam's ear, and Newnam heard Mrs Grant exclaim, "My God, what do they want?" It was Newnam's recollection that Ruby tried to calm her.

Ruby testified that after calling his sister he said, "John, I will have to leave Dallas." Ruby explained to the Commission:

> I don't know why I said that, but it is a funny reaction that
> you feel; the city is terribly let down by the tragedy that
> happened. And I said, "John, I am not opening up
> tonight." And I don't know what else transpired. I know
> people were just heartbroken . . . I left the building and I
> went down and I got in my car and I couldn't stop crying . . .

Newnam estimated that Ruby departed from the *Morning News* at about 1.30 pm, but other testimony indicated that Ruby may have left earlier.

Ruby's alleged visit to Parkland Hospital

The Commission has investigated claims that Jack Ruby was at Parkland Hospital at about 1.30 pm, when a presidential press secretary, Malcolm Kilduff, announced that President Kennedy was dead. Seth Kantor, a newspaperman who had previously met Ruby in Dallas, reported and later testified that Jack Ruby stopped him momentarily inside the main entrance to Parkland Hospital some time between

1.30 and 2 pm, Friday, November 22, 1963. The only other person besides Kantor who recalled seeing Ruby at the hospital did not make known her observation until April 1964, had never seen Ruby before, allegedly saw him only briefly then, had an obstructed view, and was uncertain of the time. Ruby has firmly denied going to Parkland and has stated that he went to the Carousel Club upon leaving the *Morning News*. Video tapes of the scene at Parkland do not show Ruby there, although Kantor can be seen.

Investigation has limited the period during which Kantor could have met Ruby at Parkland Hospital on Friday to a few minutes before and after 1.30 pm. Telephone company records and the testimony of Andrew Armstrong established that Ruby arrived at the Carousel Club no later than 1.45 pm and probably a few minutes earlier. Kantor was engaged in a long-distance telephone call to his Washington office from 1.02 pm until 1.27 pm. Kantor testified that, after completing that call, he immediately left the building from which he had been telephoning, traveled perhaps 100 yards, and entered the main entrance of the hospital. It was there, as he walked through a small doorway, that he believed he saw Jack Ruby, who, Kantor said, tugged at his coat-tails and asked, "Should I close my places for the next three nights, do you think?" Kantor recalled that he turned briefly to Ruby and proceeded to the press conference at which the president's death was announced. Kantor was certain he encountered Ruby at Parkland but had doubts about the exact time and place.

Kantor probably did not see Ruby at Parkland Hospital in the few minutes before or after 1.30 pm, the only time it would have been possible for Kantor to have done so. If Ruby immediately returned to the Carousel Club after Kantor saw him, it would have been necessary for him to have covered the distance from Parkland in approximately 10 or 15 minutes in order to have arrived at the club before

1.45 pm, when a telephone call was placed at Ruby's request to his entertainer, Karen Bennett Carlin. At a normal driving speed under normal conditions the trip can be made in 9 or 10 minutes. However, it is likely that congested traffic conditions on November 22 would have extended the driving time. Even if Ruby had been able to drive from Parkland to the Carousel in 15 minutes, his presence at the Dallas *Morning News* until after 1 pm, and at the Carousel prior to 1.45 pm, would have made his visit at Parkland exceedingly brief. Since Ruby was observed at the Dallas Police Department during a two hour period after 11 pm on Friday, when Kantor was also present, and since Kantor did not remember seeing Ruby there, Kantor may have been mistaken about both the time and the place that he saw Ruby. When seeing Ruby, Kantor was preoccupied with the important event that a press conference represented. Both Ruby and Kantor were present at another important event, a press conference held about midnight, November 22, in the assembly room of the Dallas Police Department. It is conceivable that Kantor's encounter with Ruby occurred at that time, perhaps near the small doorway there.

Ruby's decision to close his clubs
Upon arriving at the Carousel Club shortly before 1.45 pm, Ruby instructed Andrew Armstrong, the Carousel's bartender, to notify employees that the club would be closed that night. During much of the next hour Ruby talked by telephone to several persons who were or had been especially close to him, and the remainder of the time he watched television and spoke with Armstrong and Larry Crafard about the assassination. At 1.51 pm, Ruby telephoned Ralph Paul in Arlington, Texas, to say that he was going to close his clubs. He urged Paul to do likewise with his drive-in restaurant. Unable to reach Alice Nichols, a

former girlfriend, who was at lunch, Ruby telephoned his sister, Eileen Kaminsky, in Chicago. Mrs Kaminsky described her brother as completely unnerved and crying about President Kennedy's death. To Mrs Nichols, whose return call caused Ruby to cut short his conversation with Mrs Kaminsky, Ruby expressed shock over the assassination. Although Mrs Nichols had dated Ruby for nearly 11 years, she was surprised to hear from him on November 22 since they had not seen one another socially for some time. Thereafter, Ruby telephoned at 2.37 pm to Alex Gruber, a boyhood friend from Chicago who was living in Los Angeles. Gruber recalled that in their three-minute conversation Ruby talked about a dog he had promised to send Gruber, a carwash business Gruber had considered starting, and the assassination. Ruby apparently lost his self-control during the conversation and terminated it. However, two minutes after that call ended, Ruby telephoned again to Ralph Paul.

Upon leaving the Carousel Club at about 3.15 pm, Ruby drove to Eva Grant's home but left soon after he arrived, to obtain some weekend food for his sister and himself. He first returned to the Carousel Club and directed Larry Crafard to prepare a sign indicating that the club would be closed; however, Ruby instructed Crafard not to post the sign until later in the evening to avoid informing his competitors that he would be closed. Before leaving the club, Ruby telephoned Mrs Grant who reminded him to purchase food. As a result he went to the Ritz Delicatessen, about two blocks from the Carousel Club, and bought a great quantity of cold cuts.

Ruby probably arrived a second time at his sister's home close to 5.30 pm and remained for about two hours. He continued his rapid rate of telephone calls, ate sparingly, became ill, and attempted to get some rest. While at the apartment, Ruby decided to close his clubs for three days.

He testified that after talking to Don Saffran, a columnist for the Dallas *Times-Herald*:

> I put the receiver down and talked to my sister, and I said "Eva, what shall we do?" And she said, "Jack, let's close for the three days." She said, "We don't have anything anyway, but we owe it to" (chokes up.) So I called Don Saffran back immediately and I said, "Don, we decided to close for Friday, Saturday, and Sunday." And he said, "Okay."

Ruby then telephoned the Dallas *Morning News* to cancel his advertisement and, when unable to do so, he changed his ad to read that his clubs would be closed for the weekend. Ruby also telephoned Cecil Hamlin, a friend of many years. Sounding very "broken up", he told Hamlin that he had closed the clubs since he thought most people would not be in the mood to visit them and that he felt concern for President Kennedy's "kids." Thereafter he made two calls to ascertain when services at Temple Shearith Israel would be held. He placed a second call to Alice Nichols to tell her of his intention to attend those services and phoned Larry Crafard at the Carousel to ask whether he had received any messages. Eva Grant testified:

> When he was leaving, he looked pretty bad. This I remember. I can't explain it to you. He looked too broken, a broken man already. He did make the remark, he said, "I never felt so bad in my life, even when Ma or Pa died." So I said, "Well, Pa was an old man. He was almost 89 years..."

Friday evening
Ruby is uncertain whether he went directly from his sister's home to his apartment or possibly first to his club. At least five witnesses recall seeing a man they believe was Ruby on the third floor of police headquarters at times they have

estimated between 6 and 9 pm; however, it is not clear that Ruby was present at the Police and Courts Building before 11 pm. With respect to three of the witnesses, it is doubtful that the man observed was Ruby. Two of those persons had not known Ruby previously and described him wearing apparel which differed both from Ruby's known dress that night and from his known wardrobe. The third, who viewed from the rear the person he believed was Ruby, said the man unsuccessfully attempted to enter the homicide office. Of the police officers on duty near homicide at the time of the alleged event, only one remembered the episode, and he said the man in question definitely was not Ruby. The remaining witnesses knew or talked with Ruby, and their testimony leaves little doubt that they did see him on the third floor at some point on Friday night; however the possibility remains that they observed Ruby later in the evening, when his presence is conclusively established. Ruby has denied being at the police department Friday night before approximately 11.15 pm.

In any event, Ruby eventually returned to his own apartment before 9 pm. There he telephoned Ralph Paul but was unable to persuade Paul to join him at synagogue services. Shortly after 9 pm, Ruby called the Chicago home of his oldest brother, Hyman Rubenstein, and two of his sisters, Marion Carroll and Ann Volpert. Hyman Rubenstein testified that, during the call, his brother was so disturbed about the situation in Dallas that he mentioned selling his business and returning to Chicago. From his apartment, Ruby drove to Temple Shearith Israel, arriving near the end of a two-hour service which had begun at 8 pm. Rabbi Hillel Silverman, who greeted him among the crowd leaving the services was surprised that Ruby, who appeared depressed, mentioned only his sister's recent illness and said nothing about the assassination.

Ruby related that, after joining in the post-service refreshments, he drove by some night clubs, noticing whether or not they had been closed as his were. He testified that, as he drove toward town, a radio announcement that the Dallas police were working overtime prompted the thought that he might bring those at police headquarters something to eat. At about 10.30 pm, he stopped at a delicatessen near the Vegas Club and purchased eight kosher sandwiches and 10 soft drinks. From the delicatessen, he called the police department but was told that the officers had already eaten. He said he then tried to offer the food to employees at radio station KLIF but failed in several attempts to obtain the private night line number to the station. On three occasions between phone calls, Ruby spoke with a group of students whom he did not know, lamenting the president's death, teasing one of the young men about being too young for his clubs, borrowing their copy of the Dallas *Times-Herald* to see how his advertisements had been run, and stating that his clubs were the only ones that had closed because of the assassination. He also expressed the opinion, as he had earlier in the day, that the assassination would be harmful to the convention business in Dallas. Upon leaving the delicatessen with his purchases, Ruby gave the counterman as a tip a card granting free admission to his clubs. He drove downtown to the police station where he has said he hoped to find an employee from KLIF who could give him the "hot line" phone number for the radio station.

The third floor of police headquarters

Ruby is known to have made his way, by about 11.30 pm, to the third floor of the Dallas Police Department where reporters were congregated near the homicide bureau. Newsman John Rutledge, one of those who may well have been mistaken as to time, gave the following description of his first encounter with Ruby at the police station:

I saw Jack and two out-of-state reporters, whom I did not know, leave the elevator door and proceed toward those television cameras, to go around the corner where Captain Fritz' office was. Jack walked between them. These two out-of-state reporters had big press cards pinned on their coats, great big red ones, I think they said "President Kennedy's Visit to Dallas – Press", or something like that. And Jack didn't have one, but the men on either side of him did. And they walked pretty rapidly from the elevator area past the policeman, and Jack was bent over like this – writing on a piece of paper, and talking to one of the reporters, and pointing to something on the piece of paper, he was kind of hunched over.

Detective Augustus M. Eberhardt, who also recalled that he first saw Ruby earlier in the evening, said Ruby carried a note pad and professed to be a translator for the Israeli press. He remembered Ruby remarking how unfortunate the assassination was for the city of Dallas and that it was "hard to realize that a complete nothing, a zero like that, could kill a man like President Kennedy..."

Video tapes confirm Ruby's statement that he was present on the third floor when Chief Jesse E. Curry and District Attorney Henry M. Wade announced that Oswald would be shown to the newsmen at a press conference in the basement. Though he has said his original purpose was only to locate a KLIF employee, Ruby has stated that while at the police station he was "carried away with the excitement of history." He accompanied the newsmen to the basement to observe Oswald. His presence at the midnight news conference is established by television tapes and by at least 12 witnesses. When Oswald arrived, Ruby, together with a number of newsmen, was standing atop a table on one side of the room. Oswald was taken from the room after a brief appearance, and Ruby remained to hear reporters question District Attorney Wade. During the press conference, Wade stated that Oswald would probably be moved to the county jail at the beginning of the next week. In answer to one question, Wade said that Oswald belonged to the "Free Cuba Committee". A few reporters spoke up correcting Wade and among the voices was that of Jack Ruby.

Ruby later followed the district attorney out of the press conference, walked up to him and, according to Wade, said "Hi Henry ... Don't you know me? ... I am Jack Ruby, I run the Vegas Club..." Ruby also introduced himself to Justice of the Peace David L. Johnston, shook his hand, gave Johnston a business card to the Carousel Club, and, upon learning Johnston's official position, shook Johnston's hand again. After talking with Johnston, he gave another card to Icarus M. Pappas, a reporter for New York radio station WNEW. From a representative of radio station KBOX in Dallas, Ruby obtained the "hot line" telephone number to KLIF. He then called the station and told one of the employees that he would like to come up to distribute the sandwiches and cold drinks he had purchased. Observing Pappas holding a telephone line open and attempting to get the attention of District Attorney Wade, Ruby directed Wade to Pappas, who proceeded to interview the district attorney. Ruby then called KLIF a second time and offered to secure an interview with Wade; he next summoned Wade to his phone, whereupon KLIF recorded a telephone interview with the district attorney. A few minutes later, Ruby encountered Russ Knight, a reporter from KLIF who had left the station for the police department at the beginning of Ruby's second telephone call. Ruby directed Knight to Wade and waited a short distance away while the reporter conducted another interview with the district attorney.

At radio station KLIF

When Ruby left police headquarters, he drove to radio station KLIF, arriving at approximately 1.45 am and remaining for about 45 minutes. After first distributing his sandwiches and soft drinks, Ruby settled in the newsroom for the 2 am newscast in which he was credited with suggesting that Russ Knight ask District Attorney Wade whether or not Oswald was sane. After the newscast, Ruby gave a Carousel card to one KLIF employee, although another did not recall that Ruby was promoting his club as he normally did. When speaking with KLIF's Danny Patrick McCurdy, Ruby mentioned that he was going to close his clubs for the weekend and that he would rather lose $1,200 or $1,500 than remain open at that time in the nation's history. McCurdy remembered that Ruby "looked rather pale to me as he was talking to me and he kept looking at the floor." To announcer Glen Duncan, Ruby expressed satisfaction that the evidence was mounting against Oswald. Duncan said that Ruby did not appear to be grieving but, instead, seemed pleased about the personal contact he had had with the investigation earlier in the evening.

Ruby left the radio station accompanied by Russ Knight. Engaging Knight in a short conversation, Ruby handed him a radio script entitled "Heroism" from a conservative radio program called "Life Line." It was apparently one of the scripts that had come into Ruby's hands a few weeks before at the Texas Products Show when Hunt Foods were including such scripts with samples of their products. The script extolled the virtues of those who embark upon risky business ventures and stand firmly for causes they believe to be correct. Ruby asked Knight's views on the script and suggested that there was a group of "radicals" in Dallas which hated President Kennedy and that the owner of the radio station should editorialize against this group. Knight could not clearly determine whether Ruby had reference to persons who sponsored programs like "Life Line" or to those who held left-wing views. Knight gained the impression that Ruby believed such persons, whoever they might be, were partially responsible for the assassination.

Early morning of November 23
At about 2.30 am, Ruby entered his automobile and departed for the Dallas *Times-Herald* building. En route, he stopped for about an hour to speak with Kay Helen Coleman, one of his dancers, and Harry Olsen, a member of the Dallas Police Department, who had hailed him from a parking garage at the corner of Jackson and Field streets. The couple were crying and extremely upset over the assassination. At one point, according to Ruby, the police officer remarked that "they should cut this guy [Oswald] inch by inch into ribbons," and the dancer said that "in England they would drag him throught the streets and would have hung him." Although Ruby failed to mention this episode during his first two FBI interviews, he later explained that his reason for failing to do so was that he did not "want to involve them in anything, because it was supposed to be a secret that he [the police officer] was going with this young lady." About six weeks after the assassination, Olsen left the Dallas Police Department and married Miss Coleman. Both Olsen and his wife testified that they were greatly upset during their lengthy conversation with Ruby early Saturday morning; but Mrs Olsen denied and Olsen did not recall the remarks ascribed to them. The Olsens claimed instead that Ruby had cursed Oswald. Mrs Olsen also mentioned that Ruby expressed sympathy for Mrs Kennedy and her children.

From Jackson and Field streets, Ruby drove to the Dallas *Times-Herald*, where he talked for about 15 minutes with composing room employee Roy Pryor, who had just finished a shift at 4 am. Ruby mentioned that he had seen Oswald earlier in the night, that he had corrected Henry Wade in connection with the Fair Play for Cuba Committee, and that he had set up a telephone interview with Wade. Pryor testified that Ruby explicitly stated to him that he believed he was in good favor with the district attorney. Recalling that Ruby described Oswald as a "little weasel of a guy" and was emotionally concerned about the president's wife and children, Pryor also was impressed by Ruby's sorrowful mood and remembered that, as he talked, Ruby shook a newspaper to emphasize his concern over the assassination.

When Pryor left the composing room, Ruby remained and continued speaking with other employees, including Arthur Watherwax and the foreman, Clyde Gadash. Ruby, who often visited the *Times-Herald* at that early morning hour in connection with his ads, sought Watherwax's views on his decision to close his clubs and indicated he was going to attempt to persuade other club owners to do likewise. Watherwax described Ruby as "pretty shaken up" about the assassination and at the same time "excited" that he had attended Oswald's Friday night press conference.

While at the *Times-Herald*, Ruby displayed to the composing room employees a "twist board" he had previously promised to Gadash. The twist board was an exercising device consisting of two pieces of hardened materials joined together by a lazy-Susan bearing so that one piece could remain stationary on the floor while a person stood atop it and swiveled to and fro. Ruby had been trying to promote sales of the board in the weeks before President Kennedy was killed. Considerable merriment developed when one of the women employees at the *Times-Herald* demonstrated the board, and Ruby himself put on a demonstration for those assembled. He later testified: "... not that I wanted to get in with the hilarity of frolicking, but he [Gadash] asked me to show him, and the other men gathered around." Gadash agreed that Ruby's general mood was one of sorrow.

At about 4.30 am, Ruby drove from the Dallas *Times-Herald* to his apartment where he awakened his roommate George Senator. During his visit in the composing room Ruby had expressed the view that the Weissman advertisement was an effort to discredit the Jews. Senator testified that when Ruby returned to the apartment, he began to discuss the Weissman advertisement and also a sign board he had seen in Dallas urging that Chief Justice Earl Warren be impeached. Shortly thereafter, Ruby telephoned Larry Crafard at the Carousel Club. He told Crafard to meet him and Senator at the Nichols Garage adjacent to the Carousel Club and to bring a Polaroid camera kept in the club. After Crafard joined Ruby and Senator, the three men drove to the "Impeach Earl Warren" sign near Hall Avenue and Central Expressway in Dallas. There Ruby instructed Crafard to take three photographs of the billboard. Believing that the sign and the Weissman newspaper ad might somehow be connected, Ruby noted on the back of an envelope a name and post office box number that appeared on the sign. According to George Senator:

> . . . when he was looking at the sign and taking pictures of
> it, and the newspaper ad . . . this is where he really wanted
> to know the whys or why these things had to be out. He
> is trying to combine these two together when I did hear
> him say, "This is the work of the John Birch Society or
> the Communist Party or maybe a combination of both."

Pursuing a possible connection between the billboard and the newspaper advertisement, Ruby drove to the post office and asked a postal employee for the name of the man who had rented the box indicated on the billboard, but the employee said that he could not provide such information. Ruby inspected the box, however, and was upset to find it stuffed with mail. The three men then drove to a coffee-shop where Ruby continued to discuss the two advertisements. After about 30 minutes, they left the coffee shop. Crafard was taken to the Carousel Club; Ruby and Senator returned to their apartment, and Ruby retired at about 6 am.

The morning and afternoon of November 23
At 8 or 8.30 am Crafard, who had been asked to feed Ruby's dogs, telephoned Ruby at his apartment to inquire about food for the animals. Ruby forgot that he had told Crafard he did not plan to go to bed and reprimanded Crafard for waking him. A few hours thereafter Crafard assembled his few belongings, took from the Carousel cash register $5 of money due him from Ruby, left a receipt and thank-you note, and began hitchhiking to Michigan. Later that day, Andrew Armstrong found the note and telephoned Ruby.

Ruby apparently did not return to bed following Crafard's call. During the morning hours, he watched a rabbi deliver on television a moving eulogy of President Kennedy. According to Ruby, the rabbi:

> went ahead and eulogized that here is a man that fought in every battle, went to every country, and had to come back to his own country to be shot in the back [starts crying] ... That created a tremendous emotional feeling for me, the way he said that. Prior to all the other times, I was carried away.

An employee from the Carousel Club who telephoned Ruby during the morning remembered that his "voice was shaking" when he spoke of the assassination.

Ruby has stated that, upon leaving his apartment some time between noon and 1.30 pm, he drove to Dealey Plaza where a police officer, who noted Ruby's solemnity, pointed out to him the window from which the rifleshots had been fired the day before. Ruby related that he inspected the wreaths that had been placed in memory of the president and became filled with emotion while speaking with the police officer. Ruby introduced himself to a reporter for radio station KRLD who was working inside a mobile news unit at the plaza; the newsman mentioned to Ruby that he had heard of Ruby's help to KLIF in obtaining an interview with Henry Wade, and Ruby pointed out to the reporter that Captain J. Will Fritz and Chief Curry were then in the vicinity. Thereafter, the newsman interviewed and photographed the officers. Ruby said that he next drove home and returned downtown to Sol's Turf Bar on Commerce Street.

The evidence indicated, however, that sometime after leaving Dealey Plaza, Ruby went to the Nichols Parking Garage adjacent to the Carousel Club, where he was seen by Garnett C. Hallmark, general manager of the garage, and Tom Brown, an attendant. Brown believed that at about 1.30 pm he heard Ruby mention Chief Curry's name in a telephone conversation from the garage. Brown also recalled that, before finally departing, Ruby asked him to inform acquaintances whom he expected to stop by the garage that the Carousel would be closed. Hallmark testified that Ruby drove into the garage at about 3 pm, walked to the telephone, inquired whether or not a competing burlesque club would be closed that night, and told Hallmark that he (Ruby) was "acting like a reporter." Hallmark then heard Ruby address someone at the other end of the telephone as "Ken" and caught portions of a conversation concerning the transfer of Oswald. Hallmark said Ruby never called Oswald by name but used the pronoun "he" and remarked to the recipient of the call, "You know I'll be there."

Ken Dowe, a KLIF announcer, to whom Ruby made at least two telephone calls within a short span of time Saturday afternoon, confirmed that he was probably the person to whom Hallmark and Brown overheard Ruby speaking. In one call to Dowe, Ruby asked whether the station knew when Oswald would be moved; and, in another, he stated he was going to attempt to locate Henry Wade. After Ruby finished his calls, he walked onto Commerce Street, passed the Carousel Club, and returned a few minutes later to get his car.

Ruby's comment that he was "acting like a reporter" and that he would be at the Oswald transfer suggests that Ruby may have spent part of Saturday afternoon shuttling back and forth from the Police and Courts Building to Dealey Plaza. Such activity would explain the fact that Tom Brown at the Nichols Garage believed he saw Ruby at 1.30 pm while Garnett Hallmark placed Ruby at the garage at 3 pm. It would also explain Ken Dowe's receiving two phone calls from Ruby. The testimony of five news reporters supports the possibility that Ruby was at the Police and Courts Building Saturday afternoon. One stated that Ruby provided sandwiches for newsmen on duty there Saturday afternoon, although no news representative has mentioned personally receiving such sandwiches. Another testified that he received a card to the Carousel Club from Ruby that afternoon at the police station. A third believed he saw Ruby enter an office in which Henry Wade was working, but no one else reported a similar event. The remaining two witnesses mentioned no specific activities. None of the persons who believed they saw Ruby at the police department on Saturday had known him previously, and no police officer has reported Ruby's presence on that day. Ruby has not mentioned such a visit. The Commission, therefore, reached no firm conclusion as to whether or not Ruby visited the Dallas Police Department on Saturday.

Shortly after 3 pm Ruby went to Sol's Turf Bar on Commerce Street where he remained for about 45 minutes. Ruby, a non-drinker, stated that he visited Sol's for the purpose of talking with his accountant, who customarily prepared the bar's payroll on Saturday afternoon. The accountant testified, however, that he saw Ruby only briefly and mentioned no business conversation with Ruby. Ruby was first noticed at the Turf Bar by jeweler Frank Bellochio, who, after seeing Ruby, began to berate the people of Dallas for the assassination. Ruby disagreed and, when Bellochio said he might close his jewelry business and leave Dallas, Ruby attempted to calm him, saying that there were many good citizens in Dallas. In response, Bellochio pointed to a copy of the Bernard Weissman advertisement. To Bellochio's bewilderment, Ruby then said he believed that the advertisement was the work of a group attempting to create anti-Semitic feelings in Dallas and that he had learned from the Dallas *Morning News* that the ad had been paid for partly in cash. Ruby thereupon produced one of the photographs he had taken Saturday morning of the "Impeach Earl Warren" sign and excitedly began to rail against the sign as if he agreed with Bellochio's original criticism of Dallas. He "seemed to be taking two sides – he wasn't coherent," Bellochio testified. When Bellochio saw Ruby's photographs, which Bellochio thought supported his argument against Dallas, he walked to the front of the bar and showed them to Tom Apple, with whom he had been previously arguing. In Apple's presence, Bellochio asked Ruby for one of the pictures but Ruby refused, mentioning that he regarded the pictures as a scoop. Bellochio testified: "I spoke to Tom and said a few more words to Tom, and Ruby was gone – never said 'Good-bye' or 'I'll be seeing you.' "

Ruby may have left in order to telephone Stanley Kaufman, a friend and attorney who had represented him in civil matters. Kaufman testified that, at approximately 4 pm, Ruby called him about the Bernard Weissman advertisement. According to Kaufman, "Jack was particularly impressed with the [black] border as being a tip-off of some sort – that this man knew the president was going to be assassinated..." Ruby told Kaufman that he had tried to locate Weissman by going to the post office and said that he was attempting to be helpful to law enforcement authorities.

Considerable confusion exists as to the place from which Ruby placed the call to Kaufman and as to his activities after leaving Sol's Turf Bar. Eva Grant stated that the call was made from her apartment about 4 pm. Ruby, however, believed it was made from the Turf Bar. He stated that from the Turf Bar he went to the Carousel and then home and has not provided additional details on his activities during the hours from about 4 to 9.30 pm. Robert Larkin saw him downtown at about 6 pm and Andrew Armstrong testified that Ruby visited the Carousel Club between 6 and 7 pm and remained about an hour.

At Eva Grant's apartment Saturday evening

Eva Grant believed that, for most of the period from 4 until 8 pm, Ruby was at her apartment. Mrs Grant testified that her brother was still disturbed about the Weissman advertisement when he arrived, showed her the photograph of the Warren sign, and recounted his argument with Bellochio about the city of Dallas. Still curious as to whether or not Weissman was Jewish, Mrs Grant asked her brother whether he had been able to find the name Bernard Weissman in the Dallas city directory, and Ruby said he had not. Their doubts about Weissman's existence having been confirmed, both began to speculate that the Weissman ad and the Warren sign were the work of either "Commies or the Birchers", and were designed to discredit the Jews. Apparently in the midst of that conversation Ruby telephoned Russ Knight at KLIF and, according to Knight, asked who Earl Warren was.

Mrs Grant has testified that Ruby eventually retired to her bedroom where he made telephone calls and slept. About 8.30 pm, Ruby telephoned Thomas J. O'Grady, a friend and former Dallas police officer who had once worked for Ruby as a bouncer. To O'Grady, Ruby mentioned closing the Carousel Club, criticized his competitors for remaining open, and complained about the "Impeach Earl Warren" sign.

Saturday evening at Ruby's apartment

By 9.30 pm, Ruby had apparently returned to his apartment where he received a telephone call from one of his striptease dancers, Karen Bennett Carlin, who, together with her husband, had been driven from Fort Worth to Dallas that evening by another dancer, Nancy Powell. All three had stopped at the Colony Club, a burlesque nightclub which competed with the Carousel. Mrs Carlin testified that, in need of money, she telephoned Ruby, asked whether the Carousel would be open that night, and requested part of her salary. According to Mrs Carlin, Ruby became angry at the suggestion that the Carousel Club might be open for business but told her he would come to the Carousel in about an hour.

Thereafter, in a depressed mood, Ruby telephoned his sister Eva Grant, who suggested he visit a friend. Possibly in response to that suggestion, Ruby called Lawrence Meyers, a friend from Chicago whom he had visited two nights previously. Meyers testified that, during their telephone conversation, Ruby asked him what he thought of this "terrible thing". Ruby then began to criticize his competitors, Abe and Barney Weinstein, for failing to close their clubs on Saturday night. In the course of his conversation about the Weinsteins and the assassination, Ruby said "I've got to do something about this." Meyers initially understood that remark to refer to the Weinsteins. Upon reflection after Oswald was shot, Meyers was uncertain whether Ruby was referring to his competitors, or to the assassination of President Kennedy; for Ruby had also spoken at length about Mrs Kennedy and had repeated "those poor people, those poor people." At the conclusion of their conversation, Meyers declined Ruby's invitation to join him for a cup of coffee but invited Ruby to join him at the motel. When Ruby also declined, the two agreed to meet for dinner the following evening.

Meanwhile, Karen Carlin and her husband grew anxious over Ruby's failure to appear with the money they had requested. After a substantial wait, they returned together to the Nichols Garage where Mr Carlin telephoned Ruby. Carlin testified that he told Ruby they needed money in order to return to Fort Worth although Nancy Powell testified that she drove the Carlins home that evening. Agreeing to advance a small sum, Ruby asked to speak to Mrs Carlin, who claimed that Ruby told her that if she needed more money she should call him on Sunday. Thereafter, at Ruby's request, garage attendant Huey Reeves gave Mrs Carlin $5, and she signed with her stage name "Little Lynn" a receipt which Reeves time-stamped 10.33 pm, November 23.

Inconsistent testimony was developed regarding Ruby's activities during the next 45 minutes. Eva Grant testified that she did not see her brother on Saturday night after 8 pm and has denied calling Ralph Paul herself that night. Nonetheless, telephone company records revealed that at 10.44 pm a call was made to Ralph Paul's Bull

Pen Drive-In in Arlington, Texas, from Mrs Grant's apartment. It was the only call to Paul from her apartment on Friday or Saturday; she recalled her brother making such a call that weekend; and Ralph Paul has testified that Ruby telephoned him Saturday night from Eva Grant's apartment and said he and his sister were there crying.

Nineteen-year-old Wanda Helmick, a former waitress at the Bull Pen Drive-In, first reported in June, 1964 that some time during the evening she saw the cashier answer the Bull Pen's pay telephone and heard her call out to Paul, "It is for you. It is Jack." Mrs Helmick claimed she overheard Paul, speaking on the telephone, mention something about a gun which, she understood from Paul's conversation, the caller had in his possession. She said she also heard Paul exclaim "Are you crazy?" She provided no other details of the conversation. Mrs Helmick claimed that on Sunday, November 24, after Oswald had been shot, she heard Paul repeat the substance of the call to other employees as she had related it and that Paul said Ruby was the caller. Ralph Paul denied the allegations of Mrs Helmick. Both Paul and Mrs Helmick agreed that Paul went home soon after the call, apparently about 11 pm.

Shortly after 11 pm, Ruby arrived at the Nichols Garage where he repaid Huey Reeves and obtained the receipt Mrs Carlin had signed. Outside the Carousel, Ruby exchanged greetings with Police Officer Harry Olsen and Kay Coleman, whom he had seen late the previous night. Going upstairs to the club, Ruby made a series of five brief long-distance phone calls, the first being to the Bull Pen Drive-In at 11.18 pm and lasting only 1 minute. Apparently unable to reach Paul there, Ruby telephoned Paul's home in Arlington, Texas, for 3 minutes. A third call was placed at 11.36 pm for 2 minutes, again to Paul's home. At 11.44 pm Ruby telephoned Breck Wall, a friend and entertainer who had gone to Galveston, Texas, when his show in Dallas suspended its performance out of respect to President Kennedy. The call lasted 2 minutes. Thereafter, Ruby immediately placed a 1-minute phone call to Paul's home.

Although Ruby has mentioned those calls, he has not provided details to the Commission; however, he has denied ever indicating to Paul or Wall that he was going to shoot Oswald and has said he did not consider such action until Sunday morning. Ralph Paul did not mention the late evening calls in his interview with FBI agents on November 24, 1963. Later Paul testified that Ruby called him from downtown to say that nobody was doing any business. Breck Wall testified that Ruby called him to determine whether or not the American Guild of Variety Artists (AGVA), which represented striptease dancers in Dallas, had met concerning a dispute Ruby was having with the union. Ruby's major difference with AGVA during the preceding two weeks had involved what Ruby considered to be AGVA's failure to enforce against his two competitors, Abe and Barney Weinstein, AGVA's ban on "striptease contests" and performances by "amateurs". As recently as Wednesday, November 20, Ruby had telephoned an AGVA representative in Chicago about that complaint and earlier in November he had unsuccessfully sought to obtain assistance from a San Francisco gambler and a Chicagoan reputed for his heavy-handed union activities. Wall testified that Ruby "was very upset the president was assassinated and he called Abe Weinstein or Bernie Weinstein ... some names for staying open ..." Wall added, "he was very upset ... that they did not have the decency to close on such a day and he thought out of respect they should close."

Ruby's activities after midnight

After completing the series of calls to Paul and Wall at 11.48 pm, Ruby went to the Pago Club, about a 10-minute drive from the Carousel Club. He took a table near the middle of the club and, after ordering a Coke, asked the waitress in a disapproving tone, "Why are you open?" When Robert Norton, the club's manager, joined Ruby a few minutes later he expressed to Ruby his concern as to whether or not it was proper to operate the Pago Club that evening. Ruby indicated that the Carousel was closed but did not criticize Norton for remaining open. Norton raised the topic of President Kennedy's death and said, "[W]e couldn't do enough to the person that [did] this sort of thing." Norton added, however, that "Nobody has the right to take the life of another one." Ruby expressed no strong opinion, and closed the conversation by saying he was going home because he was tired. Later, Ruby told the Commission: "He knew something was wrong with me in the certain mood I was in."

Ruby testified that he went home after speaking with Norton and went to bed about 1.30 am. By that time, George Senator claimed, he had retired for the night and did not remember Ruby's return. Eva Grant testified that her brother telephoned her at about 12.45 am to learn how she was feeling.

Sunday morning
Ruby's activities on Sunday morning are the subject of conflicting testimony. George Senator believed that Ruby did not rise until 9 or 9.30 am; both Ruby and Senator maintained that Ruby did not leave their apartment until shortly before 11.00 am, and two other witnesses have provided testimony which supports that account of Ruby's whereabouts. On the other hand, three WBAP-TV television technicians – Warren Richey, John Smith, and Ira Walker – believed they saw Ruby near the Police and Courts Building at various times between 8 am and 11 am. But there are substantial reasons to doubt the accuracy of their identifications. None had ever seen Ruby on a prior

occasion. None looked for an extended period at the man believed to be Ruby, and all were occupied with their duties and had no reason to remember the man's appearance until they saw Ruby's picture on television.

Smith, for one, was not entirely positive about his identification of Ruby as the man he saw; and Richey was looking down from atop a TV mobile unit when he observed on the sidewalk the man he believed was Ruby. In addition, Richey and Smith provided descriptions of Ruby which differ substantially from information about Ruby gathered from other sources. Smith described the man he saw as being an "unkempt person that possibly could have slept with his clothes on..." Ruby was characteristically clean and well groomed. In fact, Senator testified that Ruby shaved and dressed before leaving their apartment that morning, and at the time Ruby shot Oswald was dressed in a hat and business suit. Richey described Ruby as wearing a grayish overcoat, while investigation indicated that Ruby did not own an overcoat and was not wearing one at the time of the shooting. Although Walker's identification of Ruby is the most positive, his certainty must be contrasted with the indefinite identification made by Smith, who had seen the man on one additional occasion. Both Smith and Walker saw a man resembling Ruby when the man, on two occasions, looked through the window of their mobile news unit and once asked whether Oswald had been transferred. Both saw only the man's head, and Smith was closer to the window; yet Smith would not state positively that the man was Ruby. Finally, video tapes of scenes on Sunday morning near the NBC van show a man close to the Commerce Street entrance who might have been mistaken for Ruby.

George Senator said that when he arose, before 9 am, he began to do his laundry in the basement of the apartment building while Ruby slept. During Senator's absence, Ruby received a telephone call from his cleaning lady, Mrs Elnora Pitts, who testified that she called sometime between 8.30 and 9 am to learn whether Ruby wanted her to clean his apartment that day. Mrs Pitts remembered that Ruby "sounded terrible strange to me." She said that "there was something wrong with him the way he was talking to me." Mrs Pitts explained that, although she had regularly been cleaning Ruby's apartment on Sundays, Ruby seemed not to comprehend who she was or the reason for her call and required her to repeat herself several times. As Senator returned to the apartment after the call, he was apparently mistaken for Ruby by a neighbor, Sidney Evans, Jr. Evans had never seen Ruby before but recalled observing a man resembling Ruby, clad in trousers and T-shirt, walk upstairs from the "washateria" in the basement of their building and enter Ruby's suite with a load of laundry. Later in the morning, Malcolm Slaughter who shared an apartment with Evans, saw an individual, similarly clad, on the same floor as Ruby's apartment. Senator stated that it was not Ruby's custom to do his own washing and that Ruby did not do so that morning.

While Senator was in the apartment, Ruby watched television, made himself coffee and scrambled eggs, and received, at 10.19 am, a telephone call from his entertainer, Karen Carlin. Mrs Carlin testified that in her telephone conversation she asked Ruby for $25 inasmuch as her rent was delinquent and she needed groceries. She said that Ruby, who seemed upset, mentioned that he was going downtown anyway and that he would send the money from the Western Union office. According to George Senator, Ruby then probably took a half hour or more to bathe and dress.

Supporting the accounts given by Mrs Carlin and Mrs Pitts of Ruby's emotional state, Senator testified that during the morning Ruby:

... was even mumbling, which I didn't understand. And right after breakfast he got dressed. Then after he got dressed he was pacing the floor from the living room to the bedroom, from the bedroom to the living room, and his lips were going. What he was jabbering I don't know. But he was really pacing.

Ruby has described to the Commission his own emotions of Sunday morning as follows:

... Sunday morning ... [I] saw a letter to Caroline, two columns about a 16-inch area. Someone had written a letter to Caroline. The most heartbreaking letter. I don't remember the contents ... alongside that letter on the same sheet of paper was a small comment in the newspaper that, I don't know how it was stated, that Mrs Kennedy may have to come back for the trial of Lee Harvey Oswald...

I don't know what bug got a hold of me. I don't know what it is, but I am going to tell the truth word for word.

I am taking a pill called Preludin. It is a harmless pill, and it is very easy to get in the drugstore. It isn't a highly prescribed pill. I use it for dieting.

I don't partake of that much food. I think that was a stimulus to give me an emotional feeling that suddenly I felt, which was so stupid, that I wanted to show my love for our faith, being of the Jewish faith, and I never used the term and I don't want to go into that. Suddenly the feeling, the emotional feeling came within me that someone owed this debt to our beloved president to save her the ordeal of coming back. I don't know why that came through my mind.

Sunday morning trip to police department
Leaving his apartment a few minutes before 11 am, Ruby went to his automobile taking with him his dachshund,

Sheba, and a portable radio. He placed in his pocket a revolver which he routinely carried in a bank moneybag in the trunk of his car. Listening to the radio, he drove downtown, according to his own testimony, by a route that took him past Dealey Plaza where he observed the scattered wreaths. Ruby related that he noted the crowd that had gathered outside the county jail and assumed that Oswald had already been transferred. However, when he passed the Main Street side of the Police and Courts Building, which is situated on the same block as the Western Union office, he also noted the crowd that was gathered outside that building. Normal driving time for the trip from his apartment would have been about 15 minutes, but Ruby's possible haste and the slow movement of traffic through Dealey Plaza make a reliable estimate difficult.

Ruby parked his car in a lot directly across the street from the Western Union office. He apparently placed his keys and billfold in the trunk of the car, then locked the trunk, which contained approximately $1,000 in cash, and placed the trunk key in the glove compartment of the car. He did not lock the car doors.

With his revolver, more than $2,000 in cash, and no personal identification, Ruby walked from the parking lot across the street to the Western Union office where he filled out forms for sending $25 by telegraph to Karen Carlin. After waiting in line while one other Western Union customer completed her business, Ruby paid for the telegram and retained as a receipt one of three time-stamped documents which show that the transaction was completed at almost exactly 11.17 am, CST. The Western Union clerk who accepted Ruby's order recalls that Ruby promptly turned, walked out of the door onto Main Street, and proceeded in the direction of the police department one block away. The evidence set forth in pp. 286–291 indicates that Ruby entered the police basement through the auto ramp from Main Street and stood behind the front rank of newsmen and police officers who were crowded together at the base of the ramp awaiting the transfer of Oswald to the county jail. As Oswald emerged from a basement office at approximately 11.21 am, Ruby moved quickly forward and, without speaking, fired one fatal shot into Oswald's abdomen before being subdued by a rush of police officers.

Evaluation of activities

Examination of Ruby's activities immediately preceding and following the death of President Kennedy revealed no sign of any conduct which suggests that he was involved in the assassination. Prior to the tragedy, Ruby's activities were routine. Though persons who saw him between November 22 and 24 disagree as to whether or not he appeared more upset than others around him, his response to the assassination appears to have been one of genuine shock and grief. His indications of concern over the possible effects of the assassination upon his businesses seem consistent with other evidence of his character. During the course of the weekend, Ruby seems to have become obsessed with the possibility that the "Impeach Earl Warren" sign and the Bernard Weissman ad were somehow connected and related to the assassination. However, Ruby's interest in these public notices was openly expressed and, as discussed below, the evidence reveals no connection between him and any political organization.

Examination of Larry Crafard's sudden departure from Dallas shortly before noon on November 23 does not suggest that Ruby was involved in a conspiracy. To be sure, Crafard started hitchhiking to Michigan, where members of his family lived, with only $7 in his pocket. He made no attempt to communicate with law enforcement officials after Oswald's death; and a relative in Michigan recalled that

Crafard spoke very little of his association with Ruby. When finally located by the FBI six days later, he stated that he left Ruby's employ because he did not wish to be subjected to further verbal abuse by Ruby and that he went north to see his sister, from whom he had not heard in some time.

An investigation of Crafard's unusual behavior confirms that his departure from Dallas was innocent. After Oswald was shot, FBI agents obtained from the Carousel Club an unmailed letter drafted by Crafard to a relative in Michigan at least a week before the assassination. The letter revealed that he was considering leaving Dallas at that time. On November 17, Crafard, who had been receiving only room, board, and incidental expenses, told Ruby he wanted to stop working for him; however, Crafard agreed to remain when Ruby promised a salary. Then on the morning of November 23, Ruby and Crafard had a minor altercation over the telephone. Although Crafard did not voluntarily make known to the authorities his associations with Ruby, he spoke freely and with verifiable accuracy when questioned. The automobile driver who provided Crafard his first ride from Dallas has been located; his statement generally conforms with Crafard's story; and he did not recall any unusual or troubled behavior by Crafard during that ride.

Although Crafard's peremptory decision to leave Dallas might be unusual for most persons, such behavior does not appear to have been uncommon for him. His family residence had shifted frequently among California, Michigan, and Oregon. During his 22 years, he had earned his livelihood picking crops, working in carnivals, and taking other odd jobs throughout the country. According to his testimony, he had previously hitchhiked across the country with his then wife and two infant children. Against such a background, it is most probable that the factors motivating Crafard's departure from Dallas on November 23 were dissatisfaction with his existence in Ruby's employ, which he had never considered more than temporary, Ruby's decision to close his clubs for three days, the argument on Saturday morning, and his own desire to see his relatives in Michigan. There is no evidence to suggest any connection between Crafard's departure and the assassination of the president or the shooting of Oswald.

The allegations of Wanda Helmick raised speculation that Ruby's Saturday night phone calls to Ralph Paul and Breck Wall might have concerned the shooting of Oswald, but investigation has found nothing to indicate that the calls had conspiratorial implications. Paul was a close friend, business associate, and adviser to Jack Ruby. Ruby normally kept in close telephone contact with Paul, who had a substantial sum of money committed to the Carousel Club. Paul explained that Ruby called him Saturday evening once to point out his ads, another time to say that nobody seemed to be doing any business in downtown Dallas, and a third time to relate that both he and his sister were crying over the assassination. Between two of those phone calls to Paul, Ruby telephoned to Galveston, Texas, to speak with Wall, a friend and former business associate who was an official of the American Guild of Variety Artists. Wall related that during that call Ruby criticized the Weinsteins for failing to close their clubs.

Having earlier made the same complaint to Lawrence Meyers, to whom he mentioned a need "to do something about this", it would have been characteristic for Ruby to want to direct Breck Wall's attention, as an AGVA official, to what he regarded as the Weinsteins' improper conduct. The view that the calls to Wall and Paul could have had conspiratorial implications also is belied in large measure by the conduct of both men before and after the events of November 22–24. A check of long-distance telephone records reveals no suspicious activity by either man. Paul, in

fact, is not known to have visited Dallas during the weekend of the assassination except to appear openly in an effort
to arrange counsel for Ruby within a few hours of the
attack on Oswald. Neither the FBI nor the CIA has been
able to provide any information that Ralph Paul or Breck
Wall ever engaged in any form of subversive activity.

Moreover, Mrs Helmick's reliability is undermined by
her failure to report her information to any investigative
official until June 9, 1964. Although a sister-in-law
confirms that Mrs Helmick wrote her "something about a
gun" shortly after the shooting, the only mention of any
statement by Paul which was included in a letter written by
Mrs Helmick after the Ruby trial was that Paul believed
Ruby was "not in his right mind". No corroborating witness named by Mrs Helmick has been found who
remembers the conversations she mentioned. Both Ruby
and Paul have denied that anything was said, as Mrs
Helmick suggests, about a gun or an intent to shoot
Oswald, and Wall has stated that Ruby did not discuss such
matters with him. Even if Mrs Helmick is accurate, the
statements ascribed to Paul indicate only that he may have
heard of a possible reference by Ruby to shooting Oswald.
According to her, Paul's response was to exclaim "Are you
crazy?" But under no circumstances does the report of Mrs
Helmick or any other fact support a belief that Paul or Wall
was involved in the shooting of Oswald.

The Commission has conducted an investigation of the
telephone call Ruby received from Karen Carlin at 10.19
Sunday morning to determine whether that call was prearranged for the purpose of conveying information about
the transfer of Oswald or to provide Ruby an excuse for
being near the police department. The Commission has
examined the records of long-distance telephone calls on
Sunday morning for Jack Ruby, the Carlins, the Dallas
police, and several other persons and has found no sign of

any indirect communication to Ruby through Mr or Mrs Carlin. No other evidence showing any link between the Carlins and the shooting of Oswald has been developed.

CONCLUSION

Based upon the investigation reviewed in this chapter, the Commission concluded that there is no credible evidence that Lee Harvey Oswald was part of a conspiracy to assassinate President Kennedy. Examination of the facts of the assassination itself revealed no indication that Oswald was aided in the planning or execution of his scheme. Review of Oswald's life and activities since 1959, although productive in illuminating the character of Lee Harvey Oswald, did not produce any meaningful evidence of a conspiracy. The Commission discovered no evidence that the Soviet Union or Cuba were involved in the assassination of President Kennedy. Nor did the Commission's investigation of Jack Ruby produce any grounds for believing that Ruby's killing of Oswald was part of a conspiracy. The conclusion that there is no evidence of a conspiracy was also reached independently by Dean Rusk, the Secretary of State; Robert S. McNamara, the Secretary of Defense; C. Douglas Dillon, the Secretary of the Treasury; Robert F. Kennedy, the Attorney General; J. Edgar Hoover, the Director of the FBI; John A. McCone, the Director of the CIA; and James J. Rowley, the Chief of the Secret Service, on the basis of the information available to each of them.

THE UNANSWERED QUESTIONS

No one will ever know what passed through Oswald's mind during the week before November 22, 1963. Instead of returning to Irving on November 15 for his customary weekend visit, he remained in Dallas at his wife's suggestion because of the birthday party. He had argued with her over the use of an alias and had not called her after that argument, although he usually telephoned once or twice a day. Then on Thursday morning, November 21, he asked Frazier for a ride to Irving that night, stating falsely that he wanted to pick up some curtain rods to put in an apartment.

He must have planned his attack at the very latest prior to Thursday morning when he spoke to Frazier. There is, of course, no way to determine the degree to which he was committed to his plan at that time. While there is no way to tell when he first began to think specifically of assassinating the president it should be noted that mention of the Trade Mart as the expected site of the presidential luncheon appeared in the Dallas *Times-Herald* on November 15, 1963. The next day that paper announced the final approval of the Trade Mart as the luncheon site and stated that the motorcade "apparently will loop through the downtown area, probably on Main Street, en route from Dallas Love Field" on its way to the Trade Mart on Stemmons Freeway. Anyone who was familiar with that area of Dallas would have known that the motorcade would probably pass the Texas School Book Depository to get from Main Street onto the Stemmons Freeway. That fact was made precisely clear in subsequent news stories on November 19, 20, and 22.

On November 15, 1963, the same day that his wife told him not to come to Irving, Oswald could have assumed that the presidential motorcade would pass in front of his place of work. Whether he thought about assassinating the president over the weekend can never be known, but it is reasonably certain that over the weekend he did think about his wife's request that he not come to Irving, which was prompted by the birthday party being held at the Paine home. Oswald had a highly exaggerated sense of his own importance, but he had failed at almost everything he had ever tried to do. He had great difficulty in establishing meaningful relations with other people. Except for his family he was completely alone. Even though he had searched – in the Marine Corps, in his ideal of communism, in the Soviet Union and in his attempt to get to Cuba – he had never found anything to which he felt he could really belong.

After he returned from his trip to Mexico where his application to go to Cuba had been sharply rejected, it must have appeared to him that he was unable to command even the attention of his family. He could not keep them with him in Dallas, where at least he could see his children whom, several witnesses testified, he seemed to love. His family lived with Mrs Paine, ostensibly because Oswald could not afford to keep an apartment in Dallas, but it was also, at least in part, because his wife did not want to live there with him. Now it appeared that he was not welcome at the Paine home, where he had spent every previous weekend since his return from Mexico and his wife was once again calling into question his judgment, this time concerning his use of an alias.

The conversation on Monday, November 18, 1963, ended when Marina Oswald hung up and refused to talk to him. Although he may long before have decided on the course he was to follow and may have told his wife the things he did on the evening of November 21, 1963, merely to disarm her and to provide a justification of sorts, both she and Mrs Paine thought he had come home to make up after the fight on Monday. Thoughts of his personal difficulties must have been at least partly on his mind when he went to Irving on Thursday night and told his wife that he was lonely, that he wanted to make peace with her and bring his family to Dallas where they could live with him again.

The Commission does not believe that the relations between Oswald and his wife caused him to assassinate the president. It is unlikely that the motivation was that simple. The feelings of hostility and aggression which seem to have played such an important part in Oswald's life were part of his character long before he met his wife and such a favorable opportunity to strike at a figure as great as the president would probably never have come to him again.

Oswald's behavior after the assassination throws little light on his motives. The fact that he took so little money with him when he left Irving in the morning indicates that he did not expect to get very far from Dallas on his own and suggests the possibility, as did his note to his wife just prior to the attempt on General Walker, that he did not expect to escape at all. On the other hand, he could have traveled some distance with the money he did have and he did return to his room where he obtained his revolver. He then killed Patrolman Tippit when that police officer apparently tried to question him after he had left his rooming house and he vigorously resisted arrest when he was finally apprehended in the Texas Theater. Although it is not fully corroborated by others who were present, two officers have testified that at the time of his arrest Oswald said something to the effect that "It's all over now."

Oswald was overbearing and arrogant throughout much of the time between his arrest and his own death. He consistently refused to admit involvement in the assassination or in the killing of Patrolman Tippit. While he did become enraged at least one point in his interrogation, the testimony of the officers present indicates that he handled himself with considerable composure during his questioning. He admitted nothing that would damage him but discussed other matters quite freely. His denials under questioning, which have no probative value in view of the many readily demonstrable lies he told at that time and in the face of the overwhelming evidence against him which has been set forth above, only served to prolong the period during which he was the center of the attention of the entire world.

CONCLUSION

Many factors were undoubtedly involved in Oswald's motivation for the assassination, and the Commission does not believe that it can ascribe to him any one motive or group of motives. It is apparent, however, that Oswald was moved by an overriding hostility to his environment. He does not appear to have been able to establish meaningful relationships with other people. He was perpetually discontented with the world around him. Long before the assassination he expressed his hatred for American society and acted in protest against it. Oswald's search for what he conceived to be the perfect society was doomed from the start. He sought for himself a place in history – a role as the "great man" who would be recognized as having been in advance of his times. His commitment to Marxism and communism appears to have been another important factor in his motivation. He also had demonstrated a capacity to act decisively and without regard to the consequences when such action would further his aims of the moment. Out of these and the many other factors which may have molded the character of Lee Harvey Oswald there emerged a man capable of assassinating President Kennedy.

Jack Ruby's conviction for the murder of Lee Harvey Oswald was overturned by a Texas appeals court in 1966. However, before a new trial could be held, Ruby died of cancer, in January 1967.

New titles in the series

The Compendiums

Each book in this handsome series consists of three key historical accounts, and is illustrated with maps and photographs.

The World War I Collection

The official inquiry into the disastrous military campaign at Gallipoli, plus the despatches of British generals at the front during the first nine months of the war, are presented here.

The Dardanelles Commission, 1914–16

Examines why, when British troops were already heavily deployed in France, the leaders of the day saw fit to launch a major offensive in the eastern Mediterranean.

British Battles of World War I, 1914–15

A collection of despatches written by British commanders in the field, mainly in northern France.

ISBN 0 11 702466 X   Price UK £14.99 US $19.95

The World War II Collection

Consists of three accounts of major milestones of World War II, written by the statesmen and military leaders of the day.

War 1939: Dealing with Adolf Hitler

Describes the policies of both Hitler and the British government in the months leading up to the outbreak of war.

D Day to VE Day: General Eisenhower's Report

General Eisenhower's personal account of the invasion of Europe, from June 1944 to May 1945.

The Judgment of Nuremberg, 1946

Focuses on the first trial of 21 major war criminals. The text describes the entire history, purpose and method of the Nazi party.

ISBN 0 11 702463 5   Price UK £14.99 US $19.95

The Siege Collection

The stories of four sieges involving British troops in the days of British Empire are presented here.

The Siege of Kars, 1855

This little-known siege lasted five months and took place during the Crimean War, in the mountains of eastern Turkey.

The Boer War: Ladysmith and Mafeking, 1900

Contains despatches describing the siege and relief of both Ladysmith and Mafeking, as reported by the commanders in the field. The reverses suffered at Spion Kop are included.

The Siege of the Peking Embassy, 1900

Tells the story of how the diplomatic staff in Peking, China, were besieged by the Boxers in 1900.

ISBN 0 11 702464 3   Price UK £14.99 US $19.95

Tragic Journeys

Features three of the most tragic journeys of the 20th century.

The Loss of the Titanic, 1912

The official inquiry presented here is the same report that was published in 1912. Also included is a reappraisal of the evidence relating to the SS *Californian*, the ship that failed to come to the rescue of the *Titanic*.

R.101: The Airship Disaster, 1930

In its heyday, the airship R.101 was considered as glamorous as the *Titanic*. Sadly, its fate was equally tragic, as she crashed on her maiden flight to India. The official inquiry investigates why it all went so disastrously wrong.

The Munich Air Crash, 1958

Eight key players from the Manchester United football team died in this tragic accident at Munich airport in 1958. Included here are the official inquiries into the causes.

ISBN 0 11 702465 1   Price UK £14.99 US $19.95

The War Facsimiles

The War Facsimiles are exact reproductions of illustrated books that were published during the war years. They were produced by the British government to inform people about the progress of the war and the home-defence operations.

The Battle of Britain, August–October 1940

On 8 August 1940, the Germans launched the first of a series of mass air attacks on Britain in broad daylight. For almost three months, British and German aircraft were locked in fierce and prolonged combat in what has become known as the Battle of Britain. In 1941 the government published *The Battle of Britain* to explain the strategy and tactics behind the fighting that had taken place high in the sky over London and south-east England. Such was the public interest in this document, with its graphic maps and photographs, that sales had reached two million by the end of the war.

ISBN 0 11 702536 4   Price £4.99 US $8.95

The Battle of Egypt, 1942

Often referred to as the Battle of El Alamein, this battle was one of the major turning points for the Allies in World War II. The British, commanded by General Montgomery, were defending Egypt while the Germans under Rommel were attacking. This was a campaign the British could not afford to lose, because not only would it leave Egypt wide open for invasion, but it would also mean the loss of the Suez Canal and the oil fields. First published in 1943, *The Battle of Egypt* is an astonishing contemporary report of one of the most famous military victories in British history.

ISBN 0 11 702542 9   Price £5.99 US $10.95

Bomber Command: the Air Ministry account of Bomber Command's offensive against the Axis, September 1939–July 1941

Churchill declared on 22 June 1941: "We shall bomb Germany by day as well as by night in ever-increasing measure." Bomber Command of the RAF was to translate those words into action, beginning its attacks on Germany in May 1940, and steadily increasing its efforts as the war progressed. Published in 1941 at the height of World War II, *Bomber Command* tells the story of this fighting force during those early years.

ISBN 0 11 702540 2   Price £5.99 US $11.95

East of Malta, West of Suez: the Admiralty account of the naval war in the eastern Mediterranean, September 1939 to March 1941

This is the story of the British Navy in action in the eastern Mediterranean from September 1939 to March 1941 and their bid to seize control. During this time British supremacy was vigorously asserted at Taranto and Matapan. This facsimile edition contains contemporary maps, air reconnaissance photographs of the fleets and photographs of them in action.

ISBN 0 11 702538 0   Price £4.99 US $8.95

Fleet Air Arm: the Admiralty account of naval air operations, 1943

The Fleet Air Arm was established in 1939 as the Royal Navy's own flying branch. With its vast aircraft carriers bearing squadrons of fighter pilots, its main role was to protect a fleet or convoy from attack, or to escort an air striking force into battle. In *Fleet Air Arm*, published in 1943, the public could read for the first time of the expeditions of these great ships as they pursued and sank enemy warships such as the *Bismarck*.

ISBN 0 11 702539 9   Price £5.99 US $11.95

Land at War: the official story of British farming 1939–1944

Land at War was published by the Ministry of Information in 1945 as a tribute to those who had contributed to the war effort at home. It explains how 300,000 farms, pinpointed by an extensive farm survey, had been expected to increase their production dramatically, putting an extra 6.5 million acres of grassland under the plough. This is a book not just about rural life, but of the determination of a people to survive the rigours of war.

ISBN 0 11 702 537 2   Price £5.99 US $11.95

Ocean Front: the story of the war in the Pacific, 1941–44

Ocean Front tells the story of the Allies' war against Japan in the central and western Pacific. Starting with Pearl Harbor in December 1941, this fascinating book recounts the Allies' counter-offensive, from the battles of the Coral Sea and Midway, to the recapture of the Aleutian Islands and the final invasion of the Philippines. Illustrated throughout with amazing photographs of land and sea warfare, *Ocean Front* provides a unique record of the American, Australian and New Zealand fighting forces in action.

ISBN 0 11 702543 7   Price £5.99 US $11.95

Roof over Britain: the official story of Britain's anti-aircraft defences, 1939–1942

Largely untold, *Roof over Britain* is the story of Britain's ground defences against the attacks of the German air force during the Battle of Britain in the autumn of 1940. First published in 1943, it describes how the static defences – the AA guns, searchlights and balloons – were organised, manned and supplied in order to support the work of the RAF.

ISBN 0 11 702541 0   Price £5.99 US $11.95

Uncovered editions: how to order

FOR CUSTOMERS IN THE UK
Ordering is easy. Simply follow one of these five ways:

Online
Visit www.clicktso.com

By telephone
Please call 0870 600 5522, with book details to hand.

By fax
Fax details of the books you wish to order (title, ISBN,
quantity and price) to: 0870 600 5533.
Please include details of your credit/debit card plus
expiry date, your name and address and telephone
number, and expect a handling charge of £3.00.

By post
Post the details listed above (under 'By fax') to:
The Stationery Office
PO Box 29
Norwich NR3 1GN
You can send a cheque if you prefer by this method
(made payable to The Stationery Office). Please include
a handling charge of £3 on the final amount.

TSO bookshops
Visit your local TSO bookshop (or any good bookshop).

FOR CUSTOMERS IN THE UNITED STATES
Uncovered editions are available through all major
wholesalers and bookstores, and are distributed to the
trade by Midpoint Trade Books.
Phone 913 831 2233 for single copy prepaid orders
which can be fulfilled on the spot, or simply for more
information.
Fax 913 362 7401